FRONTIER SPIRIT
THE STORY OF WYOMING
Craig Sodaro and Randy Adams

Johnson Books: Boulder

To our families for their patience, encouragement and love.

   2   3   4   5   6   7   8   9

The cover painting is "Fort Laramie or Sublette's Fort," by Alfred Jacob
Miller. Reproduced by permission of the Enron Art Foundation, Joslyn
Art Museum, Omaha, Nebraska.

Maps by Michael McNierney

ISBN 1-55566-007-X

LCCCN 86-82084

Printed in the United States of America by
Johnson Publishing Company
1880 South 57th Court
Boulder, Colorado 80301

Contents

Acknowledgements

In the three years that it has taken to complete *Frontier Spirit: The Story of Wyoming*, a number of people have helped us over the rough spots. We would be remiss if we did not acknowledge their contributions to this text.

First, without the help of Paul Novak, the Assistant Superintendent of Goshen County Schools, the late superintendent, Ron Schliske, and the school board, we would not have had the opportunity to begin this project. The Goshen County School's Special Project Program funded our research and the production of the preliminary copies of *Frontier Spirit: The Story of Wyoming*.

Second, we deeply appreciate the assistance of Jean Brainerd at the Division of Historical Research, Wyoming State Archives, in locating much of the material we used in this book.

Third, we are grateful to Charles Sharp, Jack McDermott, Joyce Maeder, Vivian Hills, John Burns, Rick Lemmers, Gaithel Gilchreist, and Don Hodgson, who spent many an hour reading and criticizing the manuscript, providing us with innumerable suggestions. In addition we thank Bill Barton of the Wyoming State Archives, Museum, and Historical Department for offering much helpful criticism after a careful reading of the manuscript.

Fourth, thanks to the 1984 eighth grade social studies classes at Torrington Middle School, who read and studied the initial chapters of the book, providing valuable comments and criticisms from the student point of view.

Special thanks go to Frank Stamm, computer instructor at Torrington Middle School, who spent hours teaching two old dogs new tricks about word processing. More than once he rescued our words when they seemed hopelessly lost somewhere on a floppy disc.

Our thanks also go to our editor, Michael McNierney, who has been a tremendous guide in transferring our words from typewritten to typeset.

Most importantly, we are grateful to our families. While they endured absent husbands and fathers more often than they should, they were always encouraging and helpful in every way. Without their support, *Frontier Spirit: The Story of Wyoming* would still be a dream.

1
Physical Wyoming

Location

Wyoming is located in the western half of the United States from 41 to 45 degrees north latitude and from 104 to 111 degrees west longitude. It is the ninth largest state with an area of 97,914 square miles or 6.27 million acres. Rectangular, it measures approximately 275 miles north to south and approximately 355 miles east to west. It is bounded on the north by Montana, on the east by Nebraska and South Dakota, on the south by Colorado and Utah, and on the west by Idaho and Utah.

Elevation

Wyoming's elevation varies from a low point of 3,125 feet above sea level in the northeast corner of the state to 13,785 feet at Gannett Peak in the Wind River Range. The average elevation of over 6,700 feet makes Wyoming the second highest state in the union after Colorado.

The Continental Divide cuts through the state from north to south. East of the divide water flows to the Atlantic Ocean, while on the west it flows to the Pacific.

Three North American regions make up physical Wyoming. The eastern third is on the edge of the Great Plains. The Rocky Mountains extend from the northwest corner to the middle of the southern boundary. The southwest corner of Wyoming is part of the Great Basin region.

Landforms

There are ten major and several minor ranges making up the Rocky Mountains in Wyoming. The major ranges include the Laramie Range in

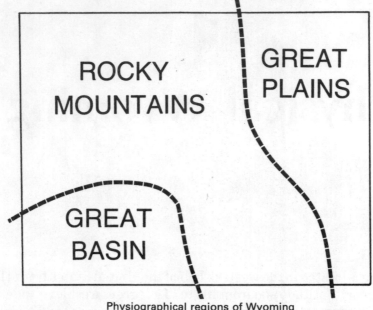

ROCKY
MOUNTAINS

GREAT
PLAINS

GREAT
BASIN

Physiographical regions of Wyoming

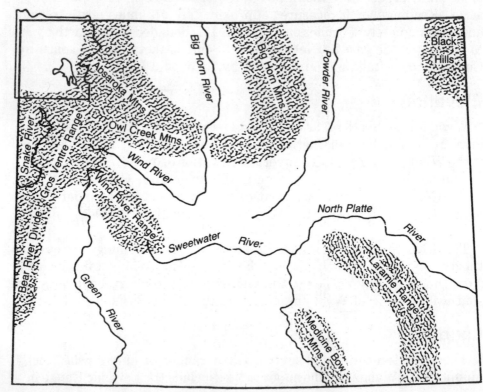

Physical Wyoming

Devil's Tower (Wyoming State Archives)

the southwest corner of the state, the Medicine Bow and Sierra Madre ranges along the south central border, and the Salt River and Teton ranges along the western edge. The Wind River and Absaroka ranges angle to the northwest corner, and the Big Horns circle from the north central border into the center of the state.

Several unusual natural features are found in Wyoming. In the center of the state, erosion has carved a miniature Grand Canyon called Hell's Half Acre. In the northeast corner the inner core of an eroded volcano stands as Devil's Tower.

The most spectacular of all the natural features of Wyoming is the most famous park in the world—Yellowstone National Park. Over three thousand square miles of unparalleled beauty with thermal pools, geysers (such as Old Faithful), and unusual formations greet visitors each year.

The Tetons offer breathtaking views as they rise vertically over seven thousand feet from the Jackson Hole area south of Yellowstone.

Water

Wyoming is justifiably known as a dry state. With an average rainfall that rarely exceeds fourteen inches and a very high evaporation rate, most of Wyoming flirts with being a desert.

The five major rivers, therefore, are small and miles apart. The Green River, a tributary of the Colorado, flows south out of the Absaroka and Salt River ranges. The Big Horn River (actually a combination of Wind River and the Big Horn) flows north through the Big Horn Basin to become a tributary of the Missouri.

The Powder River flows north from central Wyoming up the east side of the Big Horn Mountains to become yet another tributary of the Missouri. The North Platte River begins in northern Colorado and flows north into

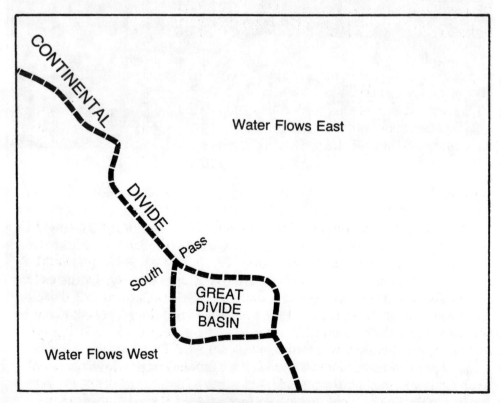

The Continental Divide

Yellowstone Falls (Wyoming
State Archives)

central Wyoming, then back to the southeast before leaving the state to
flow through central Nebraska.

The Snake River begins in the Yellowstone area and flows south through
the Jackson Hole region and then back to the west, leaving the state to
become a tributary of the Columbia River.

Climate

A resident's usual comment about Wyoming's weather is, "If you don't
like it, wait a minute. It'll change!"

Wyoming has elements of continental climate, semi-arid steppe climate,
and highland mountain climate. Summer temperatures regularly soar to
one hundred degrees in the eastern and southwestern parts of the state.
In winter temperatures regularly go below 0 degrees Fahrenheit and have
plunged to 50 below. Mountain temperatures rarely exceed 80 degrees,
and in many places snow remains on the ground year round.

Wind velocities in major towns and cities across the state average about
ten miles per hour. Higher winds are common in the spring when cold
fronts from Canada meet warm air masses from the Gulf of Mexico.

Many thunderstorms and occasional tornadoes strike the eastern portion of the state. Late winter may also see chinooks (warm winds) blow in and prematurely melt snows, bringing Wyoming's citizens out of doors to enjoy the weather.

Sixteen to twenty inches of precipitation per year fall regularly in southeastern Wyoming, but less than eight inches per year is more common in the Red Desert area of southwestern Wyoming. Mountain snows reach over one hundred inches annually and provide snowmelt to fuel the state's rivers.

Late winter and spring is the wettest time of the year. Though flooding has been a problem, better control methods have made damaging floods nearly a thing of the past.

Wildlife

Wyoming's wildlife is as varied as that of any state in the nation, largely due to the different elevations and climates found within its borders.

Hunters find Wyoming a paradise filled with big game. Mule deer, white-tailed deer, elk, Rocky Mountain sheep, antelope, moose, and bear are found in abundance. Sportsmen also hunt pheasant, turkey, sage grouse, many varieties of duck, and geese during small game season.

Many other forms of wildlife are present also. Visitors to the state might see jack rabbits, cottontails, prairie dogs, ground squirrels, gophers, coyotes, bobcats, mountain lions, muskrats, porcupines, skunks, and many predatory birds such as eagles, hawks and falcons.

Several varieties of trout swim in the streams and river, and perch, walleye, bass, and other species are found in lakes and reservoirs. Depending on elevation, many different kinds of reptiles and amphibians are present, the most notorious of which is the rattlesnake.

Several forms of wildlife have played an important role in Wyoming's history. In the 1820s and 1830s the beaver brought the first people other than Indians into Wyoming. These early trappers hunted beaver for profit. The buffalo or North American bison was the mainstay of life for the Plains Indians for hundreds of years. Later, buffalo provided food for workers during the building of the transcontinental railroad. Because of the lack of concern for the buffalo, it was nearly exterminated in the late 1800s, but fortunately the buffalo was saved and now thrives in Wyoming. Today thousands of buffalo graze across the state at many public and private reserves.

2
Early Hunters in Wyoming

First People in Wyoming

The history of humans living in Wyoming begins somewhere between ten thousand and twenty thousands years ago. Most scientists believe people entered North America by crossing between Alaska and Asia during the last Ice Age when the Bering Strait was dry land. These people were hunters of big game animals such as the mammoths, giant sloths, horses, camels, mastodons, and prehistoric bison. As nomads, they were following these animals as they crossed into North America. The people then wandered south into what is now the United States but did not stay long and passed on into Central and South America.

The relatively few archeological finds that pre-date 10,000 B.C. make it nearly impossible to say when humans first became permanent residents in Wyoming. We do know that they lived in the area around Greybull twelve thousand years ago and trapped and then slaughtered over one hundred head of bison near present Casper about ten thousand years ago. Some early people mined quartzite and other minerals for their tools at the "Spanish Diggings" near Guernsey, beginning about ten thousand years ago. Other hunters butchered six immature mammoths near Worland 11,200 years ago. And we know that people were living west of the present site of Cody over nine thousand years ago.

Around 5,000 B.C. the climate changed, and Wyoming gradually became a desert. The large animals left, followed by most of the people who hunted them. For the next two thousand years Wyoming was virtually without humans.

Early Buffalo Hunters

About 2,500 years ago the climate changed somewhat, and small animals and some sparse vegetation returned. A few people returned and struggled to survive on what they could find to eat. By about 500 A.D. the climate had improved enough to support the North American bison. So from then to the late 1800s, people living in Wyoming followed and hunted the buffalo herds.

During this period the lives of Wyoming's natives began to improve. They tamed the dog and used it as a beast of burden to pull travois and haul light loads while the bands of hunters followed the buffalo herds. Approximately seven hundred years ago, the bow and arrow came into use, improving the hunter's ability to kill game. Finally, Wyoming's natives tamed horses, descended from animals brought to North America by the Spaniards. By the early 1700s, Wyoming natives were expert horsemen.

The Medicine Wheel

From the period after 1500 A.D., there are many archeological remains left by early inhabitants. Probably the most notable is the Medicine Wheel

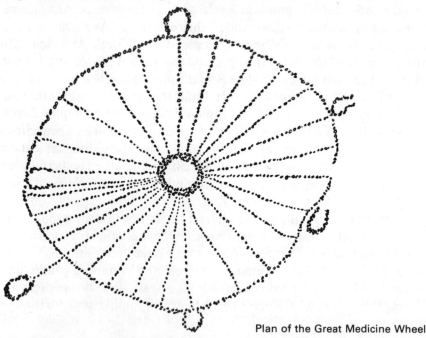

Plan of the Great Medicine Wheel

located at 12,000 feet on Medicine Bow Mountain in the Big Horn Mountains. The wheel is a circle of stones approximately seventy-five feet in diameter. Twenty-eight stone spokes radiate from the central "cairn" to the edge.

No one knows the meaning of the Medicine Wheel, though many historians and archeologists think that it has some astronomical significance and was therefore used as a primitive calendar. Research done by the University of Wyoming has shown that the wheel is probably not more than 250 years old, though the central cairn may be a bit older. Pottery shards found in the area indicate that the wheel was probably built by the Shoshone or the Crow Indians.

Nearby, at Meeteetse, is the Great Arrow. Made of stones, the sixty-foot arrow points northeast toward the Medicine Wheel, a hundred miles away.

Tribes Form in Wyoming

By the time trappers and traders began to enter Wyoming at the beginning of the nineteenth century, probably fewer than twelve thousand Indians were living in Wyoming. To the east, on the Great Plains, the climate was more favorable, making buffalo more plentiful. Therefore most Indians on the northern plains lived east of what is now Wyoming. The intertribal warfare which was very typical of Wyoming Indians also helped keep the number of inhabitants low.

In the 1700s, most of Wyoming was claimed by the Shoshone tribe. The Crows lived in the Big Horn Mountains and on the plains to the east. Beginning in the mid-1700s the Arapahoes and the Cheyennes challenged the Crows for their hunting grounds. It would not be until the 1830s that the Ogallala and the Brule Sioux were invited in from Dakota Territory to trade and hunt. Together, the Cheyennes, Arapahoes, and Sioux would drive the Crows and Shoshones to the west into the mountains and would occupy the plains area of what is now eastern Wyoming.

Tribal Culture

The Wyoming tribes all shared a common culture. Their tribal names usually came from other tribes and languages. For example, the Cheyennes called themselves *tsis tsistas*, meaning "The People." The Minnesota Sioux, unable to understand the Cheyenne language, called them *Sha hi ye na*, which means "speakers of an unintelligible language." When the

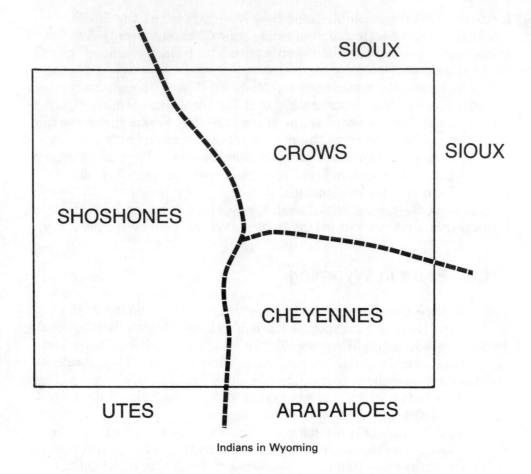

Indians in Wyoming

French heard the Sioux name for "The People," they pronounced it "Cheyenne."

Regardless of tribal names, the buffalo was the most important game animal to all Plains Indians. The animal provided not only food, but tools from the bones, and shelter and clothing from the hides. The early Plains Indians hunted buffalo on foot, but by 1870, they had acquired the horse. This made hunting easier. The hunters could mass the animals in a spiral moving to the center. Confused stragglers could then be cut out of the herd and killed by lance or arrow.

Each summer every plains tribe met for a huge hunt and tribal ceremony that united bands that had not gathered during the winter months. Following the hunts, the buffalo meat was cut into thin strips and hung up to dry. This was called jerking, and the staple food became "jerky."

The nomadic Arapahoes, Cheyennes, Crows, Bannocks, and others lived in skin lodges which could be put up quickly using tall pine poles and between six and twenty-eight buffalo hides. A fire was built in the center for warmth, but cooking was usually done outside. An opening in the top of the lodge allowed smoke to escape in the winter and created a cool updraft in the summer when the sides of the tipi were raised.

Groups of warriors formed within each band of Indians. The "contraries," for example, who said "yes" when they meant "no," were one of the Cheyennes' most powerful societies because these warriors were supposed to have magical powers.

But life was not all hunting and warfare for the Wyoming Indian tribes. Many games kept children and adults busy during times of peace. Sliding on a buffalo rib, rawhide-covered toboggan was fun in the winter. Top-spinning and a form of "football" played by girls only amused young and old alike. The children even played house using a small calf-skin tipi. This pastime was taken seriously when boys and girls turned ten years old. At that time, the children were approaching adulthood and marriage, so the game provided training.

Marriage customs of the plains tribes were very different from those of today. A young man usually "courted" the woman's parents and other relatives rather than the prospective bride. He even proposed to her parents rather than to her. The actual marriage was simple, usually the exchanging of gifts. The "groom" gave the woman's family horses, beadwork, or other goods in return for the bride.

Each tribe held firm beliefs about life after death, and these beliefs affected the way they lived. The Cheyennes, for example, believed that all the dead would go to the same afterworld. Heaven was in the sky, reached by following the "Hanging Road," what we call the Milky Way. Life after death was like life on earth except that the dead were shadows. When Indians first made contact with the camera, they were terrified since they thought the picture was really the soul of the photographed person. This also explains their early fear of mirrors, which they thought showed the soul of the individual.

Ironically, the white man made the Plains Indian "heyday" possible for a century. With the Spaniards' horses, the tribes achieved a mobility and hunting ability unsurpassed up to that time. Yet when white culture brought different values and vast changes the dominance of the Plains Indian came to a bloody end as we shall see in later chapters.

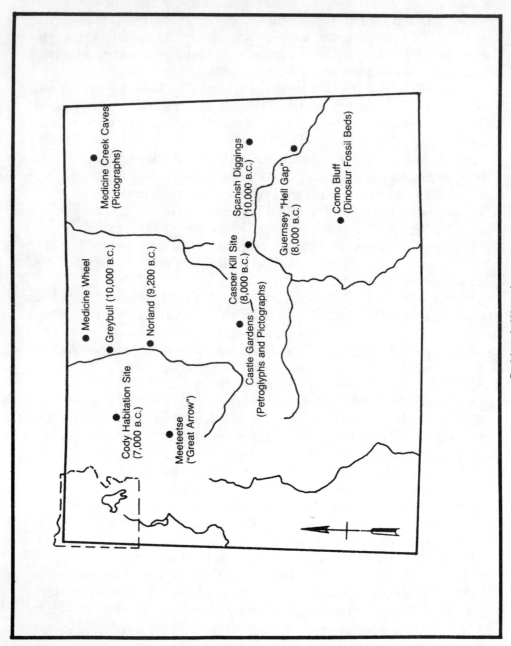

Medicine Creek Caves
(Pictographs)

Spanish Diggings
(10,000 B.C.)

Como Bluff
(Dinosaur Fossil Beds)

Guernsey "Hell Gap"
(8,000 B.C.)

Medicine Wheel

Greybull (10,000 B.C.)

Norland (9,200 B.C.)

Casper Kill Site
(8,000 B.C.)

Castle Gardens
(Petroglyphs and Pictographs)

Cody Habitation Site
(7,000 B.C.)

Meeteetse
("Great Arrow")

Prehistoric Wyoming

3

The Fur Trade

When Lewis and Clark returned from their famous expedition in 1806, they brought back tales of an abundance of wild animals found out west. Fashionable coats, hats, shoes, and other pieces of clothing were made from beaver, fox, and bear pelts. Since Wyoming was rich in such game, our earliest economy was based almost entirely on the fur trade that resulted from early exploration.

LaVerendrye—First Explorer

No one will ever know for certain which white men first entered Wyoming. Possibly they were Spaniards in their relentless search of the golden city of Cibola who marched into the unmapped territory of southeastern Wyoming.

Indeed, by the 1700s word had spread among the Canadian fur trappers of the mysterious white men who lived at the foot of "the mountains." These "iron-covered" men marched on horseback and could not be killed by arrow or musket, the Assiniboin Indians of Montana reported.

But any such Spanish visitors made no permanent settlements nor left any records of their explorations. The French would be the first to actually write about a trip to what is now Wyoming.

On July 20, 1738, six canoes carrying twenty-three men cut through the waters of Lake Superior on an expedition west. Lieutenant LaVerendrye, a company commander of the Canadian marines of New France, and his brother led the explorers. His job was to find a route across the continent to the "Western Sea" (Pacific Ocean).

LaVerendrye headed northwest to the Lake of the Woods, then west to what is now Winnipeg. Living off the land, often with friendly Indians such as the Crees and Assiniboins, LaVerendrye pieced together a route to the ocean. On Indian advice, he traveled southwest after leaving Winnipeg.

Several Frenchmen and Indians joined the explorers, and when LaVerendrye finally entered a Mandan Indian camp in what is now North Dakota, fifty-two accompanied him.

LaVerendrye spent part of the winter of 1738 in the earth lodges of the Mandans on the banks of the Missouri River. From visiting tribes he heard of distant rivers where sulfurous water flowed from "brackish . . . marshes and ponds." This might well have been the first word of Yellowstone.

In late December LaVerendrye set out west again, reaching the first "mountain" by January 9, 1739. At this point, LaVerendrye's party was in Wyoming, probably near the Big Horn Mountains. Surviving on moose and deer, the members of the expedition spent a miserable spring. LaVerendrye wrote, "I don't know how God preserves us."

LaVerendrye does not make clear in his journal what his direction was after summer finally arrived, but he does say that in midsummer he found a river flowing to the west rather than the east. This could mean that he crossed the Continental Divide before being warned not to enter western Indian territory.

Lewis and Clark Head West

Following the appearance of the LaVerendryes in Wyoming, nearly seventy years passed before anyone other than Indians entered the state.

But in 1803 President Thomas Jefferson concluded a deal with Napoleon Bonaparte in which the United States bought all of Louisiana Territory, including two thirds of Wyoming, for fifteen million dollars. Jefferson ordered Meriwether Lewis and William Clark to explore the territory and in doing so find a route to the Pacific.

Lewis and Clark hired John Colter on October 15, 1803, as a private in the expedition for a fee of $5.00 per month. Thomas James, a trapper and trader, said of Colter, "His character was that of a true American backwoodsman. His veracity was never questioned among us . . . . Danger had for him a kind of fascination."

The expedition started up the Missouri River from St. Louis on May 14, 1804. Over the next two years, Lewis and Clark traveled the Missouri River through the Dakotas and Montana and across the Continental Divide to the Columbia River and eventually to the Pacific Ocean. They were aided through this completely unexplored territory by "The Bird Woman," Sacajawea.

Colter Leaves the Expedition

On the return trip in August 1806, John Colter asked to be discharged from the expedition. Lewis and Clark reluctantly agreed. Colter soon joined with the fur trader Manuel Lisa and returned to the Yellowstone country.

In November 1807 Lisa established Fort Raymond (Manuel's Fort) at the junction of the Yellowstone and Big Horn Rivers and immediately sent Colter on a mission. Colter was to locate regions for trapping beaver and acquaint himself with the Indians, convincing them to come to the post and barter their furs. On this 500-mile mission, Colter made his historic discoveries. He kept no journal but described his route to Captain William Clark, who later published Colter's maps.

Colter Explores Wyoming

Colter followed the Big Horn River to the present site of Cody where he observed thermal activity (Colter's Hell). He then continued south along the south fork of the Shoshone River and crossed to the Wind River and the Buffalo River before entering the Jackson Hole area.

He then crossed into what is now Idaho over Teton Pass, traveled north, and then cut back into the Yellowstone Park area. He undoubtedly saw the West Thumb area of Yellowstone Lake and at least some of the thermal activity in the area. He also saw the Grand Canyon of the Yellowstone, Yellowstone Falls, and probably Tower Falls.

Colter then cut back to the east, eventually returning to Fort Raymond by way of the east fork of the Yellowstone and the Great Indian Trail.

By traveling this route, Colter earned the credit for being the first white man in the Yellowstone Park, Jackson Hole, and Big Horn Basin areas of Wyoming. Historian Hiram Chittenden explains the magnificence of this trip: "This remarkable achievement is due to the courage and hardihood of this lone adventurer and remarkable in its unexpected results in geographical discovery deserves to be classed among the most celebrated performances in the history of American exploration. Colter had now accomplished enough to entitle him to lasting distinction."

Run for Life

Colter's explorations of northwestern Wyoming made him an important historical figure as an explorer, but another incident has possibly gained him wider fame as a brave and courageous conqueror of the wilderness.

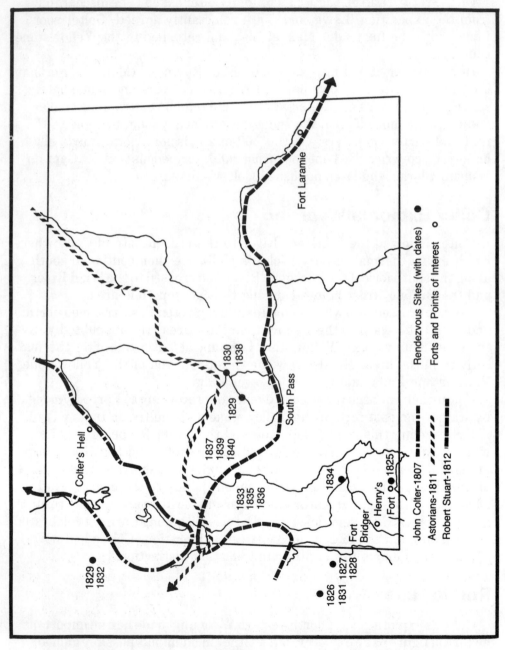

The Fur Trade in Wyoming

Rendezvous Sites (with dates) ●

Forts and Points of Interest ○

John Colter–1807

Astorians–1811

Robert Stuart–1812

Fort Laramie

South Pass

1830
1838

1829

1837
1839
1840

Colter's Hell

1833
1835
1836

1834

Fort
Bridger

Henry's
Fort 1825

1829
1832

1826 1827
1831 1828

In 1808 Colter was traveling the Three Forks of the Missouri area north of Yellowstone with another trapper, John Potts. Suddenly, Blackfeet Indians surrounded the trappers. Potts attempted to escape and was immediately, in Colter's words, "made a riddle of" by Blackfeet arrows.

Colter was captured but given a chance to save his own life. He was stripped naked, given several hundred yards head start, and allowed to run for his life. He quickly outdistanced all but one man whom he managed to "dispatch." He then ducked into a beaver dam and hid while the rest of the pursuers searched for him.

The next day, he continued his escape. He swam downstream as far as he could and then started overland, covering the three hundred miles back to Lisa's Fort Raymond in ten days, living on roots he found along the way.

Shortly thereafter, Colter vowed that if he survived in the mountains this time, he would leave and never return. True to his word, Colter left the mountains and in 1810 married a girl named Sally and settled on a farm in Missouri. He died of a liver ailment in 1813 at about thirty-five years of age.

Astor Forms Fur Company

Two years after Colter's escape, German-born businessman John Jacob Astor decided to take a chance on building a western fur trade. In 1810 he formed the Pacific Fur Company.

Managing the firm in New York, he furnished ships, goods, and ammunition for the establishment of a company headquarters on the Pacific Ocean. The headquarters would be set up at the mouth of the Columbia River in Oregon, an area rich in furs.

Astor planned two expeditions to Oregon. Wilson Price Hunt, one of his partners, was to head overland to Oregon. Meanwhile, a ship named the *Tonquin* was to sail around South America and meet the Hunt party in Oregon. The ship arrived at the Columbia River first, in April 1811, and Astoria, the company headquarters, was built.

The Hunt party, known as the "Astorians," left Macinac, Michigan in August 1810 and pushed southwest to St. Louis. At the raw, bustling frontier town, they bought supplies and made plans. Fur trappers, paid $300 each, joined the party. Knowing it would be expensive staying in St. Louis for the winter, Hunt moved his men up the Missouri River 450 miles, camping in an area rich in game.

Astorians Enter Wyoming

In spring the party broke camp and followed the Missouri and then the Yellowstone rivers. Hunt entered northeastern Wyoming near the Big Horn Mountains in late summer and struggled to find a way to cross the rugged range. Only after a desperate search did he locate an opening. Climbing to the top of a ridge with his partner, Mr. McKenzie, Hunt saw a vast plain below "dotted with innumerable head of buffalo."

Descending into the Big Horn Basin, they found plenty of food. But danger was always present. Many grizzlies lurked along the trail. More than once Hunt recorded encounters with them, such as the time John Day, a Kentucky hunter, and a young companion met up with a bear while hunting. Three times it reared up as if to attack and then strangely retreated while the men remained motionless. Finally the nervous companion fired his gun, wounding the animal. Luckily, the bear staggered back into the brush. Day scolded the younger man for being reckless because a wounded grizzly can truly be a "bully."

As they headed west water became scarce, and the buffalo disappeared. Miserable, the men continued until a group of Crow warriors galloped into their camp and invited the white men to visit their chief. A group of hide "tents" pitched in a meadow bordering a stream formed the Crow camp. Numerous horses grazed in the distance. The Crows were friendly, and the Hunt party enjoyed their hospitality for several days.

Continuing into the Wind River country, the Astorians met Shoshone and Flathead Indians. The Shoshones, Hunt recalled, were "bolder in spirit and more open and wider in their wanderings than the other Indians" he had met. They directed the travelers north.

In early fall the Astorians stood before the "remarkable" Tetons, which Hunt named the "Pilot Knobs." Just over the Tetons the party was cheered by the sight of the headwaters of the Columbia River, which they could follow to Astoria.

The Astorians finally arrived in Astoria in early January 1812. After wandering 3,500 miles they were greeted by a feast of fish, beaver, and venison complete with grog and "a grand dance that night."

Stuart Returns East

In summer it became necessary to send messages back to Astor in New York. Young, inexperienced Robert Stuart, who had sailed on the *Tonquin* to Oregon a year earlier, headed the new expedition of sixty men, two barges, and ten canoes heading east.

Retracing Hunt's route, the Stuart party stood before the Tetons looking east on October 1, 1812. As the travelers neared Wyoming, they found game in sudden abundance. One hunter, Ben Jones, killed five elk in only a few hours. Jones also ran into a grizzly but could only wound it.

Crossing the Tetons was difficult because nine inches of snow covered the path and made the mountains treacherously slippery. The elk meat dwindled and hunger began to take its toll. As they dropped into the valley, the men expected to find numerous buffalo. Instead they found the lake and river banks deserted.

After traveling for several days, Stuart spotted smoke. Hoping for an Indian camp, he sent a Canadian, LeClerc, to investigate. But the trapper returned with bad news. The smoke came from a blazing cabin. Hurrying to the site, the Astorians found a trapper named McLellan, near starvation. LeClerc, knowing now that no food was to be found, suggested they kill and eat one of their own party so the others would not starve.

Stuart and LeClerc argued. Finally Stuart threatened to shoot the Canadian if he did not withdraw the suggestion of cannibalism. LeClerc gave in, obviously not wanting to be the first item on the menu. Hungrily, the party pushed slowly east.

Buffalo skeletons were scattered far and wide, and no sign of life could be found until an "old, run-down bull" staggered before the group. Instantly the beast was "dispatched," roasted and eaten—so quickly that Stuart feared his men would eat too much too soon and become sick.

Crossing South Pass

Following Indian trails, Stuart's party moved south by east. On October 21, 1812, the men trudged across South Pass as snow spattered the area. This gentle split in the Rocky Mountains located in southwestern Wyoming would become the most convenient spot for future travelers to cross the Continental Divide. Although others may have crossed it before, Stuart is given credit for discovering South Pass.

Wintering in Wyoming

The Astorians now picked up the Sweetwater River and followed it east to the North Platte. They decided to camp near present-day Casper when severe weather hampered travel. As a shelter they built a buffalo skin "wigwam." Sitting around the fire in the evenings, Stuart and his men decided to float down the Platte in the spring.

But five weeks later they heard Indian warriors shouting. Arapahoes, painted in "warlike style," were spotted among trees surrounding the camp. Stuart invited the chief and one other Indian into the wigwam. The guests eyed the venison and buffalo meat hanging from the rafters. Being hospitable, Stuart gave them some meat, which they devoured. The Indians then asked for ammunition and promised Stuart horses in return. Stuart told them they would have the ammunition only when the horses were delivered. The Indians left, promising to be back in two weeks.

Sensing trouble, Stuart led his party farther down the Platte. They found themselves on the deserted plains of eastern Wyoming, which were blanketed with fifteen inches of snow. Food and fuel became scarce, but finally, near present-day Torrington, Stuart found a heavily wooded area where herds of buffalo could be seen at a distance.

A second wigwam was completed there on New Year's Day. The men spent the rest of the winter in peace and plenty.

On March 20 they broke camp and followed the Platte to the Missouri. They arrived in St. Louis on April 30, 1813. Stuart and the Astorians had unknowingly been the first whites to travel along the Oregon Trail, which would later become the great highway west.

Jacques LaRamee

During the next decade, however, fewer than fifty white men entered Wyoming. One of the early arrivals was Jacques LaRamee. Little information is available on LaRamee except that he was probably killed by Arapahoes somewhere on the Laramie River in 1820. He will always be associated with early Wyoming because a fort, mountain range, city, county, and town all bear his name.

Ashley Hires Trappers

In 1822 William Ashley emerged as the dominant force in establishing the fur trade in Wyoming. Forty-year-old Ashley had been a miner, surveyor, trader, land speculator, and a manufacturer of gunpowder. A militia captain in the War of 1812, he had been promoted to the rank of brigadier general.

Jim Bridger (University of Wyoming)

In 1822 an advertisement appeared in the *Missouri Gazette* asking for "100 enterprising young men" to ascend the Missouri River and trap for beaver. Ashley and his partner, Andrew Henry, obtained licenses to trap the upper part of the great muddy river. Henry set off in 1822 with two keelboats for the Yellowstone River. Among the "enterprising young men" were Milton Sublette, Hugh Glass, Jim Bridger, Jed Smith, Tom Fitzpatrick, and Jim Clyman.

Trappers Face Problems

Henry himself led the trappers up the muddy Missouri. Near Fort Osage they lost one of the boats and nearly $10,000 worth of supplies in the rugged waters. Later they were tricked out of half their horses by the Arikaras of North Dakota. Fearing the fierce Blackfeet, who eventually attacked the trappers in the spring, Henry left the Missouri and moved his men south into Wyoming that fall.

Henry broke his men into groups. His party traveled south to the Green River where he built "Henry's Fort." This small outpost became one of the first inland trading posts west of the Continental Divide.

Jed Smith led a party through the Big Horns and down through the Wind River Range to excellent beaver grounds along the Green River.

Fitzpatrick and Clyman trapped along the North Platte, and then they too found success in the Green River Valley. They returned to the Platte in 1824.

Smith and Glass Spar with Grizzlies

During these early expeditions the famous fights of Hugh Glass and Jed Smith took place. At different times and places, both famous mountain men had life and death struggles with grizzly bears.

In 1823 Hugh Glass was so badly mauled that he could not travel. His companions, positive that he would die, left nineteen-year-old Jim Bridger and another man to stay with him until he died and then bury him. Fearing for their lives, the two abandoned Glass to rejoin the party. Glass regained consciousness and somehow, probably out of anger, managed to crawl over a hundred miles to a fort where he received medical attention.

Jed Smith's encounter with the grizzly left him badly mauled about the head. His scalp was nearly torn off from his left eyebrow across to his right ear. Smith, still conscious, directed his companion Jim Clyman, to get a needle and thread and "sew him up." Clyman carried out Smith's instructions and Smith survived.

These two incidents give some appreciation for the tough qualities that were necessary to be a mountain man in Wyoming in the early 1800s.

First Rendezvous—1825

Ashley and Jed Smith led the second party of trappers from St. Louis in the spring of 1823. Along the way they were attacked by a fierce band of Arikaras. Fourteen men were killed and forty-seven injured in the ambush.

Undaunted, Ashley directed his men to meet in July of 1825 in order to pool their furs and get supplies for the next year's trapping. He chose Henry's Fort on the Green River for the meeting.

This meeting was the first "Rendezvous," a French word meaning a "get-together at a pre-planned place."

Rendezvous (Fort Laramie)

The Rendezvous System

The rendezvous system worked like this. Each summer there would be a meeting somewhere in the mountains. The site and date would be arranged at the previous year's rendezvous. At the meeting, the trappers, who had been living in the mountains, would bring their bundles of beaver skins to trade for goods brought by Ashley and Henry.

The skins were exchanged for supplies at a rate of $5 to $8 per skin. The trading would usually take from one to two days. The rest of the time would be spent drinking, gambling, fighting, dueling, racing, and in any other form of entertainment the company-starved men could think of.

The rendezvous would last anywhere from a week to a month. At the end of this time, the trappers would have been traded out of their skins and, after having been drunk, most of their possessions as well.

Battle of Pierre's Hole

Trappers were often notoriously bad decision makers. They fought when they should have talked, fled when they should have fought, and lied when they should have told the truth. The battle of Pierre's Hole stands as an example of the mountain man's attitude toward himself and his Indian friends.

The 1832 rendezvous had begun, and on July 17, approximately seven miles from the site just west of the Tetons, a party of trappers led by Milton Sublette encountered one hundred and fifty Gros Ventre Indians, mortal enemies of the trappers.

Sublette asked for a parley (meeting) and sent Antoine Godin and a Flathead warrior as his representatives. Instead of the hand of friendship, Godin ordered the Flathead to shoot the Gros Ventre negotiator.

Both sides dug in as a fight began. The trappers were quickly reinforced by two hundred more mountain men and five hundred Flatheads from the rendezvous, outnumbering the Gros Ventres seven to one. As night fell, the fighting stopped.

Under cover of darkness, the Gros Ventres slipped away after frightening the trappers with the promise that six to eight hundred reinforcements would be arriving during the night.

After the battle estimates placed the casualties at twenty-six Gros Ventres killed and thirty-two trappers and Flatheads killed. In a later fight with the Gros Ventres, mountain man Jim Bridger was wounded. He carried a barbed arrowhead in his back from this fight until Dr. Marcus Whitman cut it out in 1835.

Profits Soar

Most of the fifteen rendezvous were spent in remarkable peace, however. Ashley and Henry, as well as others who ran trading companies after them, made a good deal of money from this type of operation. On the first rendezvous alone, Ashley made $50,000.

After only two years, Ashley and Henry sold their business, having made enough money to retire from the fur trade forever as rich men. Ashley eventually served as a member of the United States House of Representatives from 1831 to 1837, where his experience in the West was valued by other members.

Fur Trade Declines

The rendezvous system began a gradual decline in the mid-1830s, mainly because of the dwindling supply of beaver. As early as 1826, Ashley warned the trappers not to overtrap any area or they would destroy the beaver. His prediction proved correct. With fewer beaver pelts to be had, the trappers' profits declined. At the same time, the demand for beaver pelts declined. Most had been used to make hats, but fashion changed, and men began to prefer silk hats.

A new approach to the fur trade system also began in the 1830s. The idea of building a fort that would be open year round for trading instead of once a year began to attract attention.

In 1834 William Sublette built a fur trading post, in part financed by Robert Campbell, at the junction of the Laramie and North Platte Rivers. The fort was named Fort William after Sublette. In 1835 Campbell and Sublette sold the fort to Jim Bridger, Thomas Fitzpatrick, and Milton Sublette, and a year later these men sold out to the American Fur Company.

Forts Replace Rendezvous

The forts were more efficient than rendezvous for several reasons. First, forts such as Fort William were built at sites which were midway between St. Louis and the fur trapping areas. Therefore the distance traveled to bring supplies was shorter and much less hazardous. Second, the forts

Fort William (Fort Laramie)

were open year round, and the mountain man who needed supplies did not have to wait an entire year. Third, the forts served as a place of protection from the dangers of the wilderness, a place where a trapper might be able to return to some semblance of civilization.

With the success of Fort William and Fort Bridger, the rendezvous system gradually dwindled until the final rendezvous was held in 1840.

When the rendezvous system ended, so did the era of the mountain man. Most trappers either became guides for emigrant parties, ran trading posts, served as army scouts against the Indians, or left the West forever. They were a colorful group of men, and although they dominated the scene for only thirty to forty years, they contributed greatly to our knowledge of the West and of Wyoming in particular.

Jim Baker (University of Wyoming)

Joe Meek (University of Wyoming)

4
Trails Through Wyoming

Important Discovery

During the Fur Trade period from 1810 to 1840, the mountain men learned much about Wyoming.

They learned about the wildlife of our state. They saw millions of buffalo roaming north and south, followed by the nomadic Plains Indians on the hunt.

They learned of resources hidden among the majestic natural features: coal, iron, copper, and other minerals; precious water in lakes and streams; timber; clean air; and magnificent views.

But the most important thing they learned was the location of a route through the Rockies that was passable not only by a man on foot or horseback but also by wagon. This route crossed South Pass, where at 7,550 feet above sea level, the crossing of the Continental Divide is barely noticeable. South Pass made it possible for pioneers searching for a better life to cross the continent, thus helping Wyoming grow during the middle of the nineteenth century.

Fremont Sent to Study Wyoming

The government was very interested in this vast new territory, but little was actually known about it in Washington. To learn more about the possibilities of overland travel to the West Coast, John C. Fremont, an officer in the corps of topographical engineers, was ordered to explore and report on the "country between the frontiers of the Missouri and

South Pass in the Rocky Mountains." He was to study and map the trail to and through Wyoming.

Fremont and a party of twenty-one men, including several Canadian trappers, left St. Louis on May 22, 1842, on the first scientific expedition across Wyoming. Carrying weather equipment and mapmaking devices, Fremont was determined to learn all he could about the weather, terrain, and wildlife of the new territory. This way people other than mountain men and courageous explorers could use the road west.

Along the way Fremont hired new adventurers. Charles Preuss, a member of the party, joked on June 28 as the group approached Wyoming, "Have just heard . . . Fremont hired on the men we met yesterday . . . we are now twenty-eight head, including two stupid boys who really have none [i.e., heads]."

Troubles with the Indians

On July 8 Fremont met with trappers led by Jim Bridger. "They tell stories about the Sioux," Preuss wrote, "who are said to hide out above Fort Laramie to waylay white travelers."

Fremont arrived at Fort Laramie at 4:00 P.M. on July 13. "We were cordially received," he recalled later, "We pitched our camp a little above the Fort on the bank of the Laramie River." He described the Fort as a "quadrangle structure" made of clay. The walls were fifteen feet high. On top was a wooden walkway called a "palisade." There were two entrances, and on two corners were lookout towers called "bastions."

At the fort Fremont learned that the Cheyennes and Sioux had become angry at the number of white men entering their territory. Since there had been several outbreaks of violence west of Fort Laramie, Fremont recommended in his report that the U.S. Army take over the fort to offer protection to travelers on the trail. But with no protection for his own party, Fremont continued his expedition west.

Less than a hundred miles from Fort Laramie, Fremont met a Sioux war party near Laramie Peak. The meeting was peaceful because, as Fremont put it, "the Sioux couldn't decide to attack the wagon train."

Near Casper Fremont ran into a second party of Indians, but this band was different. They were starving because a grasshopper plague had driven the buffalo from their land. They wanted mules and horses for food.

Supplies Dwindle as Terrain Rises

By August 1 Fremont's party rested at Independence Rock. A week later they had reached South Pass. But spirits were low. The grasshopper plague had indeed scattered the buffalo Fremont had hoped to use as food. Only old jerky, "hard as wood and tasting like bark" kept the men going. A small cache of "maccaroni [sic]" and coffee sustained the men as they climbed through the Wind River Range.

Fremont scaled a mountain later named after him, thinking it was the tallest. But it was not. Gannett Peak, towering a few miles away is actually Wyoming's tallest point.

By August 15 Fremont had reached the "Trois Teton," then began a return trip that retraced his own steps. The grass had grown back now, and the buffalo were returning, so the trip back was uneventful. Fremont and his men compiled accurate weather data and elaborate reports on the wildlife and plant life along the Oregon Trail. They even used a rubber boat to float down the Platte—the first recorded tubing of a Wyoming river.

When he returned to Washington, Fremont wrote a book with the help of his wife about his travels west and presented all his scientific data. This lengthy, interesting, and thorough report became popular reading. And his practical advice on how to travel west would help many a pioneer over the new trail.

Importance of South Pass

Within twenty-five years of the announcement of South Pass by Ashley's men in 1825, the number of people crossing grew from a trickle to over 50,000 "emigrants" a year. Though crossings could be made elsewhere, the journey would necessarily have been more difficult and far longer, so most pioneers trekked westward over Robert Stuart's trail along the Platte to the Sweetwater River and over South Pass.

The first wheeled vehicle over the pass was a two-wheeled cannon pulled by Ashley's men to a rendezvous in 1827. William Sublette took the first wagons to carry trade goods to the 1830 rendezvous site. The first wagon train to cross the pass was Captain Bonneville's expedition in 1832. And the first women to cross South Pass arrived on the summit in 1836. By the 1840s the numbers increased dramatically.

Oregon Holds Promise

Where were all the people who traveled over South Pass going? Most were going to the West Coast. Some headed to the Willamette Valley in Oregon Territory where rich soil, plentiful moisture, and lush crops were

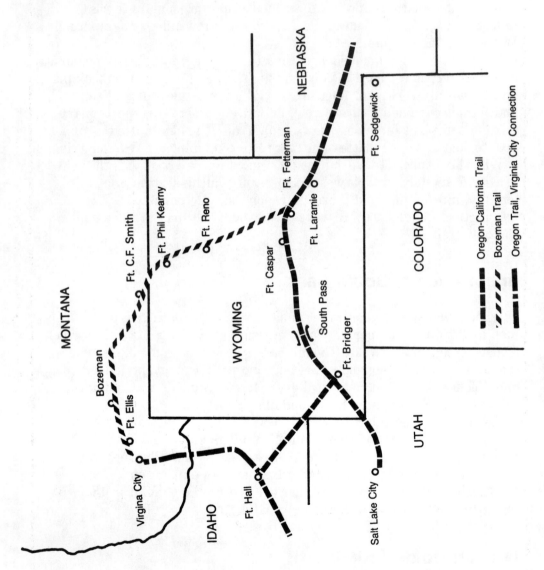

Forts and trails in Wyoming

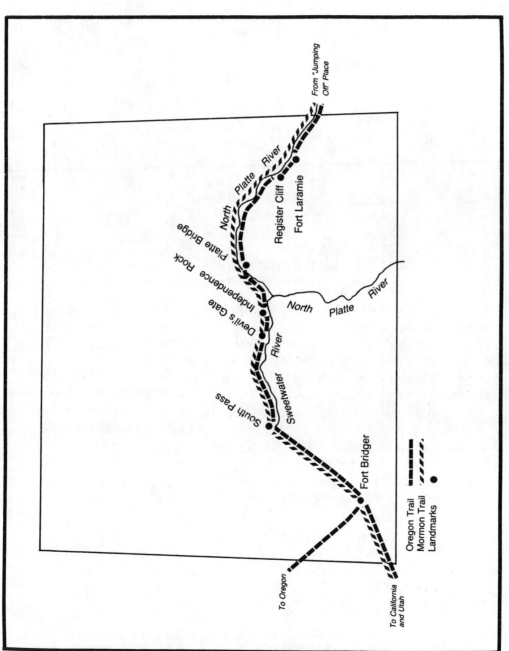

Emigrant trails through Wyoming

Trappers crossing South Pass (Fort Laramie)

promised. Said one pioneer of the valley, "Oregon is a pioneer's paradise, where the pigs are running around under the great acorn trees, round and fat, and already cooked, with knives and forks sticking out of them so you can cut off a slice whenever you're hungry!"

Some pioneers were heading to California where visitors to the Spanish territory had long bragged about the perpetually sunny climate. No one, it seemed, ever got sick in California. One trapper even joked, "But one man in California ever got a chill there, and that was such a matter of wonderment that folks went thirteen miles into the country just to see him shake."

It seemed to the troubled Easterners that land on the west coast of North America was warm, sunny, rich, and wonderful—literally, a paradise for the taking.

Even with such glowing reports exciting people's imaginations, a journey of two thousand miles across unknown territory filled with danger seemed foolhardy. Yet families sold everything they had and headed west.

Manifest Destiny

There were many reasons why people were willing to leave the civilized East and head west in the 1840s, 1850s, and 1860s. The first was a combination of feelings which stir nearly all people at one time or another in their lives. The spirit of adventure, combined with the hunger for free land was enough to make the young, untied, and restless head out with nothing to lose and everything to gain.

The national feeling of "Manifest Destiny" also became a strong force in the westward movement. "Manifest Destiny" was the belief that the United States was destined to govern all land from the Atlantic to the Pacific Ocean.

Hard Times in the East

But the remaining reasons were not nearly so romantic. Life in the so-called "Civilized East" had its problems in the mid-nineteenth century.

Following the presidency of Andrew Jackson, a financial panic spread throughout the East in 1837. It was the result of poor banking management and speculation in public lands. A depression enveloped the nation, resulting in poor agricultural prices. Literally thousands of people lost their savings, their farms, their businesses, their livelihoods. To these, the dangerous trip through the Rockies seemed worth the risk.

Another reason for migration was a series of epidemics. These quick-spreading diseases killed thousands of people, particularly in the large cities of the East. More people, for example, died of typhoid, dysentary, tuberculosis, scarlet fever, and malaria than from any other cause. Each of these diseases spreads quickly in any heavily populated area. In the towns along the Mississippi River Valley, yellow fever caused the death rate to exceed the birth rate. Beginning in 1830, cholera came to be a killer, causing 30,000 deaths a year by 1850. The clean, pure air of California and Oregon was an easy alternative to dying of disease.

Move Against Slavery

Beginning in the early 1800s, many people, particularly Northerners became sickened by legalized slavery practiced in the United States. Those who wanted slavery stamped out were called "abolitionists." Many abolitionists preferred to pull up stakes and head for a new land where slavery was not practiced.

Early Missionaries Head West

Some left the East for religious reasons. In fact, some of the first travelers in the state were missionaries on their way to establish churches, hospitals, and schools in Oregon and the far west.

Jason Lee, a thirty year old Methodist minister, and his nephew, Daniel, crossed Wyoming in the summer of 1834. The Methodist Board of Missions had ordered the Lees to Oregon to work with the "brutish Flatheads." Lee, who finally settled in the Willamette Valley, helped lure emigrants to Oregon with his reports of rich, abundant farmland.

Marcus Whitman Attends a Rendezvous

That same year the likable, strong-willed Dr. Marcus Whitman from New York asked the American Board of Missionaries to let him go to Oregon as a doctor and teacher. The board agreed to have Whitman and Reverend Samuel Parker head west to decide how suitable Oregon would be for mission work. They joined Tom Fitzpatrick's pack train bound for the 1835 rendezvous.

When Whitman and Parker arrived at Horse Creek, they found themselves out of place among the rough, hard-drinking trappers and traders. But soon Whitman met young Jim Bridger, who had an arrowhead lodged in his back. Though Bridger managed with the injury, it caused him some pain. Being a doctor, Whitman removed the arrow in an open-air operation much to Bridger's pleasure. This established Whitman's reputation as "a great medicine man" among the mountain men and Indians alike.

Although he had not made it to Oregon, Whitman left Parker when the rendezvous ended and returned to the East. There he asked Narcissa Prentis, a religious young woman, to marry him and return with him to Oregon. She accepted, and in 1836 the newlyweds headed west with the straight-laced Reverend Henry Spalding and his wife, Eliza.

Whitman's Second Trip

The trip was difficult for the Spaldings, but the Whitmans relished the journey. Their days across Wyoming, while long and tough, were exhilarating for Marcus and Narcissa. In her diary, Narcissa wrote, "We are ready to start at six, travel til eleven, camp, rest, start again at two and travel til six." The party ate "dried buffalo meat and tea for breakfast and tea and dried buffalo meat for supper." Eliza Spalding, who hated buffalo, existed on "odor of camphor and spirits of turpentine."

The party spent an uneventful week at Fort Laramie, where post trader Luciene Fontenelle lent them his apartment. It was the first civilized place the women had seen in three months and consisted of a bed and two chairs.

Narcissa Whitman (University of Wyoming)

Although Narcissa only recalled washing clothes at the fort, mountain man Joe Meek, "never lost an opportunity to be in the presence of Mrs. Whitman." Apparently she was unimpressed by the attentions of a trapper who called her husband "Doc Sawbones."

On July 4 Narcissa wrote at South Pass, "It is a reality that after four months of painful travel I am alive and actually standing on the summit of the Rocky Mountains where the foot of a white woman has never trod before."

On July 6 Narcissa and Eliza also became the first white women to attend a rendezvous—this one at Green River. Over two thousand Indians, three hundred trappers, and several important army officers and explorers had gathered for what Mrs. Spalding called "hours relieved by horsemanship, foot races, wrestling, jumping, and pounding noses by boasting and counterboasting."

The white women intrigued the Indians very much. They generously piled trout, venison, and elk meat at the opening of the Whitman tent. In honor of the women, the Indians mounted six hundred horses in a lavish spectacle of horsemanship. "We ladies were such a curiosity," Narcissa wrote, "they would come and stand around our tent—peep in and grin in their astonishment." The Indian women particularly liked Eliza because they could dote on the sickly, frail missionary.

Narcissa, however, was more interested in the trappers and hunters who came to enjoy her company. As she passed Bibles amongst the ruffians, she impressed them with her beauty and determination.

Following the rendezvous, the Whitmans left Wyoming. Marcus returned only once more in 1843. In 1847 both Marcus and Narcissa were massacred by the Cayuse Indians at the mission they had built in Oregon.

Father DeSmet—Blackrobe of the Rockies

A Catholic priest was one of the first missionaries to stay among the Rocky Mountain tribes rather than traveling to the West Coast. In 1840 the Flathead and Nez Perce Indians sent tribal members Pierre Garches and Ignaces to St. Louis asking for missionaries. Catholic Bishop Rosati promised them a priest. That spring Pierre Jean DeSmet, a Belgian priest born in 1801, volunteered for the duty. DeSmet had already worked with the Potowatami and Sioux Indians, establishing peace between their nations in the woodlands of Wisconsin and Minnesota.

On March 27 DeSmet left St. Louis, joining the annual expedition to the American Fur Company. Arriving at Green River, DeSmet attended the final rendezvous, then headed north. Near Yellowstone, he met members of the Blackfeet nation. "The whole village," he wrote, "was in commotion. Men, women, and children all came to meet me and shake hands."

The Indians came to call him "Blackrobe" because of his long black robe, which signified to the northern Plains tribes one who spoke with the Great Spirit. DeSmet stayed in the Rocky Mountain region for a number of years working among the various tribes. He returned to St. Louis in 1846 but was called west by the government in 1851 and 1858 to help negotiate peace with various Indian tribes.

Mormons Face Persecution

One of the biggest religious migrations in United States history was the flow of Mormons into the Salt Lake area. The Church of Jesus Christ of Latter Day Saints had been founded in 1830 by Joseph Smith and five followers. Through hard work and missionary zeal Smith spread his doctrines throughout the country and into Europe by 1840. But the

Mormons found persecution at every turn. Finally Smith began a Mormon town at Nauvoo, Illinois. Administered well by Smith, the town prospered, much to the dislike of the non-Mormons living in the surrounding area.

In 1844 hatred of the Mormons became violent. In June Smith and his brother Hyrum, were murdered in the Carthage County, Illinois, courthouse by a mob. Brigham Young, Smith's elected successor, decided to move his people west where they could practice their religion free from persecution.

In 1846 Henry Chatelain, O.P. Gleason, Niles Bragg, J.P. Johnson, Sol Siver, and Win Hall headed to the Great Salt Lake to see if Mormon settlement would be possible there. Young had read Fremont's description of the lake and thought it would be isolated enough for his people.

Brigham Young Leads His People West

When conditions proved favorable, Brigham Young led hundreds of Mormons from Nauvoo to winter quarters at Omaha. The following spring, he led the first 143 men, three women, and two children with seventy-three

Brigham Young (Wyoming State Archives)

wagons west. They traveled on the north side of the Platte River avoiding non-Mormon travelers on the south side.

It took two days to cross the North Platte at Fort Laramie, where wagons were fixed and supplies for the continuing journey were loaded. Traveling thirteen to twenty miles a day, the party soon reached Platte River Crossing near present day Casper, where Young built two ferries so the wagons could cross the treacherous river. When all the Mormons had ferried the torrent, Young left several men to aid other travelers using the ferries. Mormons were allowed to cross free, while non-Mormons paid a toll for the service.

By June 21 the party reached Independence Rock. On the anniversary of Joseph Smith's martyrdom, June 27, they crossed South Pass and began the descent into the Salt Lake region. By July Brigham Young's party left Wyoming and entered Utah, where, in the middle of the month, they sighted their Zion, the Great Salt Lake. Thousands followed, using what became known as the Mormon Trail.

Gold Rush

In 1848 gold was discovered on land owned by John Sutter in California. Word spread like wildfire, and soon "gold fever" caused thousands to go west. Travel reached a peak in 1850 when 53,000 emigrants traveled the trail.

In the 1860s many fled the East because of the tragedy of the Civil War. Many left to escape participation. Others came west after the war ended to forget and rebuild.

Regardless of the reasons, from 1825 until 1869, when the transcontinental railroad was completed, no less than 350,000 emigrants had traveled west along the trail, averaging 10,000 to 20,000 per year during the peak years of the middle-1840s through the 1860s.

The men, women, and children who trudged west, often with only hope and determination to draw them on, became known as pioneers or "emigrants"—those leaving one country or region for another. Remember, at this time Wyoming was not a state, but part of a vast territory. Because most early emigrants headed to Oregon on Robert Stuart's trail, the route became known as the "Oregon Trail."

Packing the Wagon

Making the journey from Missouri to either Oregon or California was a serious undertaking. Important decisions had to be made about what supplies to take and what to leave behind. A wagon of the finest quality was necessary and, if one could afford them, the tools required to keep it solid. Spare wheels, tongues, axles, and jacks were also an absolute necessity.

Experienced guides suggested that oxen rather than horses or mules be purchased to pull the wagon. They were cheaper, required less food and attention, seldom strayed, and were less likely to stampede.

Pioneers also needed good quality kitchen supplies: pots, pans, forks, knives, all designed to pack in the smallest space. One large and very durable Dutch oven was indispensable, for in it the pioneer housewife would cook everything from stew to bread. Large amounts of flour, coffee, sugar, beans, salt, bacon sides or salt pork, vinegar, and dried fruit were needed. Water barrels, axle grease, leather harnesses, and supplies to keep the leather in shape left little room in a wagon for personal items.

Once supplied, the pioneer family was ready for the journey. Life for the pioneer family would soon change, never to be the same again. At the jumping off place, they would join a wagon train and probably help select a wagon master. A wagon train would consist of twenty to eighty wagons, sometimes as many as two thousand head of livestock, and literally hundreds of people. A good guide and a wagon master with a gift of common sense were absolutely necessary for the perilous undertaking.

Following the Oregon Trail

The Oregon Trail began for most pioneers at one of the "jumping off" places (sites where wagon trains were formed and journeys west began). St. Joseph and Independence, Missouri, were typical of these places. From there the wagons struck west following the Kansas River, then cut to the north across the prairies to find the Platte River. The trail joined the Platte just east of the present site of Fort Kearny, Nebraska, and followed the north fork of one river all the way into central Wyoming near the present site of Casper. From there the Sweetwater River was the guide to South Pass. From South Pass the pioneers traveled to the Green River. They then either headed northwest along the Snake River and Columbia River to Oregon Territory or southwest following the Humbolt (in present Nevada) across the high Sierras and into California.

Landmarks in Wyoming

Entering what is now Wyoming approximately eight miles southeast of present-day Torrington, pioneers encountered many landmarks along the

Fort Laramie, 1853, with Fort John visible in foreground (Fort Laramie)

trail. In the previous fifty miles they had visited the now famous sites of Ash Hollow, Courthouse and Jailhouse Rocks, Chimney Rock, and Scott's Bluff, all in present-day Nebraska.

The first significant landmark after Scott's Bluff was Fort John (Fort Laramie after 1849). Fort John was the most important stopping place on the Oregon Trail. For most pioneers, it was the first sign of civilized life for over three hundred miles. It was also approximately the half-way point on the trail. Here pioneers replenished their supplies, repaired damaged wagons and tools, and traded worn and tired oxen for fresh ones from the American Fur Company traders. After 1849 Fort Laramie also served as a place of refuge and protection, as it was purchased by the United States government, and soldiers were stationed there for the support of the pioneers.

From Fort Laramie, the next major landmark was Laramie Peak. It is the highest peak in the Laramie Range, visible on a clear day from up to one hundred miles away. Between Fort Laramie and Laramie Peak, emigrants passed Register Cliff where they carved their names and the dates of their passing. From there, past Warm Springs where the warm water for laundry was enjoyed as a luxury, the pioneers stayed south and west of the North Platte River, skirting the northern end of the Laramie Range. Platte River crossing, near present Casper, was the next significant landmark. A bridge was built by 1852 and later defended by the army, which placed a fort at the site.

From Platte River Bridge, the emigrants headed west along the Sweetwater River and encountered their next landmark, Independence Rock. So named because July 4, 1830, was celebrated there by a group of mountain men, it is a dome of granite a mile in circumference. Once again, the pioneers carved their names in the rock, as they had done at Register Cliff. Just a short distance away is Devil's Gate. A split in a three-hundred-foot-high vertical rock cliff through which the Sweetwater River flows gave the pioneers a stirring sight.

Wagon train camps near
Independence Rock
(Wyoming State Archives)

Beyond Devil's Gate and the Sweetwater, the pioneers reached South Pass, crossed it, and headed toward the next major site, Fort Bridger. Build by Jim Bridger originally for the fur trade, Fort Bridger became important as a layover site and supply point where those emigrants going to California and those going to Oregon parted company.

Hazards on the Trail

During the next four to five months, approximately two thousand miles were covered. Hazards along the way were numerous. The most obvious dangers were those supplied by nature. The weather posed many difficulties. Leaving the "jumping off" place in April, the pioneers found themselves in mud up to their axles many times during their first month on the trail. Along with the rain came the threat of flash floods, swollen streams, and hidden dangers at river crossings that cost many lives.

At times along the trail the weather could also turn very dry. Storms, accompanied by lightning and thunder, continually set the prairies on fire. Prairie fires, sometimes covering hundreds of square miles, posed a serious danger during the dry months. Severe thunderstorms could also be accompanied by tornadoes that forced hapless pioneers to take cover as best they could.

Mother Nature also provided animal life that threatened the pioneers. Bears, wolves, and other large animals were not the only problem. Others came in much smaller packages. Mosquitoes, flies, locusts, and grasshoppers continually plagued the travelers, making life on the trail miserable. The rattlesnake, not well-known among Easterners, sparked terror on the trail when more than a few emigrants died painful deaths after being bitten.

The fear of disease was a constant companion, especially until the pioneers reached Fort Laramie. Climate and elevation virtually eliminated cholera west of the fort, but from the Mississippi Valley to Wyoming it was the most vicious killer on the trail. Cholera's horror included diarrhea, vomiting, fever, convulsions, and almost certain death. "Died of Cholera" was the most common epitaph on graves along the trail.

Stampedes were a serious threat to life and limb. Whether a stampede of the domestic animals belonging to the train or a stampede of thousands of head of buffalo, something or someone was sure to be damaged, broken, or killed. Stampedes within the herds belonging to the pioneers were usually the result of thunderstorms, although occasionally they could be started by Indians looking to disrupt the normal process of wagon train life.

Indian Attacks

Probably the most romanticized and exaggerated danger along the trail was Indian attack. The fear of a savage ambush was begun and perpetuated by newspapers, magazines, and books in the East, which published dramatic accounts of incidents that seldom took place.

Between 1840 and 1860, 362 emigrants on the overland trails (not only the Oregon Trail) were killed by Indians. During the same time, 426 Indians were killed by emigrants. The emigrants' death toll indicates that one out of every thousand died as a result of Indian attack, or an average of eighteen to twenty per year. Ninety percent of these deaths took place west of South Pass, and most took place in Oregon Territory, very little of which makes up modern Wyoming.

Prior to the 1850s most encounters with Indians were friendly. The Indians were curious, usually interested in trading for tobacco or sugar. As the white migration continued, growing in magnitude, the unfriendly encounters between pioneers and Indians increased. Precautions were taken by pioneers. Wagons were drawn into a circular corral at night, and guards were posted. Almost never in all the history of western migration did an Indian war party descend upon a circle of wagons. Indians did occasionally attack a single wagon or one straggling at the end of a train.

Overall, 20,000 emigrants died en route, most from disease, fewest from Indian attacks. For every mile of Oregon Trail traveled, there were approximately ten graves, marking the place where one out of every seventeen pioneers who started the journey died.

A Crowded Highway

Another misconception that must be corrected is that the average pioneer on the trail was a lonely, isolated individual in the middle of hundreds of empty square miles. Particularly during the years 1849 to 1853 most pioneers would have preferred privacy to the dust-choked air, crowded campsites, and grassless valleys.

There were so many emigrants that one pioneer in 1850 reported from near South Pass that, "the road, from morning to night, is crowded like Pearl Street or Broadway" and that "fathers had become separated from their sons and did not meet again until they reached California."

Some emigrants kept track of the wagon traffic they encountered along the trail. James B. Persinger reported passing two hundred wagons one morning, while on another day one hundred wagons passed him and at least five hundred wagons on another! Reuben Knox, writing from Fort Kearney, Nebraska Territory, reported that one thousand wagons passed the fort on May 31, 1850.

"Crowded Highway" near South Pass (Wyoming State Archives)

With this large amount of traffic, the trail became a dry, dusty path nearly three miles wide, deeply rutted by the iron tires of the wagons. The air was choked with dust because not only wagons but thousands of head of livestock also traveled the trail. There was no grass for the stock, and wild game was scattered for at least twenty miles north and south of the trail.

For campfires, the typical pioneer used buffalo chips, mainly because the Platte Valley was devoid of trees. As the wagons traveled farther west, the trail took on the appearance of a garbage dump with trash and household possessions dumped to lighten the load for tired and trail-worn oxen. "Pleasant" would not be an accurate word for the look of the Oregon Trail as seen by an 1850s emigrant.

Overland Trail

As time passed, other western routes were developed across Wyoming. The most successful spin-off of the Oregon Trail was probably the Overland Trail.

Pioneered by Ben Holliday, who developed the Overland Stage Line to carry mail and passengers to the West Coast, the trail saw use during the 1860s and 1870s. Emigrants began to use the Overland Trail because of the many stage stations located along the road to support the stagecoach line.

Entering Wyoming south of the present site of Laramie, the trail led northwest across the Laramie plains, around the north side of Elk Mountain, and then cut to the west through Bridger Pass. The trail continued west to Fort Bridger , from where it then followed either the Oregon or California trails to the coast. It was in constant use until 1868 when the transcontinental railroad line entered Wyoming, removing forever the necessity of traveling west in a wagon.

The Pony Express

After the discovery of gold in California, the federal government wanted to link the now populous West with the East. As the clouds of the Civil War gathered, it was important for Washington to secure western votes on key issues and keep California and Oregon informed. To do this a regular year-round mail service was needed.

By the late 1850s the Oregon—California Trail was a well-traveled highway, providing a route for a mail service. All that was needed was money. Finally, in 1860 some senators persuaded the freighting firm of Russel, Majors, and Wadell to begin a mail run from St. Joseph, Missouri, to Sacramento, California, over the Oregon—California trail. They called their service the Pony Express.

General Manager William Russel advertised for "wiry, young" riders of less than one hundred pounds. He then secured old stage stations along the route and arranged for a ceremonial opening in St. Joe's and Sacramento on April 30, 1860. Carrying forty-nine letters and nine dispatches in a leather "mochilla," Johnny Frey dashed out of St. Joe's at 7:15 after a crowd heard "remarks by Major Wadell."

In Sacramento, Sam Hamilton got off to a bad start. After waiting for over two hours in a downpour, he finally received the mail from San Francisco. Then, in the early hours of the morning, he galloped through the muddy streets towards the distant mountains where a blizzard was raging. Despite the rough spring weather, the first batch of mail was delivered within ten days at both ends. The country was now linked by a vital but dangerous route.

Eighty men rode the 420 horses for the Pony Express. They covered an average of seventy-five miles, stopping about every fifteen miles at a stage station. There were thirty-nine stations dotting the 474-mile route through Wyoming. Places like Verdling's Ranch, Red Rock, Ice Springs, and Quaking Aspen meant hot food and a fresh horse for the tired riders who kept up a pace of eight to fifteen miles per hour.

Riders earned $50 to $150 per month carrying the twenty-pound mail bag, a job they described as "pretty tough!" "Just think," said Nick Wilson, the youngest rider, "of jumpin' on a horse and poundin' away full tilt for ten miles, leapin' on another, poundin' away again for the same distance!"

Riders faced severe dangers in Wyoming as well as along the rest of the 1800 mile trail. The Quaking Aspen area in the southwest corner of the state was particularly dangerous during the Paiute Indians uprising. One bullet-torn rider died at the Quaking Aspen station. J.G. Kelly then took his place. As he rode into a dense aspen grove he kept his Sharps rifle at full cock and raced through the woods "like a streak of greased lightning" as bullets flew around him.

Thieves and emigrants themselves caused further problems. Young William F. Cody, later to become "Buffalo Bill," was halted by robbers who demanded the mail mochilla. He threw a false bag at one, shot at another, and made a quick getaway. Another driver was shot at by emigrants who thought he was an Indian. Of course, winter weather caused problems for all the riders, especially those who had to cross the Rockies in Wyoming and the Sierras in California.

Despite the dangers, the Pony Express faithfully delivered letters and dispatches in as short a time as seven days and seventeen hours. During its entire run, only two drivers were killed—though many drivers had close calls—and remarkably only one mochilla was stolen and never returned.

While the Pony Express cut a glamorous path through Wyoming, it was a short lived one. In October 1861 the first transcontinental telegraph line linked East and West with instant communications. No longer needed, the Pony Express riders rode past the new telegraph wires on their last runs in November 1861.

Last ride of the Pony Express as the transcontinental telegraph is completed (Wyoming State Archives)

5
The Indian Wars

Cultural Differences

From the early 1600s when the Pilgrims first stepped onto the North American continent until the end of the nineteenth century, the white man and the Indian were almost continually at war. As settlement moved inland, Indian tribes were forced off their land. The early pioneers justified this as Cotton Mather, the famous Puritan, did at the beginning of the eighteenth century, by saying that the Indian was a "rabid animal, a veritable devil in the flesh, an agent employed by Satan himself, to overcome God's chosen people." Believing this, colonists and settlers had no scruples about taking an Indian's life, let alone his land. Each step in the westward growth of white civilization resulted in the displacement of one or more tribes of Indians, and each step brought more violent Indian resistance to the loss of hunting grounds and sacred territory. The loss of their lands and nomadic lifestyle combined with the unfair treatment imposed upon them by the government (broken treaties, unfulfilled promises, corrupt Indian agents), surely caused battle after battle.

The Indians eventually lost the war with the white man for several reasons. The Indians were not unified. They felt loyalty to their tribe only, and many other tribes were considered enemies to be preyed upon. Thus tribal numbers remained small in the face of the combined forces of the United States government.

The Indians were also less advanced technologically than their white foes. As Washakie, the greatest of Wyoming Indian chiefs, once said, "When we had bows, the whites had pistols, when we got pistols, the whites had rifles, and when we got rifles the whites had cannons." The

Indian acquired equal firepower only by theft or by recovering arms from the field of battle.

The Indians' view of land ownership differed widely from that of the whites. The Indians believed that the land belonged to all Indians to be used by them. One Indian could not own forever any piece of ground. The whites used paper, with ink writing to define ownership. Once owned, the land continued to be owned until sold or passed on after death. The practice made no sense at all to the Indians.

Finally, the Indians never had one overall leader to guide them in their efforts. A chief led by personal influence and respect only. When writing treaties with an Indian chief, the white agents felt that they were dealing with the commander-in-chief when in fact they were dealing with an individual who probably, at the most, commanded no more than five hundred followers.

Establishing the Frontier Posts

After his early expeditions into Wyoming, John C. Fremont had suggested that the government establish military posts in the region to protect emigrants. As stories drifted back to Washington in the mid 1840s, it became apparent that Fremont's suggestions should be followed. Not only were the Indians causing trouble along the trail, but the whites, still looking upon the Indians as "dirty, disgusting, and uncivilized," were taking advantage of the Indians. With each act of violence committed by either group, a vengeful act was bound to follow. It was a vicious cycle that needed to be broken to end all of the violence.

In 1845 Colonel Stephen W. Kearny held the first army-Indian council in Wyoming. At a site on the Laramie River, he warned the Indians against "disturbing the emigrants" and assured them of the "love and solicitude of the Great White Father," meaning the president of the United States.

Acting on Fremont's words and Kearny's advice, President James K. Polk signed an act in 1846 for the "establishment of Military stations on the route to Oregon." The Mexican War caused a brief interruption in the process, but in 1848 the first fort on the trail, Fort Kearny, was built along the Platte River in Nebraska Territory.

The following year, Lieutenant Daniel P. Woodbury was authorized to buy Fort John (Laramie) from the American Fur Company for $4,000, and Fort Laramie became the first military fort in Wyoming. The occupation was timely, for by August of 1850 over forty thousand people traveled the trail past the fort, and the companies of "mounted rifles" were kept busy assisting the travelers and settling disputes.

For nearly ten years, Fort Laramie was to be the only military post in Wyoming. In the summer of 1858, the government took over a military reservation at Fort Bridger in southwestern Wyoming. Originally built as a fur trading post by the famous mountain man Jim Bridger in 1845, the fort was controlled by the Mormons during the 1850s. During the Mormon War of 1857 and 1858, it was occupied by the United States army under the command of General Albert Sydney Johnson before officially becoming a United States post.

Both Fort Laramie and Fort Bridger were to see control by the United States army until 1890. They were to remain as the sole centers of civilization in Wyoming until the building of the transcontinental railroad in the late 1860s and the establishment of other forts as the Indian Wars heated up.

The Treaty of 1851

By 1850 many problems had developed over the number of whites using the Oregon Trail. What had begun as a path for the mountain men and missionaries had turned into a crowded highway. Forage had all but disappeared from the river valleys, the rivers themselves were becoming filled with debris, and worst of all, the buffalo and other game had been forced far from the trail.

The Indians had increased their harrassment of the travelers, stealing goods and livestock routinely. It became obvious that if the differences were not settled soon, open fighting would occur.

The Indians and the whites agreed to meet at Fort Laramie in September of 1851 to map out a treaty to settle all of their differences. Nearly 12,000 Indians from all of the Plains tribes converged on the fort. Sioux, Cheyennes, Arapahoes, Snakes, Bannocks, and Crows came in huge numbers. Jim Bridger, Robert Campbell, and Tom Fitzpatrick, former mountain men and guides, represented Washington along with a large delegation from the East headed by Superintendant of Indian Affairs D.D. Mitchell.

As was the custom, gifts from the "white father" (president) were presented to the Indian leaders. When the wagon train carrying more gifts was late, the Indians waited patiently. But after several days, the treaty site had to be moved east down the Platte River. The ponies had eaten what grass there was, game was scarce, and garbage and debris

Indian encampment near Fort Laramie (Fort Laramie)

had piled up to epic proportions. Two companies of soldiers led the procession to the final treaty site near the Wyoming-Nebraska border.

Here Sioux and Cheyenne women built an arbor (circular branch-covered arena) for the council. Feasting and visiting filled the days and nights. Sometimes the feasting of one tribe or another kept the entire camp of nearly thirteen thousand awake.

Finally a cannon sounded and the negotiations began. The Indians, richly dressed in their "prairie costumes" assembled with the blackcoated dignitaries from Washington. The peace pipe was smoked and proposals were made.

Over the next few days the Indians mulled over the ideas from the East. They feasted, discussed, and settled old differences. By September 17, good will prevailed, and after some discussion the treaty was signed by the whites and several Indian chiefs.

Among its provisions, the treaty said that the Indians would allow the whites to make roads and travel them freely. The whites agreed to protect the Indians, and restitution would be made for all wrongs committed along the trail. Goods or annuities worth $50,000 per year would be provided for the Indians. This would seal a "firm and lasting peace."

The treaty gifts arrived on September 20, and in a grand ceremony, the Indians were presented with uniforms, hats, medals, beads, and other trinkets. A delegation of eleven representatives from various tribes was then taken to Washington by Tom Fitzpatrick to present the treaty to the Senate for ratification. All departed in good will.

Unfortunately, when the Senate finally ratified the treaty, the goods were cut from $50,000 a year to $10,000 per year. This move did little to secure the "firm and lasting peace" predicted by the treaty of 1851.

First Engagement with the Indians

Following the treaty signing, emigration continued to increase, and problems developed. Near Fort Laramie on the Platte River, a ferry had been built to allow travelers on the north side of the river to come to the fort. On June 15, 1853, a group of Sioux Indians seized the ferry and fired at the sergeant in charge, who recaptured it. Lieutenant Hugh Fleming, commander in charge of the fort at that time, and twenty-three men went to arrest the offenders, who had refused to surrender. In the resulting skirmish, three Indians were killed, three were wounded, and two were taken prisoner. After a period of tension between the army and the Indians, the Indians were persuaded to settle down, accept the 1851 treaty annuities, and no further hostilities took place that year.

Grattan Massacre

A year later the treaty failed a disastrous test, opening years of fighting between Indians and whites for control of the high plains.

In August of 1854, a cow belonging to Mormon emigrants strayed from the trail and lagged behind. A Minneconjou Sioux, High Forehead, shot the cow and took it back to the Brule Sioux camp located eight miles east of Fort Laramie near present-day Lingle. When the emigrants reached the fort, they demanded payment for the cow according to the treaty provisions.

Lieutenant John F. Grattan convinced the post commander, Lieutenant Hugh Fleming, to arrest the Indian and bring him to the fort where he could await the arrival of the Indian agent who would settle the matter. Lieutenant Fleming ordered Grattan, twenty-eight men, an interpreter, and two cannons to the camp where High Forehead was said to be lodging.

Unfortunately, according to fort chaplain Charles Page, Grattan "had a unwarrantable contempt of the Indian character." He added that the young West Point graduate "was in a state of extreme agitation" when he left with his detachment at 3:00 P.M. on Saturday, August 19. To complicate matters, his interpreter, Lucien Auguste, was drunk.

Grattan massacre (Fort Laramie)

After stopping to load small arms at the American Fur Company's trading post five miles east of the fort, Grattan neared the sprawling Brule camp of over a thousand Indians. Nervously, the lieutenant asked James Bordeau, a trader living nearby, to help him since Bordeau had an Indian wife and knew the chiefs.

Bordeau said later that Marto Ioway, a Brule chief, soon appeared. Grattan asked for High Forehead. Without answering, the chief went back to camp. In a few minutes, he returned with three other chiefs and a messenger following them. The messenger said High Forehead refused to give himself up.

Bordeau cautioned the furious Grattan not to approach the Indian camp. Boldly, the lieutenant ignored the trader and pushed his force within sixty yards of High Forehead's lodge. Auguste bantered with and irritated the Indians, misinterpreting for Grattan. An argument arose over Grattan's refusal to follow the Indian custom of asking four times for the renegade. As heated words flew, the soldiers gripped their rifles and took revolvers from their holsters. The Sioux warriors strung their bows and slipped arrows from their quivers.

Suddenly, a nervous soldier fired. An Indian screamed out not to fire in return. "Perhaps the whites are satisfied since an Indian has died," he shouted. "But the words were hardly out of his mouth," Bordeau later reported, "when more soldiers fired." Grattan managed two quick stray cannon shots before he was pelted with arrows. In the Sioux barrage that followed, the soldiers' guns were of little use.

Within minutes, all but one soldier was dead. That man was brought to Bordeau's fort by friendly Indians and was hidden until Monday when he was returned to Fort Laramie. Because he had his tongue severed, he was unable to warn the forty-two remaining soldiers of the danger the Indians presented. He died a few days later.

Outraged by the attack, stunned Easterners demanded that something be done. In the fall of 1855, General Harney revenged the deaths by attacking Blue Thunder's people camped at Ash Hollow, Nebraska. The high plains Indian wars had opened, and repeated conflicts would blacken Wyoming's history for the next twenty years.

Shoshones Make Early Peace

In 1862, as the Sioux, Arapahoes, Cheyennes, and other Wyoming tribes watched in growing horror and anger as the whites flooded into their land, one tribe entered into a remarkable peace with the U.S. government. The Shoshones, led by Chief Washakie, agreed in 1863 at Fort Bridger to a treaty establishing peace between the two nations.

Five years later, the Shoshones and the U.S. government reached agreement on the boundaries of a reservation for the tribe. The massive 44,672,000-acre tract of land, almost the entire western half of Wyoming, included the Wind River Range—the beloved home of the tribe.

In years to come, the Shoshones would lose much of their reservation land as the government either bought or took back portions of the claim. Yet the Shoshones remained one of the strongest allies of the U.S. government during the turbulent years of the high plains Indian wars from 1865 to 1876.

Shoshone camp, Wind River Mountains, 1870 (Wyoming State Archives)

Shoshone Chief Washakie
(Wyoming State Archives)

Why did this tribe alone find peace without war? There are several reasons. For one thing, the Shoshones had long had contact with the whites in peaceful times. The first whites, mountain men, came to live among the Shoshones, adopting their ways. The coexistence between the Indians and whites was to the benefit of both, and as a result, it was peaceful. Knowing the white man's ways, the Shoshones had little fear of him. Another reason was that the bitterest enemies of the Shoshones—the Sioux, Arapahoes, and Blackfeet—were also bitter enemies of the whites. To band together with the U.S. government was to band against these age-old enemies. Also, the government was willing to give the Shoshones the territory they loved, and so the early agreements were acceptable.

The most important reason, however, was the vision of the Shoshone chief, Washakie. Washakie, a courageous warrior and respected leader saw very early that war against the whites was foolish. Though at times the Shoshone warriors grew restless and discontented, Washakie never waivered in his friendship with the United States. He managed through his long life to keep peace and spare his tribe much of the pain brought by the bloody conflicts on the Indian Wars.

More People Come to Indian Territory

With the rapid growth of the population of California and Oregon, more and more people began to cross Wyoming, leading the Indians to believe that "eventually all the whites would run out in the East" and the land would be theirs again. The Pony Express in 1860 and the building of the transcontinental telegraph line that replaced it in 1861 only brought more people to the trails. Wild game was driven further from the valleys of the Platte and the Sweetwater, the trees were cut down, and soldiers seemed to be everywhere along the trail. At about the same time that the "singing wires" of the telegraph line were bringing information from coast to coast, people were rushing to Viginia City, Montana, where gold had been discovered.

The Bozeman Trail

Of all the trails that traversed Wyoming in the nineteenth century, the most disputed was used for only five years, and during those five years only by miners and soldiers sent to protect them.

The story of the Bozeman Trail actually begins many years prior to the 1860s. It was used, beginning in the late 1700s by Indians following game to the Powder River country or "Absaroka" (Home of the Crows) as it was known to the Indians. The Crow chief Arapooish described the Powder River Basin as "the right place" given to the Crows by the Great Spirit. In the 1830s, Joe Meek, a mountain man, described the area as "the land of Canaan." But this area was valued highly by other tribes, too.

Beginning in the 1850s, the Sioux and the Cheyenne Indians began to hunt in Crow territory and by the 1860s controlled the Powder River Basin, driving the Crows to the north and west.

In 1859 a Yellowstone expedition under the command of Captain William F. Raynolds crossed the area with the purpose of determining the Indian population, finding a possible wagon route between the Oregon Trail and valleys of the Missouri Basin, and determining its resource value. Raynolds noted, "At the East basin of the mountains there is a belt of country some twenty miles in width, that is peculiarly suitable for a wagon road, and which I doubt not will become the great line of travel into the valley of the Three Forks (Virginia City area)." Raynolds's prediction would soon become painfully true.

That same year, John Bozeman left Georgia seeking his fortune as a prospector in the mines of Colorado. Finding that the best claims were already taken, Bozeman moved to Idaho territory where he became familiar with the gold fields of western Montana. While Bozeman was unsuccessfully working claims in the Idaho-Montana area, many others were following the Oregon Trail to Fort Hall in Idaho and then cutting north to the gold fields. Others rode Missouri River steamboats to the Yellowstone River where they could cut over the Rockies to Virginia City and the gold mines. Although slow and expensive, steamboats are said to have transported over ten thousand miners to the Montana mines in 1867 alone.

Hearing of Raynolds's expedition and acquiring his maps, Bozeman felt that the Powder River route would greatly shorten the journey.

In May of 1863, forty-six wagons with eighty-nine men and some women became the first wagon train on the Bozeman. By the time it arrived in the gold fields, Bozeman found that this route shortened the trip by over 350 miles. In 1864 nine wagon trains successfully navigated Bozeman's trail. The year 1864 became the year of heaviest migration on the trail.

Following the Chivington Massacre in Colorado in 1864, Cheyenne and Arapaho fugitives fled to the Powder River country where they were joined by the many divisions of the Sioux. In March of 1865, General Connor led the Powder River Expedition into the Bozeman Trail area to "smash the Powder River tribes" and in Connor's words, "to kill all male Indians over the age of twelve." Due to peace movements in the East, the expedition was not allowed to fulfill Connor's plans.

The Platte River Bridge Fight

Yet blood washed Wyoming's Platte River Valley in 1865, as the eastern tribes tried to reclaim the valley from the growing white takeover. In January the Sioux thundered down on Julesburg and a month later attacked Mud Springs. By April they regularly attacked travelers heading west of Fort Laramie.

But the Indians were by no means alone on the offensive. "The only good Indian is a dead Indian" could be overheard at any fort or settlement that waited in fear of attack. Soldiers from Fort Laramie and Fort Mitchell were kept busy retaliating for Indian attacks by raiding Sioux, Cheyenne, and Arapaho camps to the north. One extreme case of army brutality

Platte Bridge Station, later Fort Caspar (Wyoming State Archives)

occurred when Colonel Thomas Moonlight, commander of Fort Laramie, hanged two Sioux sub-chiefs for returning a white woman and her daughter who had been captured by the Cheyennes. As the ultimate insult, Moonlight hanged the Indians with chains and allowed their bodies to dangle in the open air, rotting as a warning to other "savages."

Infuriated, the Sioux, Cheyennes, and Arapahoes plotted revenge. They picked the Platte River Bridge as their target. At present-day Casper, trader John Richard had built a wooden bridge to profit from the pioneers' final crossing of the Platte. Taking this bridge would be indeed be a "useful prize" in the Indians' drive to halt settlement of the valley.

Ninety-six soldiers of the Eleventh Kansas Cavalry under Major Martin Anderson guarded the bridge at tiny Platte River Station. Though they had heard of the stepped-up Indian offensive, they were anxious to go home. After all, the Civil War had ended in April, and they said, "let the career soldiers take care of the Sioux."

Unknown to the bluecoats, by the middle of June, Cheyenne, Sioux, and Arapaho warriors began massing around the Platte Bridge area, generally hiding in the hills to the south.

On June 25, the Indians made their first move. In the early hours of the morning, several warriors paraded unexpectedly in front of the bridge. Sensing trouble, Anderson ordered the howitzer fired as a warning. Shortly after the blast, several braves attempted to steal cattle west of the garrison. A dozen troopers rode out to scatter the Indians but encountered no trouble. The Indians were merely toying with the soldiers, not wanting to "show their hand on such small game."

A third raid that afternoon drew blood. Chief High-Backed, son of Blind

Wolf, was killed in a crossfire as the Indians attempted to trap the soldiers. Feverish now with excitement, the troopers knew that Blind Wolf would not leave his son's death unavenged.

An uneasy silence fell as the sun glared at its hottest. At 4:00 P.M. Caspar Collins rode into the station. Stopping on his way west to Sweetwater Station, young Collins brought welcomed mail from Fort Laramie, 150 miles to the east.

Twenty years old, Collins was an experienced Ohio volunteer who had come out with his family in May 1862. His father was Lieutenant Colonel William O. Collins, a lawyer who had organized the Ohio volunteers at the outbreak of the Civil War. He spent that war commanding Fort Laramie, where Caspar learned to love military life. Although sickly with a persistent cough when he first came west, Caspar had regained his health. He was a striking officer, his fellow soldiers remembered, for he "played a magnificent game of poker," was "devoid of fear," and had "ambitions to have a military success."

Now after picking up his commission and a new uniform at Fort Laramie, he was ready to assume command of Sweetwater Station west of Platte River Bridge.

Officers on the porch of Bedlam at Fort Laramie, 1864 (Wyoming State Archives)

Only a gentle breeze disturbed the peace of the cool June night. But at 2:00 P.M. the next day, Captain Breteny, a friend of Collins, rode into the station with an ominous message for Anderson. He had been leading ten men to Fort Laramie to collect pay when they passed a slow-moving supply train of five wagons and twenty-five men camped at Willow Creek to the west. Having seen warriors parading atop the bluffs, Breteny warned Anderson to send a relief detachment to rescue the men.

Anderson disregarded the warning, saying it was too late in the day to do any good. The Indians, after all, would not make a move at night. As mist slowly burned off the cool Platte at dawn the next day, several warriors appeared like ghosts on the opposite bank. But there was something different about these warriors. They had donned war paint.

Anderson now agreed to send out a detachment to help the wagon train make it to the station. He ordered each of his five Kansas officers to undertake the duty. They each came up with a flimsy excuse to avoid leading the "suicide mission."

Then Anderson ordered Collins to head the detail with Captain Greer. Furious, Breteny told his friend not to go. After all, Anderson had his own men, and because Collins was not under his command, he could rightly refuse the duty. But Collins told Breteny, "a soldier's duty is to follow orders."

Incensed, Breteny stormed into Anderson's office demanding that Anderson retract the order. But Collins had already borrowed a horse from the leader of the regimental band and was saddling up with his men. In his new uniform, Collins looked every inch the leader and confidently headed his twenty-five men out on their mission. As the horses clomped over the bridge, reinforcements were readied under Captain Breteny.

Had Collins been able to see through the brush along the river bank, he would not have been so confident. He did not know that four hundred Cheyennes were crouched behind the brush, arrows ready; hundreds of Sioux lay in wait in the dry wash; Arapahoes hid by Caspar Creek, weapons ready. The Indians had positioned themselves earlier according to an effective plan. The Cheyennes would attack and contain the soldiers. As the troopers attempted to return to the bridge, the Sioux and Arapahoes would rise up and block their retreat, while the main body of a thousand Sioux would cut off escape to the north.

A half mile from the post, Collins spotted several Indians cutting the telegraph lines. The Indians mounted and charged north. Collins pursued them into the main body of Indians. The Cheyennes were ready from behind, and within seconds war whoops terrified the bluecoats. Two thousand Indians descended on the men.

At such close range, arrows were ineffective, so hatchets and knives flashed as the soldiers fired their single-shot rifles. With no time to reload, the soldiers swung their carbines as clubs, trying to battle their way back to the bridge. The soldiers were hit time and time again, but only four were killed.

Unfortunately, Collins was hit in the hip. As he joined the retreat, he heard a cry, "Don't leave me!" Turning, he saw a horseless soldier, lying wounded. Collins spun his horse around, charged towards the Indians and bent over to pick up his comrade. Suddenly, as his horse whirled toward the enemy, an arrow struck Collins in the forehead. Shots roared from his pistols, but his terrified horse charged into the main body of the Indians, a cloud of dust and war whoops encircling the young lieutenant.

The main part of the detachment had received reinforcements from Captain Breteny, who held the bridge open for retreat. The Cheyennes poured arrows at the soldiers, but because of the unusual angle of their shots, most of their arrows ended up striking the Sioux, above the soldiers on the ridge. Infuriated, the Sioux screamed a cease fire. Taking advantage of the lull, the soldiers charged to the bridge.

Anderson tried to have the telegraph line repaired, but his detachment of five men was immediately attacked by the waiting Cheyennes. Fearing for the wagon train, which was now in sight of the station, he fired the howitzer as a warning. The column prepared for an attack as quickly as they could, but the only defense they could manage before the Indians swarmed over them was to hide behind two of the wagons in a small draw. With plenty of ammunition and repeaters, the soldiers repelled the first onslaught, surprising the Indians. A second attempt also failed. Realizing that a frontal attack was hopeless, the Indians lay seige to the wagon train, patiently wearing the men down, inching closer and closer, hiding behind the rocks, digging trenches, slowly advancing.

Knowing he had neither men nor ammunition to spare, Anderson decided he could do nothing to aid the wagon train. Such a move would cost the army the post and the bridge.

After four hours, the Indians overwhelmed the weakened survivors of the wagon train. Torture and mutilation finished the job. Once the soldiers had been "dispatched," the Indians gathered their surprisingly heavy casualties on travois, set fire to the wagons, and headed north.

Silence and smoke told the men at the fort that the fight was over, so that night Anderson sent for reinforcements. Because the Indians feared additional soldiers and firepower, they abandoned their plans to seize the post. By the next day, the last warriors paraded defiantly across the bridge, then disappeared to the Powder River country.

The twenty-eight men killed—including Collins—were gathered up from the field of battle and drawn back to the station. Gloom settled over Platte River Station as reinforcements from Fort Laramie arrived. The Sioux, Cheyennes, and Arapahoes had come very close to winning back ground lost to the Oregon Trail, but never again would they get such a chance.

Fetterman Massacre

In 1866 Red Cloud, Red Leaf, Man-Afraid-of-his-Horses, Spotted Tail, and other leaders of the Powder River tribes met at Fort Laramie to discuss their problems with the government representatives. Unfortunately, Colonel Henry B. Carrington's expedition arrived at the same time with orders to establish army posts on the Bozeman Trail, which cut through the best remaining hunting grounds. Red Cloud refused to be introduced to Carrington and said the Sioux would "not give them [the whites] a road unless they whip them." While some chiefs did sign the treaty, Red Cloud left the fort angrily.

He later bitterly told Cheyennes who had come to inform him the whites were going ahead with their plans to build a road, "white man lies and steals. My lodges were many, but now they are few. The white man wants all. The white man must fight and the Indians will die where their fathers died."

As ordered, Carrington headed north and established Fort Reno, Fort C. F. Smith, and Fort Phil Kearny—Phil for short—on Little Piney Creek.

Red Cloud immediately began to make life miserable for the troops

Sioux Chief Red Cloud (Wyoming State Archives)

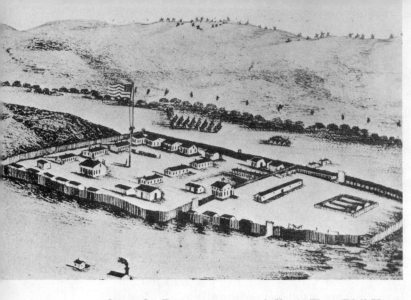

Fort Phil Kearny (Wyoming State Archives)

along the Bozeman, especially at Fort Phil Kearny. In the last five months of 1866, fifty-one attacks on the garrison took place, making the nearly four hundred inhabitants virtual prisoners inside the wooden stockade that surrounded the fort buildings. Carrington begged for reinforcements, and in November a cavalry company of sixty-three men under the command of Lieutenant Horatio Bingham arrived from Fort Laramie. Accompanying Bingham was Captain William Judd Fetterman.

From the start, Fettermen and Carrington opposed each other. A reckless Civil War veteran, Fetterman was anxious for a fight with the Sioux. Carrington, by contrast, was experienced and cautious, preferring a strong defense of the fort over any offense at all. And there was good reason for his caution. By August, supplies at Fort Phil Kearny were low, especially ammunition, and goods were very slow to arrive if they came at all.

Captain William Judd Fetterman (Wyoming State Archives)

Fetterman continued to needle Carrington, undermining his authority. "With eighty men I could ride through the Sioux nation," he told Carrington. Another time he said bitterly that what was needed was not words, but something "that even the heathen mind could understand, a prompt display of force and action."

Finally, Carrington allowed Fetterman the chance to attack the Sioux. One early November night, Fetterman hid his men in a cottonwood thicket along the Big Piney River, opposite the fort. Several mules were hobbled or tied up between the soldiers and the fort as bait. The women, children, civilians, and remaining soldiers in the stockade waited for the crack of rifles sure to sound when the Indians rode in to steal the mules and be caught in the crossfire. The only sound, though, came from the wolves howling. The Indians sensed the trap, waited until the men had given up and grown tired and cold, then stampeded a herd of cattle on the other side of the fort.

Instead of learning a lesson from this humiliation, Fetterman hardened bitterly. He wanted to try again, but Carrington refused to allow him the chance.

On December 6, however, Fetterman found an opportunity. A party had gone from the fort to cut wood—a routine, cold, and difficult job that was dangerous because the only wood was located at least a mile from

Fetterman massacre (Fort Laramie)

the fort near the river. Once out in Sullivant Wood, the soldiers were attacked.

As soon as he saw the flag signaling trouble from Pilot Knob, Carrington ordered Fetterman to relieve the wood train. Carrington took a detachment to cut off the Indians' retreat. The troopers' maneuvers were disastrous, though. Captain Fetterman and Lieutenant Bingham were lured into Indian traps. As Private John Guthrie later recalled, "the soldiers had gone out to apprehend the thieves, but were soon outnumbered, ten Indians to one soldier. We had all we could do to keep our horses from being ripped up by the horns of the cattle. The lieutenant (Bingham) was first shot and fell off his horse, shot in the head."

Now that one of his closest friends and supporters was dead, Fetterman pressed Carrington for revenge. The colonel refused but wrote to headquarters that the situation was deteriorating—supplies were dwindling, morale was low, and attacks were even more frequent.

The sun was bright and the air almost balmy on the morning of December 21. Nearly all recent snow had melted, and spirits seemed higher at the post since Christmas was coming. Parties were planned, and decorations dotted the crude houses where officers and their families lived.

As always, a wood cutting detail had to be sent out, so Carrington ordered Lieutenant Wands to head out about ten o'clock. Less than an hour later the guards on Pilot Knob began waving flags indicating an attack. The train, as Carrington wrote in his report, was "corraled and threatened on Sullivant Hill about a mile and a half from the Fort."

A relief column had to be sent out. Fetterman demanded that he be given the command. Carrington, remembering the near-disaster on December 6, refused. But Fetterman claimed the right of rank to go. His hands tied, Carrington ordered Fetterman and seventy-eight men out. Two civilians, eager for a fight—Isaac Fischer and James Wheatly—joined the column dashing through the stockade gates. Equipped with sixteen-shot Henry rifles, they were the envy of the soldiers who were each armed with a muzzle-loading Springfield and twenty rounds of ammunition.

Before leaving, Fetterman had been given a clear order by Colonel Carrington: "Support the wood train . . . Do not engage or pursue Indians at its expense. Under no circumstances pursue over Lodge Trail Ridge."

By the time Fetterman had reached the attacking Indians, the sky was clouding over, and the temperature was dropping. He scattered the warriors, who headed off toward Lodge Trail Ridge. Against orders, hot for a fight, Fetterman pursued the Indians. As the column moved onto the Bozeman Trail, the cavalrymen were so anxious to fight that they rode on ahead of the foot soldiers (infantry), allowing a gap to develop.

Suddenly, as the column passed over the hill, Indians appeared everywhere, thousands slipping from behind trees.

Gunfire cracked through the cold air as soldiers scrambled for cover. Arrows fell like rain—one thousand per minute. Fetterman's command was split, making it easy for the Indians to surround and cut down the soldiers. Wheatly and Fischer fired continuously, taking a heavy toll with their superior weapons. But the enemy numbers were so vast that it was only a matter of time. As the small amount of ammunition ran out, soldiers tried to hide to escape the inevitable. Fetterman and Lieutenant Brown, seeing the hopelessness of the situation, aimed their revolvers at one another's temples and fired.

As the gunfire died away, the Indians scalped and mutilated the soldiers, even though some were still alive. They then dragged off their own dead, about 160 in all, and picked up many of the forty thousand arrows shot in the fight.

By the time relief appeared, there was nothing to relieve. The Indians had disappeared, leaving bodies, most disfigured beyond recognition, scattered about the rocky hillside.

Wood wagons were loaded with the corpses and hurried back to the fort as snow began to fall. There was no time for grief. Fearing an attack on the fort itself, preparations had to be made. "We had orders to bar up the windows and doors, but to leave portholes in the windows to fire through," said Frank Fessenden later.

A Legendary Ride

That night Portugee Phillips, a mining partner of Wheatly and Fischer, slipped through the gate of the fort on one of Carrington's own horses. In his saddlebag, next to the hardtack and oats, was a dispatch for Fort Laramie informing them of the attack and begging for reinforcements. "May God help you," Carrington was heard to say as the rider disappeared into the blinding snow.

Although Carrington had probably ordered at least one other rider out with the same message requesting help, legends have rightly grown up around Phillip's ride of 236 miles south to Fort Laramie. Not only did he have to watch for Indians, but a full plains blizzard had developed. Because of the brightness of the snow, Phillips traveled mainly at night when he could make his way through the drifts.

With bound legs and a frosted buffalo coat, Phillips looked more like a giant grizzly bear than a man when he stumbled up the step of "Old

Bedlam" at Fort Laramie on Christmas night. Party-goers heard the news of the fight with horror, and reinforcements were sent as soon as weather permitted.

At Fort Phil Kearny, the dead were finally buried on December 26, when a trench could be dug in the frozen ground.

Disgusted and shocked, Easterners demanded an explanation for this new, terrible outbreak of hostilities. As a result, the War Department now took over the Indian affairs.

Wagon Box Fight

Following the Fetterman massacre, Chief Red Cloud of the Sioux continued his vow of running the white men out of the Powder River country with his Sioux and Cheyenne Warriors. Throughout the spring and summer of 1867, the Indians made repeated strikes at small parties of miners on the Bozeman Trail, military detachments, and army posts. Confident due to his overwhelming victory over Fetterman, Red Cloud felt he was invincible and could easily overrun equal numbers of soldiers and civilians, but he made a huge mistake.

On August 2, 1867, he attacked a military detachment under Major James Powell that was guarding a wood cutting party near Fort Phil Kearny. Unknown to Red Cloud, the soldiers had recently been issued new .50 breech-loading Springfield rifles. Prior to receiving these new weapons, the soldiers had used muzzle-loaders that could take as long as thirty seconds to reload. The Indians used this to their advantage, attacking in force after drawing fire, while the soldiers were reloading. With the new breech-loaders, the soldiers could reload in less that fifteen seconds and continue firing.

The woodcutting party had taken large army freight wagons to the area where timber was to be cut. They then removed the boxes and used the frames to haul timbers.

Red Cloud saw an opportunity for an easy victory. With as many as fifteen hundred warriors at his command, he sent a small group of between three and five hundred against those who were guarding the woodcutters' horses in a corral. The whites could see that a fight was hopeless and made a dash for the woods, most of them escaping.

Red Cloud and his lesser chief, Rain-In-The-Face, then attacked across Little Piney Creek toward Major Powell's position. The soldiers had arranged the fourteen wagon boxes in an irregular circle and set themselves up behind them. Fortunately, the soldiers had also seven thousand rounds of ammunition with them.

Wagon Box fight (Fort Laramie)

Red Cloud sent five hundred warriors at the "wagon corral," expecting to overrun the barricade when the soldiers were reloading. Instead, they met unrelenting fire that mowed the Indians down. At times the Indians got so close to the corral that some of the soldiers became rattled and threw tools into the faces of the charging enemy. Red Cloud attempted between four and six charges that day, the last coming at about 2:30 P.M. This final desperate charge was led by Red Cloud's nephew. He was killed in mid-charge and the effect of his leadership ended. Red Cloud's forces withdrew, retrieving most of their dead and wounded.

Major Powell's command suffered three killed and two wounded. The Indians' losses were estimated by Major Powell at sixty dead and one hundred wounded.

The Sioux are said to have called the Wagon Box fight the "Bad Medicine Fight" where Red Cloud had sent "the flower of his fighting warriors" against the repeating fire of the soldiers' weapons. He now knew it was useless to fight the whites. From that day on, Red Cloud sought by peaceful means and treaties to save his people. Some say, "That day Red Cloud's heart broke."

The Treaty of 1868

In late October and early November, representatives of the Sioux nation, headed by an embittered Red Cloud, again considered the proposals offered by the "Great White Father." On November 6, 1868, the Indians agreed to a new treaty in the hopes of stopping further bloodshed.

Indeed, the treaty called for both sides to stop fighting. It showed give and take on both sides. The Indians were given all territory north of the North Platte River, providing that they gave up all land to the south. Further, they could hunt both north and south of the river as long as there were buffalo. The Indians, however, agreed not to oppose construction of the railroad, carry off any white women or children, kill or scalp any white man, or oppose the building or existence of military posts.

The government agreed to close the Bozeman Trail and abandon Forts Reno, C. F. Smith, and Phil Kearny along that trail. Washington also agreed to provide for Indian reservations by building storehouses for annuity goods, providing doctors, agents, and blacksmiths along with 320 acres to any Indian family which wanted to farm.

Annuities, or goods, would also be provided. The list was very specific. All Indians settling on reservations would get one pound of meat and flour per day. Each farmer would get "one good cow" and a "well-broken pair" of oxen. Articles of clothing such as "homemade socks" were also to be given annually on August 1.

Red Cloud signed the treaty on November 6, 1868, and the United States Senate ratified it in February 1869.

Delegation from Washington and Indians meeting at Fort Laramie to sign Treaty of 1868 (Fort Laramie)

As the army withdrew from the abandoned Fort Phil Kearny, the soldiers could look back over their shoulders to see smoke rising from the burning fort. The Sioux, proud of their victory, were celebrating by burning the wooden structure to the ground.

Custer Expedition of 1874

While the Treaty of 1868 attempted to settle problems between the army and the Indians, events were already under way which would ultimately bring the conflict to a violent close.

As early as 1833, explorers spoke of the possibility of gold in the Black Hills region of Dakota Territory. The first exploration of the Hills took place in 1852, and by 1861 miners were actively searching for signs of precious metals.

In 1867, Major General William T. Sherman, commander of the army in the Plains area, issued an order forbidding all whites to enter the Black Hills. The government, as you remember, promised to keep all miners and explorers out of the Hills area in order to secure safety for those involved in the building of the Northern Pacific Railroad scheduled for completion in the early 1880s.

As the 1870s dawned it was becoming apparent to all concerned that there was great value in the Black Hills. By treaty, though, no one could enter the area legally. A movement began to "run down" the Indians for not using the Hills. "An area so rich and so beautiful should be developed," an eastern newspaper insisted. "Why should the Indians, who are not using it, be allowed to keep it soley as a religious shrine?"

In 1874, under pressure from miners and developers, the government ordered Lieutenant Colonel George Armstrong Custer to lead the Seventh United States Cavalry on an official exploration of the Black Hills, heart of the Indians' reservation created by the treaty of 1868. In the exploratory party were 951 soldiers and teamsters. The official purpose of the mission, according to the army, was to check on supposed Indian treaty violations. The army claimed it was not a violation of the treaty for the exploratory party to enter the region because it was not searching for gold.

The headlines of the *Bismark Tribune* on August 12, 1874, showed that the army had lied. Custer's official report stated that "fifty pieces of gold as large as pin heads from one pan could be taken" from streams. When the news spread, hordes of gold seekers invaded the forbidden region.

The Indians saw that their treaty guarantees meant nothing to these men. They saw the government try unsuccessfully to stem the invasion of miners into their land. When the army threw out hundreds of miners, thousands more came to take their place.

Finally, the Indians grew convinced that the government had broken the treaty. They fled their reservations and listened to chiefs who wanted to renew fighting the white man.

By the fall of 1874, the Indians had already begun to call the trail leading from Fort Laramie north to the Black Hills, the "Thieves Road," and incidents of hostility on the trail were reported with increased frequency.

In 1875 another expedition entered the Black Hills. The "Jenney Expedition's" job was to establish how much gold was there so that the government would know how much to offer the Indians for the Black Hills. A figure of six million dollars or $400,000 per year was proposed for a lease.

Already, though, the government was justifying invading the Hills by blaming the Indians for treaty violations.

Because of these violations, the army ordered the Indians to return to their reservations by January 1, 1876. All those who did not return would be considered hostile. It was impossible for the Indians to comply with the new law because they did not know the northern boundary of their reservation, and communications were so poor that most Indians never discovered that they were in violation.

Bowing to increased pressure to control the hostile Indians and secure safety for those in the Black Hills, Generals Sherman and Sheridan decided that an all-out campaign should be made to "crush" the Indian resistance.

'76 Offensive

In the spring of 1876 a three-fronted attack was planned. Four hundred and fifty soldiers under Colonel John Gibbon would advance east from Fort Ellis, Montana. Advancing north from Fort Fetterman (near present day Douglas) were one thousand men under the command of Brigadier General George Crook. A third column commanded by Major General Alfred Terry, including George Armstrong Custer at the head of the Seventh Cavalry, would move west from Fort Abraham Lincoln, in Dakota Territory. The three groups would surround the Indian hostiles somewhere in the northeastern Wyoming–southeastern Montana area.

On June 17, 1876, on Rosebud Creek, near present-day Lodge-Grass, Montana, General Crook's column encountered a strong force of Sioux and Cheyenne warriors largely under the command of Crazy Horse. A day-long battle ensued. For the first time in Indian Wars history, the Indians changed their tactics. In all previous fights with the army, the Indians made "hit and run" attacks, never standing their ground. Under the leadership of Crazy Horse, the Indians decided to "stand and fight." Believing there were "too many Indians" on the Rosebud for one column of soldiers, Crook retreated south to await reinforcements. As a result Crook could not complete his third of the plan to "crush" the Indians.

After the battle on the Rosebud, the confident Indian chiefs decided to move west to the valley of the Little Big Horn (Greasy Grass) where ample game and plenty of grass for their horses were available.

The total number of Indians in the valley will never be known exactly, but no fewer than ten to twelve thousand were there, including four to five thousand warriors. Among the chiefs were Red Cloud, Crazy Horse, Sitting Bull, Gall, Low Dog, Crow King, and Two Moon.

Custer's and Gibbon's columns received reports from Crow scouts of a large body of Indians encamped somewhere between them. Colonel Gibbon and Custer's immediate superior, General Alfred Terry, planned to attack the main body of Indians on June 26, 1876.

Little Big Horn

Upon approaching the Indian's camp Custer sent a message for reinforcements. It read: "Benteen. Come on. Big Village—be quick—bring packs. P.S. bring pacs." The message was too late. Custer made a fatal mistake, attacking on June 25, one day ahead of schedule. He and 261 men of the Seventh Cavalry were killed by the combined forces of the Sioux, Cheyennes, and Arapahoes. The battle lasted only about an hour, leaving no survivors but a single horse.

The Battle of the Little Big Horn or "Custer's Last Stand" is a classic example of "winning the battle, but losing the war." The months and years following Custer's defeat saw the defeat of all the plains tribes. As public opinion, particularly in the East, swung against the Indians, a movement to "wipe them out" gathered strength. People known as "Custer Avengers" joined the army in great numbers simply to "kill Indians." The government increased the size of the army and concentrated the soldiers at the frontier posts. In 1877 over seven hundred soldiers were stationed at Fort Laramie alone.

For the first time in frontier history, the Indians had banded together against a common enemy to obtain a common goal, but never again would such a large number camp together. After the battle the large village broke up. Feeding ten thousand people and thirty to forty thousand horses at one camp was impossible.

A Battle Won, a War Lost

The government's plan following Custer's defeat was to put enough soldiers into the field to keep the Indians on the move, never allowing them to hunt and amass food supplies for the winter. The Indian Appropriation Act of 1876 withheld food from Indians on reservations until those on the warpath came in; all claims to the Black Hills would have to be given up. Red Cloud and Spotted Tail, principal reservation chiefs of the Sioux, signed the act without really knowing what it said. The government took this sign to mean that all the Indians had given up their rights to the riches of the Black Hills.

A Summer of Fighting

Several battles were fought in the months immediately after the battle of the Little Big Horn, with the Indians "taking it on the chin." On July 17, 1876, a group of soldiers under the command of Colonel Wesley Merrit attacked the Northern Cheyennes at War Bonnet Creek in northeastern Nebraska. William F. Cody (Buffalo Bill) acted as scout and guide during the march. During this battle, Buffalo Bill won his heroic fight to the death with Yellow Hand, Chief of the Cheyennes. After singlehandedly killing the Indian, Buffalo Bill took his scalp. The press called this the "first scalp for Custer."

Later that summer Colonel Anson Mills attacked a Sioux village at Slim Buttes, scattering the inhabitants. Meanwhile General George Crook scoured the Bozeman Trail–Powder River Basin area for Crazy Horse, and General Nelson Miles chased Sitting Bull across the stretches of Montana.

Dull Knife Battle

On November 14, 1876, Colonel R. S. MacKenzie was ordered out of Fort Fetterman with over one thousand soldiers and four hundred Shoshone and Arapaho scouts to seek out any remaining hostile Indian bands. The column spread out over several miles and included 168 wagons, eight ambulances, and a pack of over 400 mules.

On November 18, a severe snow storm halted the column, socking the men in for two days. On the twenty-fourth, excited Indian scouts rode up to MacKenzie and reported Dull Knife's camp about thirty miles ahead

Cheyenne Chief Dull Knife (Wyoming State Archives)

near present-day Kaycee. There were nearly two hundred lodges, the scouts said, along with many, many ponies. The news excited the anxious soldiers. "There was no shouting, cheering, or loud talking to show excitement," a member of the expedition recalled, "but any old soldier would have known that the news passed along was enough to stir a civilian's blood."

MacKenzie decided to follow a night march with a surprise attack at dawn.

In the moonlit, frigid night, the column moved through the Big Horns toward the village. Because rough terrain slowed them up, the soldiers reached the Indian camp a half hour after sunrise. The Cheyennes were still awake, celebrating a victory over the Shoshones, so complete surprise was impossible. When the Indians saw the soldiers, their drums stopped. Immediately the troopers got the order: "Gallop!"

The soldiers swooped down on the Cheyennes, who hurried women and children to the surrounding mountains for safety and then fought using crevices and crags for cover.

MacKenzie decided not to pursue the Indians into the mountains, so sporadic fighting occurred throughout the day as the army rounded up five hundred ponies and burned the lodges.

As night fell, the temperature plunged to thirty below. Still huddled in the foothills as their village burned in the dark, the Indians suffered greatly. Some of them gave themselves up to be transferred to a reservation; others hid and set out in the morning to find safety with another band; still others froze to death.

At dawn the soldiers marched away, leaving Cheyenne women wailing in grief over the ruins of the village. Some of the remaining warriors and the chief, Dull Knife, escaped and found their way to Crazy Horse's camp on the Tongue River. But the bitterness of the winter and the lack of food and ammunition forced Dull Knife and his remaining people to surrender to General Crook in the spring. The gallant Northern Cheyenne chief led his band to the Cheyenne-Arapaho reservation near old Fort Reno in August 1877.

Crazy Horse and Sitting Bull Surrender

On May 6, 1877, Crazy Horse himself surrendered his winter-weakened warriors and their families at Fort Robinson, Nebraska. Fearing Crazy Horse, Crook ordered the warrior arrested. During his arrest by Agency Indian Police, Crazy Horse was stabbed and killed.

Sitting Bull took his band north hoping to find sanctuary in Canada, but the government of Canada refused. He finally surrendered to General Alfred Terry in July of 1881.

The defeated Cheyennes were forced onto reservations in Oklahoma, and the Sioux were placed on the Pine Ridge, Standing Rock, and Rosebud reservations in South Dakota.

The Ghost Dance and Tragedy of Wounded Knee

The late 1880s provided a last gasp effort of the Plains Indians. The "Ghost Dance" religion began in Utah and spread hope throughout the West. In October 1890, the Sioux learned of the religion in which all dead Indians would return and all Indians who wore the special "Ghost Shirt" would be protected from the white man's bullets.

Fearing another uprising, General Miles ordered Sitting Bull's arrest. In a nervous confrontation between forty-three Indian policemen and over one hundred "Ghost Dancers" outside Sitting Bull's cabin, a shot was fired, and the Sioux chief was killed.

In December 1890, Big Foot and the remains of his Sioux followers (120 men and 230 women and children) were camped at Wounded Knee on the Pine Ridge reservation. Colonel James Forsyth was ordered to arrest the entire band and send them to military prison in Omaha. After the soldiers surrounded the camp, the Indians were ordered to stack their arms and surrender. During the search for weapons supposedly hidden, a shot was fired and general shooting broke out in which 300 to 350 Indians were massacred.

Wounded Knee represents the last major conflict of the Indian Wars. After January 1, 1891, there were only minor confrontations with the Utes and Crows, but never again would a full scale battle be fought between the army and the Plains Indians.

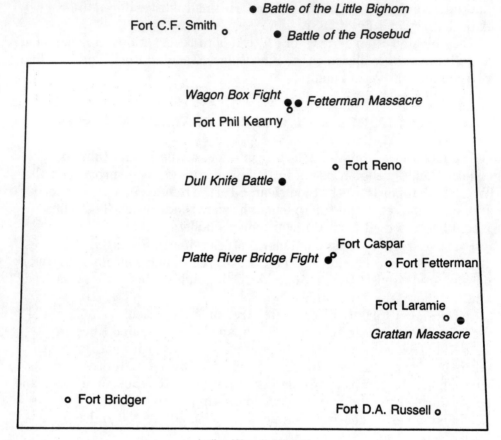

Indian Wars in Wyoming

6
The Transcontinental Railroad

People Come To Stay

If a student of western history should ask the question "Why did Wyoming become a state?" many answers could be offered. Only one answer, though, will bear the test of time. Wyoming became a territory and state only after the transcontinental railroad passed through the southwestern part of what, at that time, was Dakota Territory.

Until the 1860s and the coming of the railroad, Wyoming did not contain enough people to be considered for territorial status. People are necessary, by law, in order to establish a territory. The Northwest Ordinance of 1787, set the required number at 5,000 citizens. For statehood, 60,000 are required.

The fur trading period from 1820-1840 brought less than a thousand people to the area. From 1840 through the 1860s, thousands of emigrants entered Wyoming moving westward up the Platte valley. Unfortunately most of them passed on through to the rich soils of Oregon or the gold mines of California. Only the railroad brought enough people into the territory to make it necessary for rules to live by. The railroad entered Wyoming in the fall of 1867, and less than one year later, Wyoming Territory was organized.

Beginnings of the Railroad

The story of the railroad in Wyoming really begins much earlier than the 1860s. California officially became a territory of the United States in

1848 after the Mexican War. Many Americans were already living along the coasts and in the lush valleys there. In 1848 James Marshall, foreman for a sawmilling operation owned by land baron John Sutter, found gold in a small stream above present-day Sacramento. This discovery caused a huge rush of people to California to search for gold. California became a state in 1850 as its population soared. It was obvious that a railroad link between the eastern states and California was necessary.

During the 1850s, Secretary of War Jefferson Davis ordered four major surveys of possible routes to the West Coast. None of these was chosen. The route eventually used was basically the same as that used by the emigrants' wagon trains in previous years.

Unfortunately the railroads could not be built during the 1850s because the United States was deeply divided by strong "sectionalism" just before the Civil War (1861-1865). Neither the North nor South could agree where it should be built. Each side could see the advantages of having the West Coast connected to itself, so neither would approve a plan for its opposing section.

The Pacific Railroad Act

After the South seceded from the Union in 1861, the problem of where to build the railroad eased. It would now be built with a northern connection. On July 1, 1862, President Abraham Lincoln signed into law the Pacific Railroad Act. The act provided for the following: 1) Construction by two subsidized companies, the Central Pacific, building from the West Coast over the Sierra Nevada Mountains east, and the Union Pacific building from Council Bluffs, Iowa, west over the Rocky Mountains; 2) A grant of land to the two companies at a rate of ten square miles for every mile of track laid (a later act passed in 1864 doubled the land grant to twenty square miles for every mile of track laid); 3) Low interest loans collectable by the railroad companies after the first forty miles of track had been laid; this money was paid to the companies at a rate of $16,000 per mile on the plains of Nebraska as far as Cheyenne, $32,000 per mile for difficult terrain not including the mountains, and $48,000 per mile over the mountains.

Southern Route Chosen

Construction began in Omaha, Nebraska, in 1865 when forty miles of track were laid. Crews laid 260 miles of track in 1866 and another 240 miles in 1867, reaching the new city of Cheyenne on November 13 of that year.

The Oregon Trail over South Pass was discussed as a possible route through Wyoming because of its gentle slope and low summit at the Continental Divide. But the southern route was picked for three reasons. First, it had better coal deposits, and timber areas for the cutting of ties were closer and more desirable. Second, the route was forty miles shorter than the emigrant route. Third, it was closer to Denver, the growing city to the south.

Several people were important in the building of the transcontinental railroad through Wyoming. Thomas C. Durant, vice-president and general manager of the Union Pacific Railroad Company, was the brains behind the company. The chief engineer was a military man, General Grenville Dodge. He organized materials and administered operations. He also served as a public relations officer, continually keeping the Union Pacific name respected by the moneyed interests in the East. Superintendant of Construction was Samual B. Reed. It was Reed who actually oversaw the building of the railroad. Directly under Reed were the Casement brothers, Jack and Dan, who held the track-laying contracts.

Problems Solved

Laying the rails across Wyoming as part of the transcontinental railroad has been called one of the most incredible engineering feats of all time. Many problems had to be overcome in order to span the continent with a thin band of iron rails.

The first problem was that the starting point of the railroad at Omaha, Nebraska, had no railroad connections with eastern cities that would supply materials for construction. Just to lay one mile of track required some forty railroad carloads of supplies. But the factories that manufac-

Union Pacific Railroad Commission showing General Grenville Dodge (seated third from left) and Major General Rawlins (seated second from left) (Wyoming State Archives)

tured them were located in the populated areas to the east. As a result, all materials to be used in construction had to be shipped via freight wagon or brought up the Missouri River by steamboat. Therefore, the cost of getting supplies to the construction areas was staggering.

Another problem was the number of workmen needed to complete the project. At times, ten thousand men were working either directly or indirectly on the transcontinental railroad. Keeping these men on the job supplied with shelter and materials to work with and safe from Indian attack, accident, and prairie fire was to be an awesome task.

Providing food alone required unusual measures. A hunter hired by the railroad, William F. Cody, earned the name "Buffalo Bill" because he killed 4,280 buffalo in eighteen months to feed the workers. In Wyoming "Bible Back" Brown supplied much game for the hungry construction crews crossing Wyoming.

In order to overcome the difficulties of such a complex operation, a military approach was necessary, and an ex-military man was hired for the job. Jack Casement had been a general in the Civil War. This tough boss of construction gangs prided himself on the discipline of his forces. He organized his men with military precision and kept a completely stocked construction train "at the front" (end of track).

Construction Begins

Building the railroad was not just a matter of laying the track and then waiting for the train. Six stages were necessary to get a locomotive across the country.

First came the survey crews. They were made up from eighteen to twenty-two men with a hunter for food. Usually they were able to survey eight to twelve miles per day on level ground but only one mile per day in the mountains. Most of the Indian problems encountered involved the surveyors because they were the first railroad men in the area. Many of the surveys had to be redone because the surveyors were killed and their valuable information lost.

Following the survey crews came the graders whose job was to scrape off the high spots, fill in the low spots, and provide a smooth, flat area for the track layer to follow. Care had to be taken by the surveyors and graders because specifications for safety had to be closely followed. The track could not rise more than 116 feet in a mile, graders (through Wyoming) had to provide a roadbed no less than fourteen feet wide, and curves had to be gentle enough to keep the cars on the tracks. Grading

Building the railroad at
Carmichael's Cut near Bitter
Creek (University of Wyoming)

Dale Creek Bridge, 1868 (Wyoming State Archives)

work was done with picks and shovels. Earth was moved by horse and mule-drawn scrapers and wagons, and gunpowder blasted away what could not be moved by human and animal muscle power.

Next came the bridge builders. Their task was to span every gap that could not be filled by the grading crews. Due to the speed at which they had to move, they could not build the quality into the bridges that they would have liked. Therefore many of the bridges looked as if they would not support a man, let alone a fully loaded train. Many of these flimsy bridges were replaced shortly after completion of the transcontinental line when the atmosphere of a race no longer speeded the construction. The bridge builders usually worked between five and twenty miles ahead of the track laying crew.

Laying the Track

Once the route had been surveyed, the graders had smoothed the roadbed, and the bridges had been built, the line was ready for the tracklayers. The end of track was the busiest, most confusing, yet most exciting stage involved in building the road. This point found Casement's fully loaded construction train, one hundred teams of horses and mules, and over a thousand men. Among these were former Union and Confederate soldiers, Irish immigrants seeking a foothold in America, and, unfortunately, undesirables (ex-convicts, criminals escaping prosecution, gamblers, extortionists, and deserters from the frontier army). Together, they did an admirable job under the guidance of Jack Casement. Averaging approximately two miles a day, the railroad stretched across Wyoming.

Mr. W. A. Bell, a writer who had the opportunity to visit the end of track during construction wrote the following description of what he saw:

On they came. A light car, drawn by a single horse, gallops up to the front with its load of rails. Two men seize the end of the rail and start forward, the rest of the gang taking hold by twos, until it is clear of the car. They came forward on a run. At the word of command the rail is dropped in its place, right side up with care, while the same process goes on at the other side of the car. Less than thirty seconds to a rail for each gang and so four rails go down in a minute. Quick work you say, but the fellows on the Union Pacific are tremendously in earnest. The moment the car is empty, it is tipped over on the side of the track to let the loaded car go past, and then it is tipped back again; and it is a sight to see it go flying back for another load, propelled by a horse a full gallop at the end of 60 or 80 feet of rope, ridden by some young Jehu, who drives furiously. Close behind the first gang come the gauger, spikers, and bolsters, and a lively time they make of it. It is a grand 'anvil chorus' that those sturdy sledges are playing across the plains. It is in a triple time, three strokes to the spike. There are ten spikes to a rail, 100 rails to the mile, 1800 miles to San Francisco—21,000,000 times are those sledges to be swung; 21,000,000 times are they to come down with their sharp punctuation before the great work of modern America is complete.

The first tracks arrived in Cheyenne, Dakota Territory, on November 13, 1867. The crews began working again the following spring and pushed west. On December 16, 1868, just over one year after entering the state, the construction crews left. Behind them were the beginnings of towns, a railroad, a newly organized territory, and most important of all, people.

Towns Are Born

Throughout Wyoming the force behind the establishment of towns was nearly always the railroads and the first real settlements of any size came with the transcontinental railroad line. Before that, the closest thing you could find to a town were military forts, such as Fort Laramie, Fort Bridger, and Fort Caspar, which were located on the Oregon Trail. In time connections between the railroad and these forts were made, providing towns at those points. Later, other towns grew in Wyoming at other sites primarily because of the railroad access. Few Wyoming towns were located away from the railroad. Those that were developed because of mining, recreation, or as junction points connecting already established towns.

As the railroad sped across Wyoming, "end of track" towns sprang up in the tracklayers' path. Some of these towns, such as Cheyenne, Laramie, and Green River, took root and survived to become centers of population today. Others eventually withered and died as they lost their usefulness, or the route was later changed, bypassing them in favor of better locations. Benton, Bryon, and Bear River City are all railroad ghost towns.

All "end of track" towns tended to be similar, at least in their beginnings. They were constructed of canvas and board frame buildings, some with false fronts. The people who ran businesses usually provided services that brought in quick money without regard for the people they served. After

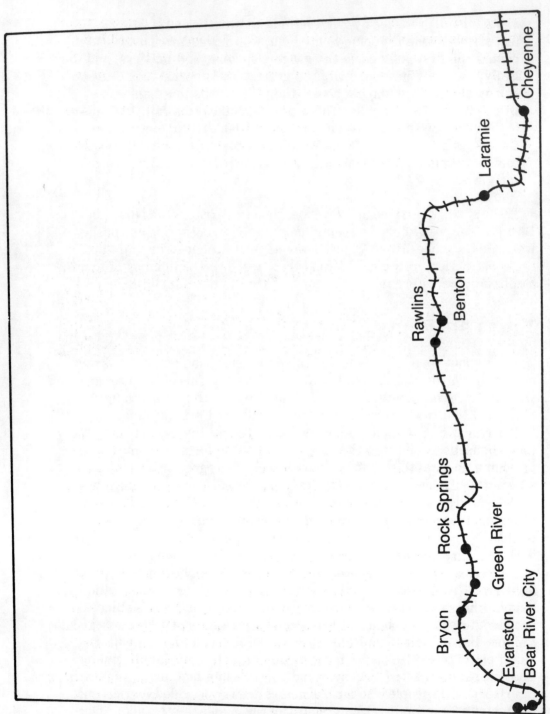

Transcontinental railroad through Wyoming

visiting a town, the noted author and journalist, Henry Stanley, wrote: "As the construction crews pushed westward, canvas and board front towns sprouted at whatever point happened to be the 'end of the track.' Gamblers and saloon keepers were their mainstay and payday for the construction crews was the high point of the week."

Six "end of track" towns developed into important Wyoming cities. They are Cheyenne, Laramie, Rawlins, Rock Springs, Green River, and Evanston. Each of these cities owes its beginnings to the railroad, but each also progressed in its own direction.

Sixteenth Street, Cheyenne, 1867 (Wyoming State Archives)

Cheyenne

Cheyenne was named by General Dodge when he established a division point on the transcontinental railroad in July 1867 at a site 516 miles west of Omaha. Between this date and the arrival of tracklayers on November 13, General Dodge laid out the city, making provisions for various land donations. When the tracklayers arrived, there were 3,000 residents already in Cheyenne. A newspaper, the *Daily Leader*, was quickly published. Two months later population was guessed to be over 5,000, with approximately 300 assorted businesses.

Unfortunately Cheyenne was still in Dakota Territory, hundreds of miles from Yankton, the territorial seat of government. As a result, the town lacked peace officers and had to resort to vigilance committees to preserve even a semblance of law and order. Cheyenne's population dropped by half in the spring of 1868 when construction crews moved on, but the new Union Pacific shops and a promised spur line to Denver held hope for the future. In 1869 Cheyenne was designated as the territorial capital of the newly established Wyoming Territory and became the state capital in 1890 when Wyoming became a state.

Cheyenne's reputation as a "hell on wheels" town of the 1870s was entirely justified. Frank Leslie, a newspaper journalist of the period wrote: "This city of the plains has a reputation for vice and crime far in excess of any existing facts . . . Every careless street takes on the aspect of prowling assassins, and the very dogs are clothed in mystery. Keno signs in blue and red abound. It boasts two dailies [newspapers], three hotels, two theatres, five churches, one school, and twenty gambling saloons."

In the 1870s Cheyenne became an outfitting point for expeditions north through Fort Laramie into Indian territory as soldiers, horses, supplies, and weapons arrived daily via the railroad. The discovery of gold in the Black Hills made Cheyenne a terminus of stagecoach and shipping companies. During the open range period late in the 1800s Cheyenne became the center of Wyoming's livestock industry.

Laramie

The next major town on the transcontinental line was Laramie, approximately forty-five miles west of Cheyenne. Building the railroad across this short span was in itself a major accomplishment because the Laramie Mountains separated the sites. General Grenville Dodge had earlier (1866) discovered a route called "the Gangplank" that avoided steep grades to the summit over Sherman Pass and back down the west slope into the plain between Laramie and the Medicine Bow Mountains. Crossing this range forced the builders to span wide canyons (Dale Creek Bridge was 128 feet high and 530 feet long) and blast away huge amounts of rock. The summit, called Sherman, was the highest point on the transcontinental line at 8,236 feet above sea level.

Railroad Hotel, Laramie, 1868 (Wyoming State Archives)

Asa Moore, Con Wager, and "Big Ed" hanged by vigilantes in Laramie, 1868 (Wyoming State Archives)

The first construction train arrived in Laramie on May 9, 1868. Already a tent city and a fort (Fort John Buford) awaited the tracklayers. The people of Laramie were typical "end of track" types. Ruthless and lawless, they were better organized than some and managed to run off what there was of city government. The army moved with the tracklayers and left the town without law and order for nearly five months. Frank Leslie of *Leslie's Illustrated*, interviewed a Laramie citizen during this time in lawless Laramie: "Thar was a time when it was mighty unsafe to kill a man out yer, but its gettin' easier nowadays. Murder's done with impunity now. I tell you, young fellers, there never was but one judge that made no mistake and that was Judge Lynch and we didn't gain much by gettin' rid of him."

In October 1868 a vigilante committee was formed and in a Hollywood style shoot-out, five outlaws were killed, fifteen were wounded, and four others, including "Long" Steve Young, were hanged from handy telegraph poles. Even with this, law and order did not return, and the city of Laramie was put under federal court rule until 1874, when the order was lifted.

Things settled down somewhat in 1869 after a school and four churches with congregations praying for civilization were built. During the 1870s cattlemen grazed their herds on the Laramie Plains, and many centered their businesses and built their mansions in Laramie.

The Union Pacific built its rolling mills (rail forming) in Laramie during the 1870s, thus assuring Laramie an economic future. In 1886 the University of Wyoming was established in Laramie and remains to this day.

Rawlins

As tracklayers skirted the northern end of the Medicine Bow Mountains around Elk Mountain and then headed west, they entered a region much different from the ones they had previously crossed. This region, called the "Great Basin," is a dry windy plain extending west through southwestern Wyoming. Water was a key resource here, and it led to the founding of the city of Rawlins.

West of the northward flowing Platte River, the country becomes very dry. General Grenville Dodge was assisted in his explorations for a railroad route by General John A. Rawlins. At one point General Rawlins became very thirsty. A scout with the group, Ballard Dunn, recounted: "We started out to find running water, and I discovered a spring in a draw near where the town of Rawlins now stands. General Rawlins was very appreciative. General Dodge then said, 'We will name this Rawlins Spring.'"

Later General Dodge wrote: "The end of one of the divisions happened to be close to the spring, and I named the station Rawlins, which has grown into quite a town and division point of the Union Pacific road."

Rawlins was typical of end of track towns except that very little wood was available, so buildings were made mostly of sod or cloth.

Soon it was discovered that the Rawlins area provided excellent grazing for sheep. As a result the city eventually became known as a wool growing center.

Rawlins had its wild and wooly days. During the late 1870s outlaws "Dutch" Charley Burris and "Big Nose" George Parrott tried to derail and rob a train. After killing two deputies while trying to escape, they spent some time in jail. Burris was lynched after being taken from a train where he was recognized. Parrott was tried, found guilty, and sentenced to death. While in jail, he tried to escape, was slowed by the jailor's wife, and was captured and hanged by vigilantes. The vigilantes then ordered twenty-four other "badmen" out of town under threat of the same treatment. The next morning, they were gone.

Rawlins became the site of the state prison after statehood in 1890, replacing the territorial prison in Laramie, which served during much of the lawless period in Wyoming.

Rock Springs

Rock Springs had modest beginnings when a government surveyor, Captain Howard Stansbury, took notes on the huge coal seams in the hills overlooking what would later become Rock Springs in September 1852. In 1861 the location became a station for the Pony Express and the Overland Stage. In an attempt to avoid pursuing Indians, an Express rider "holed up" in a rocky outcropping from which a stream flowed. In 1866 Archie and Duncan Blair settled near the springs. When transcontinental railroad tracks reached this point in mid 1868 the Blairs opened the first coal mine. The site was originally named Camp Blairtown but was later changed to the more historically significant name of Rock Springs.

Owned by the Union Pacific, the Rock Springs coal mines soon became the largest in the West. Much of the coal was used to fuel the huge locomotives developed near the end of the nineteenth century, but some contributed to the growth of industrial cities of the West where it was used to fuel factories.

Because of the need for cheap labor in the mines, many nationalities of people soon lived in Rock Springs. By 1885 a thousand Chinese lived in the area along with nearly two thousand Irish, Welsh, Scots, Greeks, Italians, and Poles.

In that year racial prejudice and dissatisfaction with the operation of the Union Pacific mines erupted in violence. Unemployed white miners, "tramps and outlaws" as they were called by Governor Francis E. Warren, killed twenty-eight Chinese, wounded fifteen others, chased hundreds out of town, and destroyed property valued at nearly $150,000. Chinese workers had been brought in to break a strike against the Union Pacific mines. As a result, Governor Warren called in troops from Camp Murray, Utah, to calm the atmosphere. Sixteen men were arrested, but no indictments were served. No one was punished. The troops stayed in Rock Springs until 1898, when they were called away to fight in the Spanish-American War.

During the first half of the twentieth century, coal remained the chief industry, and the population neared 10,000. When the demand for coal was replaced by oil and gas, unemployment caused the population to decline.

Massacre of the Chinese, Rock Springs, 1885 (Wyoming State Archives)

Green River

Green River owes its existence to the transcontinental railroad twice. When the tracklayers arrived in 1868, speculators had preceded them. There were 2,000 townspeople in residence. The railroad was in a hurry to chew up as many miles as possible and did not tarry long in Green River. The town nearly died in the next few months. However, the Union Pacific realized the importance of the site, and after the line was completed to Promontory, the company made Green River a division point on the transcontinental line.

Green River did not suffer the problems of vice and crime so common to many railroad town and had a relatively civilized history.

Green River became the connection point for the Oregon Short Line Railroad and the Union Pacific, thus assuring the town a continued existence.

Evanston

Like Green River, Evanston came to life twice as a result of the railroad moving ahead and then coming back to give it life again. Named after the

Union Pacific surveyor who plotted the town, the Uinta County seat was blessed by the proximity of several coal mines. Like Rock Springs, Evanston boasted a very large number of Chinese during the mining period, but they drifted away after the Rock Springs massacre.

The Wyoming State Hospital for the mentally ill, founded in 1888, was located just outside the city limits. It, along with the railroad, insured Evanston of a strong future.

Impact on the Future

Having crossed Wyoming, the Union Pacific pressed on into Utah and met with the Central Pacific pressing east from Sacramento. They met at an unlikely spot north of Great Salt Lake called Promontory Point (summit) on May 10, 1869. With this meeting, the industrial East was tied to the rapidly growing West Coast.

Overland Limited (Wyoming State Archives)

As the construction crews left Wyoming so did the population. A census taken in early summer of 1869 showed a population of only 8,104 people. Future generations owed their existence in Wyoming to the railroad. It was responsible for the first towns, the first mines, the first lumber operations, and most importantly, for the creation of Wyoming Territory and later, statehood.

With the railroad's presence in southern Wyoming, it became economically possible to raise and ship cattle and sheep to population centers in the East. Unfortunately though, animals that were on the scene prior to the railroad suffered greatly. The buffalo, which once roamed the Great Plains region in herds numbering in the millions, were killed by hired hunters to feed the construction workers and nearly exterminated.

Few events have had a greater impact on the development of a state than the building of the transcontinental railroad had on Wyoming. It provided employment, transportation, shipping, adventure, and growth unparallelled since that time.

7
Territorial Wyoming

With the building of the transcontinental railroad beginning in 1865, it became apparent that very soon the southwestern part of Dakota Teritory would see some vast changes. After all, Dakota Territory in the 1860s was obviously too large for successful management. The people responsible for running the territory could see that reducing its size could only improve the situation.

The same year as construction began on the railroad, Ohio Congressman J. M. Ashley introduced a bill to provide a "temporary government for the Territory of Wyoming" to be formed from parts of Dakota, Utah, and Idaho territories. The bill stayed in the committee on territories until 1868. Had it passed, Wyoming would have included what is now the Nebraska panhandle and the Black Hills of South Dakota.

In December 1867 the governor of Dakota Territory, A. J. Faulk, suggested the creation of a new territory when he addressed the Dakota Territorial Legislature. Dakota's legislature then petitioned Congress to make a separate territory out of the southwest part of its own territory.

Reasons for Creating Wyoming Territory

In its petition to Congress, the legislature gave several reasons favoring the creation of the new territory. First, the southwestern part was many miles from the territorial capital, Yankton, located in southeastern South Dakota north of Omaha. Second, Dakota Territory's population was split into two parts: that east of the Missouri River and that along the newly established transcontinental railroad right-of-way. Between these two areas of population lay thousands of square miles of hostile Indian territory. Third, no form of communication existed between the two parts. Last, two different lifestyles existed in the two sections. Eastern Dakota Territory was already a region of tidy farms and small towns. The western part contained rip-roaring mining camps, railhead towns, and occasional Indian uprisings. Neither section cared about the other.

Shortly thereafter, more bills were proposed to create the new territory. Had some passed, we might be living in the state of "Lincoln" instead of Wyoming. Others proposed a variety of names debated by members of Congress. Some favored naming the territory after Indian tribes (Sioux, Pawnee, Arapaho, Cheyenne, or Shoshone). Others favored rivers (Yellowstone, Platte, or Sweetwater). As Congressional debate continued, though, the name "Wyoming" gained favor after the meanings of this eastern Indian word became well known. The word "Wyoming" is Delaware Indian in origin and was adapted from two words, "Mecheweami—ing." It meant "at the big flats" from which the whites derived "large plains" or "end of the plains."

Early Territorial Organization

Finally, on July 25, 1868, Congress created Wyoming Territory, but it took until May 19, 1869, before the territorial government could be organized. Ulysses S. Grant won the presidential election in November 1868 and took the oath of office in March 1869. He wasted no time in appointing officials to run the government of Wyoming Territory. On April 3, 1869, he appointed John A. Campbell governor, Edwin M. Lee secretary, and Joseph M. Carey United States marshal. They were quickly confirmed by the Senate.

Both Governor Campbell and Secretary Lee served as brigadier generals during the Civil War. Lee had been captured and served one year in a prisoner of war camp. After his release he received the Silver Star for his service. Campbell had served as assistant secretary of war of the United States until his appointment as territorial governor.

The officers arrived in Cheyenne on May 7 and quickly took charge of the territory. Later that month Campbell sent troops to quell problems with the Indians as one of his first official acts. He also designated Cheyenne as the temporary capital and arranged for persons convicted of crimes to be sent to the Detroit House of Corrections for confinement.

Campbell also arranged for an accurate census to be taken. The total population of Wyoming Territory was 8,014 people, most living along the Union Pacific right-of-way in the several towns that had sprung up there.

MONTANA TERRITORY

IDAHO
TERRITORY

DAKOTA ⋮ TERRITORY

NEBRASKA TERRITORY

UTAH
TERRITORY

COLORADO
TERRITORY

Western territories

At the time that Wyoming Territory was being organized, four counties already existed, having been created by the Dakota legislature. They were Laramie, Carter, Carbon, and Albany. They extended all the way from the northern border to the southern border of the state. In 1869 when the government of the territory was organized, a part of Utah and a part of Idaho became Uinta Country.

Women Win the Vote

Among the routine business matters facing the tiny legislature of the new territory in November 1869 was a small handwritten law that granted voting rights to women. The bill surprisingly passed, making Wyoming a first—the first territory in the world to consider women politically equal to men.

A no more unlikely place could have been found for the birthplace of women's suffrage than Wyoming. Conservative by nature, the population then consisted mainly of miners, ranchers, railroad workers, cattlemen, trappers, and some businessmen—almost all men. Less than 1,863 women lived in the territory. Nowhere in the country were women allowed to vote or hold office. Even property rights for women were heavily restricted.

Yet because of the isolation of Wyoming, barriers between men and women never really existed. A woman, for example, could easily become a widow and be left with a ranch or business to run unaided by any male relatives. On the trail, women's and men's jobs often became indistinguishable. Further, men depended on women not only as homemakers, but as partners.

Nationally, the passage of the Thirteenth Amendment after the Civil War influenced Wyoming's lawmakers. This amendment granted suffrage (voting rights) to all minorities. Now men of all races could cast ballots, and to some people it seemed odd that women still could not vote.

Among those people were Colonel William Bright, Edward Lee, and Esther Morris, three leaders of the suffrage movement in Wyoming. Bright was president of the Legislative Council of Wyoming. Living in South Pass City at the time, Bright represented Carter County. A colleague characterized him as "not a statesman of the highest order or he would not have run a saloon and kept a bull dog." Despite such criticism, though, Bright was a capable, self-made man who hadn't the fortune of a formal education. Bright, who had served in the Civil War (hence his title "Colonel"), had married a woman he considered his intellectual superior. Julia Bright was a suffragette long before it became popular, and for many years her husband thought it was unfair not to have his wife vote when he himself could.

Esther Morris, in contrast to Julia Bright, was an "old, manish woman" who came from Spencer, New York, by way of Illinois. She had a history of standing up for the rights of the downtrodden. In fact, before the Civil War she had been a courageous abolitionist in Illinois. She moved to South Pass City with her husband and three sons in 1869.

As legend has it, in this mountain town of 2,000, Mrs. Morris hosted a tea party on September 2, 1869. Being interested in the upcoming elections for the first territorial legislature, she invited two candidates. The democrat was William H. Bright and the republican was H. G. Nickerson. As Nickerson remembered, Mrs. Morris at one point stood and said, "One (of these men) is sure to be elected and we would desire . . . a public pledge that whichever is elected will introduce and work for passage of a bill granting the right of suffrage to all women." The men pledged themselves to the applause of the forty people present.

Women Gain Property Rights

When Bright won, as did all the democrats, he was elected president of the Territorial Council. One of the first bills considered was a law granting women the right to acquire and hold any kind of property in their own name. Up until this time, laws restricted what property they could consider theirs. But the legislature decided quickly that women in Wyoming should be free to own their own property to protect them from "shiftless and improvident husbands." After all, one Cheyenne paper asked, "The moral right of a wife to protection in property exists. Why not make this right a legal one?"

While this act was being debated and passed, a number of suffragette leaders such as Anna Dickinson and Redelia Bates visited Cheyenne. The territorial press covered their well-attended lectures carefully.

The stage was being set, with Colonel Bright being influenced from many sides to make a move. First, of course, there was his commitment made in his hometown. His wife undoubtedly was twisting his arm to introduce a bill. Increased interest in suffrage among the general public and the press worked on him. Equally important was the pressure now coming from Edward Lee, secretary of the legislature.

Lee had introduced a suffrage bill in the Connecticut legislature in 1867. Though the bill lost, Lee remained an ardent supporter of the movement to the point that he introduced the nationally known Anna Dickinson when she spoke in September and wrote in favor of suffrage in the *Cheyenne Tribune*.

On November 12 Colonel Bright called another member of the legislature to his chair and said he would be introducing a suffrage bill within two weeks. During that time Bright came up with a simple clearly written bill that granted women over the age of eighteen the right to vote. Some say it was Edward Lee who wrote the bill, but it was definitely Bright who introduced it on November 27.

There was apparently little surprise in the council, and on November 30 it passed six to one with one abstention. In the House of Representatives, however, it did cause some lively discussion. After a special committee recommended the bill, opponents struggled to block its passage. Ben Sheeks tried to amend the bill twice, and his second amendment, changing eighteen to twenty-one, passed. He recalled that while the bill was not introduced as a joke, its final passage of seven to four was. "I remember distinctly," he wrote later, "a lot of my friends laughing, saying they thought it would be a good joke to pass the bill!"

Joke or not, Governor Campbell, who had been a women's rights advocate, got the speaker to sign the bill that night. This took the bill out of the House before any possibility of reconsideration. Four days later, on December 10, 1869, Campbell signed the bill into law. The *Daily Leader* commented the next day: "We now expect quite an immigration of ladies to Wyoming. We say, Come on!"

What prompted the Council members and the House of Representatives to approve giving women the right to vote? For one thing, Bright himself campaigned for its passage. He told democrats that the republican governor would certainly veto the bill, so it would look good if the democrats at least sponsored such a liberal measure. He then told the Republicans they would look good if they would back this liberal measure which the democrats themselves were going to defeat.

According to one of the Council members, "One man told me he thought it was right and just to give women the vote. Another said he thought it would be a good advertisement for the territory, still another said he voted to please someone else, and so on . . . So you see, it does not appear there was much of a high and mighty impulse about the thing."

Nevertheless, Wyoming had become the feather in the cap of the women's suffrage movement, the "pet lamb of the flock" according to the *Daily Leader*. The paper further stated that the "rightists" in the East "are rejoicing over the redemption of Wyoming, a converted sinner."

Mama's on the Jury

At first it was thought Wyoming women would not exercise their newly won right to vote. But in the first election following passage, September 1870, most of them cast their ballots.

In granting women the right to vote, the lawmakers had extended other privileges and duties to the newly "enfranchised" or voting citizens. One of the most notable duties of any citizen in a democracy is serving on a jury. And within four months of passage of the suffrage bill, women in Wyoming broke down another barrier by sitting on the jury for the first time in history.

The crime was a classic, one committed a thousand times in the lawless railhead towns along the Union Pacific. It occurred late one night at the Sherman Hotel in Laramie. Law-abiding, handsome, quiet Andrew Howie had gone to sleep in an upstairs room above the rowdy Sherman saloon.

Sometime after midnight, a "local badman and famous shot" named Hoctor had gambled and drunk his way into a violent, destructive fit. The screaming, breaking glasses, and flying chairs woke Howie, who went downstairs to investigate, gun in hand. He found Hoctor standing in the middle of the room.

Hoctor pointed his gun at Howie, and some say he hissed, "I'm gonna shoot you!"

Two shots rang out. Due to his own careless drinking, Hoctor could not draw first and fell dead on the saloon floor. The next day Howie confessed, hoping to be granted protection "from mob violence."

Chief Justice John Howe had by now had enough of such routine violence in the new territory. He had seen men hang for stealing a horse but walk away from a gunfight since it was considered self-defense if the loser merely had his gun out of its holster. In an effort to bring new meaning to law and order, Judge Howe appointed six women to the grand jury.

Howe knew what would happen, for in his charge to the women he said, "You shall not be driven by the sneers and jeers and insults of a lively crowd from the temple of justice."

The moment the word of the jury leaked out, reporters, photographers, and cartoonists descended on Wyoming to cover the event.

The women had to go to the courtroom heavily veiled, according to Sarah Pease, one of the jurors, because "we feared that some special artist would make hasty sketches of us. Of course we were caricatured in a most hideous manner."

"Baby, Baby, don't get in a hurry, Your mama's gone to sit on the jury" became the chant of anti-feminists.

Undaunted by the publicity, the women—Eliza Stewart, Amelia Hatcher, C. H. Hilton, Mary Mackel, Agnes Baker, and Sarah Pease—returned a murder indictment against Howie.

Judge Howe now appointed six women and six men to the trial jury and furthered the women's rights movement by appointing Martha Atkinson bailiff, the first woman ever to hold that position.

The trial stirred as much interest as the grand jury had. The jurors were sequestered in the Old Union Pacific Hotel, next to the depot. Following the testimony, they spent two days considering the verdict.

During this time the *Cheyenne Daily Leader* speculated on the health of the women, saying they "were fatigued almost beyond endurance." The paper shuddered with fear: "It will be a miracle if some of the delicate women who are going through this painful ordeal do not sink . . . and return . . . home with shattered nerves and ruined health."

The women, however, all survived nicely, nerves intact, and with the men had agreed on a verdict: guilty of manslaughter.

Judge Howe sentenced Howie to ten years at hard labor in Detroit, since the territorial prison had not yet been built. Two years later Howie was paroled and then disappeared. This verdict, however, was a first step in the long road of establishing true law and order in the new territory.

First Woman Justice

At this same time, Esther Morris, who had hosted the legendary tea party in South Pass City, herself became a first. Perhaps to reward her efforts on behalf of the women's rights movement or to add to its victories, Secretary and then acting Governor Edward Lee commissioned the fifty-six year old woman to be the first justice of the peace in her area.

Mrs. Morris "was a commanding presence with a mind well-stored with knowledge and experiences of life," said one of her admirers. The *Chicago Post*, however, said that "Her worship is fifty-seven years old and weighs 180 pounds." Regardless of the description, Judge Morris tried about fifty cases in her year in office, and to her credit no higher court ever overturned her decisions.

Wyoming had been the first to grant women the right to vote, serve on a jury, and hold public office, but many opposed these moves. The *Daily Leader* complained of this "reform against nature." The paper viciously attacked the feminists and called for a repeal of the law saying, "it is contrary to propriety, to decency, to common sense, and to the order of nature. The sooner it dies (and die it must) the earlier our people may congratulate themselves on having escaped one of the most unnatural and dangerous innovations ever projected in this or any other age!"

A Move To Repeal

On November 14, 1871, Mr. Castle of Uinta County introduced a bill to repeal women's suffrage in Wyoming. The House passed the repeal nine to three. The Council then passed it eight to zero, but Governor Campbell vetoed the bill. The House, adamantly against suffrage, voted to override the veto. The Council was recommended to override, but the final five-to-four vote was not a two-thirds majority, and the bill was lost. The original suffrage law had passed its final test in Wyoming.

In the years to come both sides of the suffrage question would look to Wyoming as an example of how suffrage either failed or succeeded. In general, though, the "experiment" was a success. As one writer put it, "no divorces or elopements or other domestic calamities have been known to result from women's introduction to the jury box." Most men, once used to the idea, wanted women to vote. "Women everywhere are always in favor of law and order," one Wyoming rancher said. "It is owing to the women's vote that our young state where the cowboy still flourishes, has stringent laws against gambling. Women here read of the state affairs, notice what their congressmen are doing at Washington. Does it unsex them? No. It is good to see intelligence flash from their eyes."

When Wyoming became a state in 1890, the nickname "Equality State" would become official, in recognition of the major steps that Wyoming daringly took in 1869 to insure equality for all its citizens.

Territorial Industries Begin

For any territory to draw people to settle within its borders some type of industry or way of making a living must be available. Though the Union Pacific was a major industry, two other uses of Wyoming land began to flourish during the territorial years, drawing thousands into the state.

One was the cattle industry, and the other was agriculture, spurred on by the homesteading movement of the late nineteenth and early twentieth centuries.

A Fortunate Accident

If legends can be believed, livestock raising in Wyoming began by accident. It is said a group of emigrants drove five oxen into Wyoming late in the season during the early years of the westward migration. As winter hit suddenly, they abandoned the oxen and wintered at a fort. A year later they found their stock alive and well. Dumbfounded, the emigrants discovered that the proteins of the range grass crystalized during the winter so that the oxen could thrive year round.

Even if the story is not true, it does point up two important facts. First, the cattle industry in Wyoming is nearly as old as the written history of the state. And second, Wyoming is well-suited for raising livestock.

Early Herds In Wyoming

William Sublette brought the first recorded domestic cattle into Wyoming in 1830. Heading for the rendezvous to be held on July 16, he drove one milk cow along with four oxen to pull loads. After the rendezvous, he sold the cattle to travelers heading back to St. Louis. Captain Bonneville also brought a cow and a calf with him on his Wyoming expedition in 1832.

Mormons brought the first breeding cattle in 1847 when "142 men and three courageous women driving a small herd of cattle before them" entered Wyoming on their way to Utah. These Durham and Devon cattle, well-bred milk and meat animals, soon spread "to every nook and corner" of Utah and by 1853 had spilled over into western Wyoming when the Mormons colonized Camp Supply, south of Ft. Bridger.

Other early pioneers and forty-niners brought cattle from the East. By the time they reached Wyoming, the animals were usually "footsore and gaunt," so the owners traded or sold them for fresh oxen. Thus small herds began at "way stations" along the Oregon Trail.

Alexander Majors, who later helped organize the Pony Express, was forced to winter three hundred head of cattle in 1854. He had shipped over a hundred thousand pounds of supplies to Ft. Laramie in November. Too late to return east before winter, he turned his stock loose near Wheatland.

"They came out in the spring," he wrote, "in the very finest working condition . . . without losing one." So pleased was Majors that for the next ten years he wintered his cattle in the same area. Majors claimed to have started the first breeding herd in Wyoming in 1862 at Pumpkin Creek. But troublesome Indians made his venture short-lived. Fearing "they would murder my herders," Majors sold off his herd and left the territory.

The First Great Cattle Drive

Four years later in 1866, the cattle industry began in earnest. Nelson Story, an Ohio adventurer, came west to look for gold during the Montana gold rush. He was one of the lucky ones who struck it rich—to the tune of $100,000. Not wanting to fritter away his new fortune, he decided to invest in cattle. So he headed to Texas where he bought 1,500 head of tall long-horn Texas steers. Since the Texas ranges were overstocked already he decided to move them to the Montana he had fallen in love with.

He could not have picked a worse time to drive a herd north. Infuriated with the traffic over the Bozeman Trail that cut through the heart of his hunting grounds, Red Cloud was on the warpath, making life difficult for travelers to the gold fields. At Fort Laramie officers tried to convince Story that Red Cloud would take his cattle and his scalp, but the intrepid trail boss equipped his men with Remington rapid fire breech loaders and kept on course.

Texas longhorns (Wyoming State Archives)

Near Fort Reno a war party of Sioux attacked the cattle drive. Though two drovers were wounded, Story continued. By October he made it to Fort Phil Kearny, where the cautious Colonel Carrington ordered Story to halt. Knowing he must act soon to avoid winter, an angry Story called his men together. They voted to move on, and under cover of darkness Story headed the herd back to the trail.

Moving at night to avoid raids, Story made good progress through the mercifully mild fall and early winter. In December he finally reached Virginia City, where he made his home and established his herd.

With Story's success, sharp businessmen turned their eyes to the vast northern plains. Even though buffalo still spotted the grasslands and Indians held firmly to their hunting grounds, those with money to invest could see cattle in the future.

Over the next two decades, three major cattle trails cut through Wyoming. The Texas Trail, pioneered by Story, cut across the eastern half of the state. The Goodnight Trail cut into Wyoming from the south and ended on the Laramie Plains. Finally the Oregon Cattle Trail entered from both the west and north, ending in Wyoming's great basin.

Driving Cattle On The Texas Trail

Two years after Nelson Story's herd carved out the Texas Trail, John Iliff, a successful cattleman in Colorado, brought a herd from the Snyder Brothers in Fort Worth, Texas. He drove the herd to Cheyenne to sell to local butchers. By this time the railroad had connected Cheyenne to the East, so the enterprising Iliff shipped some of the butchered meat back to Chicago. Businessmen readily saw the beginnings of a profitable venture.

By October 1868, the Texas Trail had become a highway of cattle with 300,000 head being driven north each year. Some of the herds would mature on the northern grasslands, free for the grazing. Some of the cattle were driven to Cheyenne for shipment east. But most of the herds were delivered to owners who were establishing the cattle industry in Wyoming, Montana, Nebraska, and the Dakotas.

A herd of cattle numbered between two to three thousand head. Herds would begin flowing through the state in May and continue in a steady stream until late August. All types of cattle were moved on the trail except calves. Early Wyoming Governor John Kendrick, who drove cattle on the Texas Trail in his youth, recalled that calves were given away or destroyed in order to save trouble and avoid delaying the movement of the herd. Many of these calves were given to homesteaders, which helped develop small herds up and down the trail.

Kendrick noted a moderate loss of cattle along the way. One herd for example numbered 3,470 head when it left Texas, and 3,430 were finally

Trail drive (Wyoming State Archives)

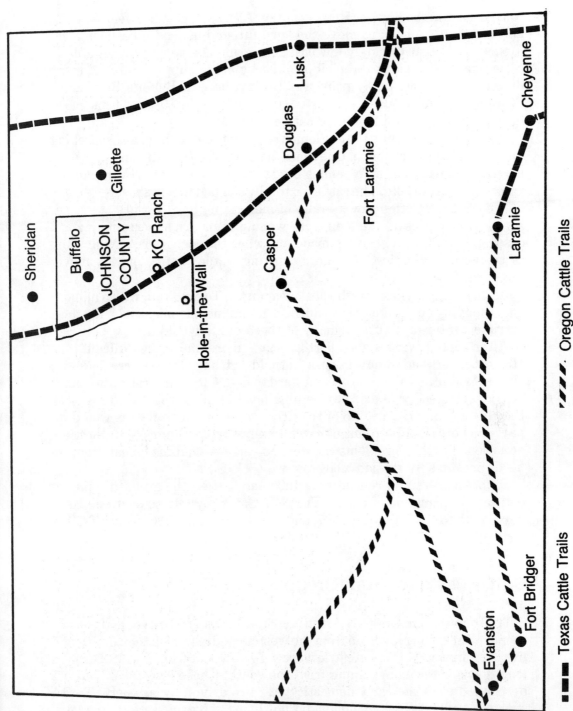

Texas Cattle Trails

Oregon Cattle Trails

Wyoming cattle country

turned loose in the Powder River country. All told, it cost between forty and fifty cents a head to move the herd fifteen hundred miles along the Texas Trail, a surprisingly low cost that made the venture profitable.

Several towns along the trail profited by being supply centers for the drives. One major supply point was Lusk, where at Baker's Brothers Store cooks could load up supplies—300 lbs. of flour for $9.75, 200 lbs. of bacon for $28.00, and 25 lbs. of oatmeal for $1.25.

Water was something the cattlemen could not readily buy, and searching for it was always a problem. One time Charles Coffee was driving a herd north when just over the Wyoming border he and the other drovers came across a beautiful lake. The cattle gratefully slurped the fresh water, but in the distance Coffee saw a group of men riding hard toward the herd. As they drew closer, the men were waving their arms, screaming and cussing. Finally, the drovers made out what the men were saying: the cattle were wading in Cheyenne's drinking water. Coffee quickly moved the herd.

Eighteen eighty-six was the peak year on the Texas Trail, with a million cattle moving up the dusty road during the summer. Ironically during the terrible winter of that year many of these cattle would die.

After 1886 driving a herd north became more and more difficult. Homesteaders had by now taken a foothold, settling along the creeks and rivers. Water for the herds became hard to find. Often the trail boss would pay a homesteader one or two cents a head to allow the herd to water, but this cut into the profits of the drive. At times a trail boss would not pay, or a homesteader refused the water anyway, and angry confrontations occurred. Further problems came when cattle would disappear from the herd, presumably rustled along the way.

Homesteaders and ranchers by 1890 had settled the area, bringing an end to the migration of cattle. The XIT Cattle Syndicate sent one last herd north to deliver in July 1897, and the dust settled on the Texas Trail forever.

Cattle Move in From Oregon

Trail drives from Oregon started after the Texas Trail drives and ended sooner. Yet cattle moving in from the west helped establish the Wyoming livestock industry. Oregon cattle were very different from the tall Texas long horns entering Wyoming from the south. These "westerns" were descended from the early domesticated cows driven by pioneers. Their shorter legs and stockier builds did not hamper travel. In fact, feeders and shippers liked them better than long horns because they could be kept in closer quarters without "horn damage."

Why were cattle driven into Wyoming from Oregon? One reason is that the Northwest was overstocked. It had more cattle than its small population could use. Also, it was cheaper to drive the cattle east than transport them around South America by ship. And finally, the defeat of the Plains Indians in 1876 removed restrictions on grazing cattle on the rich grasslands in northeastern and central Wyoming.

The earliest herds from Oregon entered Wyoming in the vicinity of Star Valley in 1876. One of the first herds that traveled the 1,600 miles was then shipped east from Cheyenne.

In 1877, fifty thousand head of "Oregon natives" arrived in Wyoming. This figure doubled a year later. These drives snaked along the old Oregon Trail, following the Sweetwater and Platte rivers. Some of the cattle were sold to such Wyoming ranchers as J.H. Douglas and William Sartoris. Henry and Will Swan brought Oregon cattle into the Saratoga Valley in the 1880s.

In 1879 the Searight Brothers of Cheyenne traveled to Oregon and bought fourteen thousand head of cattle. They also bought 285 horses to be used in one of the biggest cattle drives in history. In order to drive the cattle to Wyoming, they split the gigantic herd into seven herds of two thousand head each. A foreman, eight riders, a wrangler, and a cook were hired to move each herd. By May 20, all seven were on the way toward Wyoming. It was a difficult drive, but the westerns were delivered to the Goose Egg Ranch on the Platte by late summer.

It was important that cattle arrive in Wyoming by late summer so they could be "seasoned." This meant the cattle would be in their wintering area soon enough to get them used to the altitude and climate. N.R. Davis brought a herd in in 1879 that did not have a chance to "recruit from their long journey." An early winter caused nearly nine hundred head to starve and freeze to death since they were not used to the range.

During 1885 a record number of cattle were driven into Wyoming from Oregon. By now the last of the open ranges near the south fork of the Stinking Water (Shoshone) River was being taken up by cattle interests. Jim Redfern, a drover who brought a herd into Wyoming by way of Montana that year, recalled: "We were constantly meeting cattle . . . also we became acquainted with other cowboys."

Redfern remembered how well trail towns advertised their wares for the cowboys during that peak year. Outside "rough, wild" Arland, located near Cody, the trail boss (or ramrod) halted the drive for the day. He told his men he did not want them heading to town since the cattle were due for delivery in a few days, and he did not want any trouble to delay them.

No sooner had the cattle been bedded than two men, "tinhorns" in suits and spats, and a lady rode into camp. The drovers were quite taken with the woman, named "Blue." "She was easy to look at," Redfern remembered. After eating, the "tinhorns" took out whiskey and offered drinks to the men.

Angered at this growing temptation, the ramrod told the strangers to get out of camp. Good-naturedly the men persisted, telling the drovers of a dance at Arland as they passed the bottle around. Finally the ramrod had had enough. He grabbed the bottle, tossed it at the tinhorns, and ordered the trio out of camp at the point of his gun. None of the drovers trailed their dust back to Arland or possible trouble. Not surprisingly, the cattle were delivered ahead of schedule.

The Oregon Trail drives were fraught with the same dangers as the Texas Trail drives. Billy Johnson, who drove cattle for Tom Sun in 1882, recalled striking poison—larkspur—just after entering Wyoming. Two hundred head of cattle died. Jim Redfern remembered another danger all too well. Just over the Wyoming border from Montana, he came across a cowboy who had been struck by lightning. The man's yellow slicker raincoat lay over him, shredded to ribbons, while the soles of his boots had been burned off. Still other drovers, ramrods, cooks, and wranglers drowned in treacherous North Platte crossings. The "mile wide, inch deep" river was notorious for being swift and uneven, a torrent that often frightened cattle into swirling about, dragging horse riders under.

By 1890 the last of the Oregon cattle entered Wyoming as the open range disappeared and the railroad reached the Northwest, providing cheaper and easier shipment.

Earliest Ranches Begin Permanent Cattle Industry

While cattle drives added a great deal of romance to the history of Wyoming, they were also vital to the growth of the territory. They helped establish ranching and livestock raising as one of the biggest industries in Wyoming, for it did not take long for drovers and ramrods, businessmen and tinhorns to see that permanent herds could grow fat in Wyoming.

The earliest ranch in Wyoming was actually built before Nelson Story's historic drive in 1866. Cattle, as mentioned before, had wintered for years in the Sybille area near Wheatland and at both forts Laramie and Bridger. But it was the Myers Brothers who built the first ranch, on the Little Bear River south of Evanston in 1857. They constructed a house and corrals for a year-round herd and sold cattle frequently at Fort Bridger.

Cowpunchers at Hunter Ranch (Wyoming State Archives)

Gradually herds began to grow up around the few permanent settlements in Wyoming, but they were small and the meat was used locally. There was not much point in raising cattle unless they could be shipped to a population center for use, and the Oregon Trail itself was hardly a profitable route for shipping. Besides, the Indians, particularly in the northeast, frightened many potential ranchers away.

But in 1867, the Union Pacific completed its line to Cheyenne. This meant that even at the high price of $7.00 per head, cattle could now be shipped to Chicago. It didn't take long for ranchers to settle in areas safe from the Sioux, mainly in the southeast. John Iliff, who had driven an early herd into Cheyenne in 1868, started a permanent herd and became one of the early "Cattle Kings" of Wyoming. W.G. Bullock and B.B. Mills both began ranches in 1868 as well.

Building a ranch required an incredible amount of energy, skill, and money. Ranch houses were often dug into a hillside with only the south exposed. Some were made of lime grout, a local cement, while others were made of stone. A few ranchers managed to build houses of wood, but it was scarce.

Ranches were built near streams and rivers so water would be available for cattle. Some corrals were built, but cattle generally roamed free over the land, grazing wherever they could find grass. Allowing the cattle to roam freely over unowned government land is called "open range." It was one of the main reasons ranching grew so quickly in Wyoming. As early northwest rancher Victor Arland wrote to a Frenchman in 1884, "The cattle live in almost a wild state." With no fences to contain them, the cattle could wander many miles from the ranch. One unlucky rancher found his cattle had migrated 150 miles southeast after a particularly severe winter.

Usually twice a year roundups were held—in the spring and fall. At the roundup, cowboys would brand calves and count the cattle. Arland commented: "The only care that is taken of them is to brand the calves each season with a red-hot iron. For this purpose, the cattle raisers employ cowboys whose work consists of gathering together the cattle in certain places, then lassoing the calves and branding them with the owners's brand." Once the branding was done, any cattle to be sold would be rounded up and driven to a shipping point, usually Cheyenne or Ogallala, Nebraska. Despite the work, raising cattle was profitable since the price of beef rose steadily in the 1870s.

Cowpunchers around the chuckwagon at mealtime (Wyoming State Archives)

A few ranches were begun by "tenderfeet" or newcomers to the territory who had money to invest or a hankering for adventure. Most, however, were former drovers and ramrods who wanted to put down roots in a business they knew well. Charles Coffee, for example, drove 1,500 head in 1871 and then settled on a ranch just south of the North Platte River. He recalled that the Cheyenne Indians "kept us stirred up for five or six years," frequently raiding the herd that grazed close to the 1868 Indian Territory. But as the Sioux and Cheyenne fled the high plains of Wyoming in the late 1870s, ranchers spilled into their hunting grounds, replacing tipis with ranch houses and buffalo with cattle.

The Great Grass Bonanza

The next decade, 1876 to 1886, became known as the "Great Grass Bonanza." Raising beef was tremendously profitable for the big ranches because prices were so high and grazing land was free. It did not take long for Easterners and foreign businessmen to begin investing in Wyoming cattle. Huge corporations formed, and between 1879 and 1890, over two hundred cattle companies operated in Wyoming. Twelve were foreign-owned, mainly by British, Irish, or Scottish investment groups. Seventy-six were owned by out-of-state businessmen. And seventeen corporations were worth well over one million dollars.

Swan Brothers (Wyoming
State Archives)

HENRY SWAN   WILLIAM F. SWAN   THOMAS "BLACK TOM" SWAN   ALEXANDER H. SWAN

The biggest of the cattle companies was the Swan Land and Cattle Company. It was founded by Tom, Henry, and Alexander Swan, three brothers who had been successful farmers and stockmen in Pennsylvania and Ohio before heading west. They settled at Chugwater, bought three thousand head, and in 1873 formed a corporation. Henry withdrew from the firm quickly and Tom took on the role of advisor, leaving Alexander to run the business. And run it he did. Through careful management, good prices, and hard work, he built up the herd to 33,000 head by 1882.

In 1883 he sold the corporation to Scottish investors for $3,750,000. He remained manager and organized four other cattle companies, all of which he managed at one time or another. During his reign as the "Cattle King" of Wyoming, he introduced the Hereford breed to Wyoming rangeland, built the stockyards at Omaha, and made Cheyenne a cosmopolitan city with international interests. The corporation's holdings covered half a million acres, thirty-two ranches, and so many brands the company published its own book for employees.

Problems Plague the Industry

But problems in controlling such a huge empire began to haunt Swan. Rustlers and poor management took their tolls. In 1884, for example, the company released 11,400 steers on the open range of Goshen County. In the spring roundup of 1885 only 480 could be found. The Scottish investors soon learned "that the caprices of weather and markets, as well as incidental problems like fencing, range wars, feuds, nesters, water rights, and blizzards could lessen the chances of profits."

By 1886 over 1,500,000 head of cattle worth $45,000,000 roamed the Wyoming rangeland in the greatest year of the bonanza. But this was far more cattle than the range could handle at the time. Raising cattle is a gamble, and the investors were dealt a losing hand when overstocking, and the terrible winter of 1886-87 combined to ruin many a fortune. It began in early October when temperatures plunged as the snow piled up. It killed man and beast alike and tried the spirit of every rancher, homesteader, or city slicker in the territory.

"While cattle were starving and freezing to death by the hundreds in our yard, I was trying to keep my babies warm and well," recalled Martha Waln who ranched and homesteaded in the Cody area that winter. She added, "The thermometer outside was standing at -50 degrees to -60 degrees for weeks and the snow three and four feet deep."

Otto Franc, prominent rancher of the Cody area, noted that on January

28, 1887, it was "blowing a hurricane . . . snow drifts are on a level with the roof of the shed."

On February 7, Franc said that "Big Charlie" came to "get a beef" from Dye and brought news that "Oldis" had probably frozen to death on his way from Billings to the Franc ranch. Franc offered $25 to anyone discovering the body. It was found the next day in the Kyle Cabin on Sage Creek. Eight days later Franc grimly noted "Oldis' body has thawed sufficiently to bend his arms and we lay him in the coffin."

When grass finally began to poke through the melting snow, ranchers and cattle companies counted up their losses due to starvation, cold, and worst of all, thirst. Thousands of head were dead, and those that did survive were almost too scrawny to sell. Cattle barons were dealt a blow from which few recovered. Alexander Swan, for one, was sued by his corporation and disqualified as director of the company. He finally fled Cheyenne, dying in obscurity in an asylum a few years later.

Those ranchers who were not ruined that winter learned that though cattle could survive on a open range for a winter, there was no guarantee that they would. To help control losses, ranchers began growing hay so the cattle would have food during the winter. Pure breeds were introduced because they were heartier than range cattle, and herd size decreased to make the cattle manageable.

Range Conflicts Begin

Smaller herds meant that fewer cowboys were needed to work them. Ranchers began to lay off many of their men. A few ranchers tried to keep the men on. Otto Franc offered to cut wages twenty-five percent to $30, as he wrote in his diary on December 5, 1888, "All the men quit because I reduced wages."

Because these men had spent their lives working with cattle, they had few other skills to fall back on. So they began small ranches on their own. They were called "nesters." While some succeeded, others were bitter toward the big cattle companies and ranchers for having taken their jobs. They took revenge by rustling "mavericks"—unbranded calves.

The Wyoming Stock Growers Association, founded in 1871 in Laramie as a power base for cattle (and originally wool-growers) interests, began to receive more than the usual number of reports of rustling throughout the state.

To combat the problem, the Association hired cattle detectives to check brands and investigate accusations of rustling. The first detective was W.

C. Lykens, who had been hired back in 1877. By 1888 there were a number of detectives who would figure prominently in the growing conflict between the small and large ranch interests.

The Association received hundreds of letters from ranchers, such as one from Hulette: "Lee More and Ed Fitch are gathering all the mavericks and strays in this country and selling them to the railroad contractors . . . and to anyone that will buy them. You stockmen had better look after it." As a sign of growing tension, the rancher added at the bottom of the note, "Burn this!"

While range detectives did bring accused rustlers in, it was not easy to get a conviction because juries were mostly sympathetic to the small rancher or homesteader who was from the same area. And of course members of the juries knew thefts worked both ways. Many times nesters fell prey to the big cattle "outfits." One woman remembered how her father lost part of his small herd when "they went by and took two calves and there wasn't anything that could be done." A big herd passing could easily pick up a small herd, and a nester would be out of business. Sometimes the cattlemen tried to drive the small ranchers and homesteaders off their land, particularly if a water claim had been staked. The big outfits might fence off a stream or river or, in extreme cases, poison a source of water so no one could use it.

Bitterness on both sides grew. Martha Waln said later, "I do not imagine that many men in the Basin at the time felt it wrong or beneath them to partake in the spoils."

As statehood dawned in the late 1880s, the range conflict worsened. Violence, so long threatened, would erupt in a tragic climax in the early 1890s.

Homesteading Act Invites Settlers

The cattle industry was dominant during Wyoming's territorial days, but agriculture was another major industry beginning to take root, thanks to homesteading.

There was some interest in settling parts of Wyoming not on the Oregon and U.P. trails as early as the 1850s, but not much happened until Congress passed the Homestead Act in 1862. Although President Buchanan had vetoed the bill a few years earlier, Abraham Lincoln foresaw that settling the West would become important after the Civil War.

The Homestead Act gave 160 acres of government land to settlers. To own the land, the settlers had to live on the homestead and improve it within five years. Improvements included building a house, digging a well, planting a crop, establishing a herd, or irrigating a dry section of land.

Daniel Freeman filed for the first homestead claim under the new law, settling on farmland at Beatrice, Nebraska, in 1863. Most early claims in Wyoming were filed by ranchers seeking to control land along rivers and streams. After the hard times experienced by the cattle industry in the late 1880s forced unemployed drovers to file claims interest grew in homesteading Wyoming for agricultural and small ranching purposes. Certainly the Union Pacific helped make the dream of owning land a reality for many would-be homesteaders by providing transportation and shipping to the remote territory.

Scientific advances also stirred interest in homesteading. The inventions of the prairie plow, which dug furrows easily, and barbed wire, which fenced in stock, helped the farmer and rancher control his land. New strains of hearty hybrid wheat provided a good dryland crop to grow in the arid territory where less than twenty acres of rain fell annually.

It is a small wonder then that those who dreamed of owning a farm or ranch would gamble on heading west. The lure of 160 free acres offered a chance to start a new, exciting life for many. "To me," homesteader Elinor Pruitt Stewart wrote, "homesteading is the solution to all poverty's problems. Any woman who can stand her own company, loves growing things and is willing to put in . . . careful labor will have independence, plenty to eat all the time, and a home of her own in the end."

Who Were the Homesteaders?

But who were these early homesteaders who settled Wyoming from the late 1870s on?

They were men and women who wanted a better way of life. Some were adventurers seeking more independence than they had in the East, where times were hard. Others were Civil War veterans who came home from battle to find no job waiting for them. Many were soldiers at western forts who decided to stay west when their enlistment was up. Still others were drovers laid off from cattle drives which had begun to diminish by the 1880s. And many were farmers hoping to find better or more land than they already had.

Finally, immigrants were arriving from all points on the globe, hoping to start a life in the new world. Scandanavians and Germans formed the largest number of immigrants, but many English, Irish, Slavic, and Basque people settled the territory as well. In fact, Mrs. Margaret Dolan, an Irish mother of six, filed for the first homestead in Wyoming. She settled on the "Muddy" at Egbert, just west of the Nebraska border after traveling all the way from Florida. By 1900 nearly 25% of all Wyoming's homesteaders were foreign born.

Staking A Claim

While the train brought some homesteaders to Wyoming—special fares were offered on weekdays for new settlers—many homesteaders drove their wagons west. In wagons they could bring their plows, tools, and supplies—anything to get an edge on their environment. Once they reached the state, they followed a time-consuming claims ritual to take over their land.

The first step was to pick a site. The earliest homesteaders, usually ranchers and former cowboys, took the land in the river valleys where plenty of surface water flowed. Later homesteaders had to take high ground where deep wells had to be dug.

Jud Harvey, who homesteaded near Cheyenne, recalled that his brother took a train to Wyoming, bringing only a few possessions. With no horse, he walked the prairies until he found a suitable site. Jud, who was nearly blind, followed his brother to Wyoming by stowing away in a wooden chest shipped by train to Cheyenne. He, too, eventually picked a site and homesteaded.

Once a homesteader selected a spot, he claimed the land by driving stakes at the corners or by plowing furrows around his property. Then came the filing. And often it was a long journey to the claims office.

Jud Harvey's brother had to walk from Burns to Cheyenne, a distance of about thirty-five miles, to file his claim. Elinor Pruitt Stewart traveled sixty miles to file her claim in Green River. "It took us a whole week to go and come," she wrote. At the claims office, she was greeted by a "taciturn old man" who ignored her until she kicked over a chair. He then confessed he thought she was a book salesman. "Fancy me, a fat, comfortable widow, trying to sell books," she quipped. She then paid the required $14 filing fee, signed the appropriate papers, and headed back home.

With the claim filed, the homesteader had to "take up residence" on the land. This meant building a house, the first improvement settlers made. What kind of houses were built? Some were made of sod, called "soddies." One homesteader remarked, "The real heavy fellows built soddies," made from chunks of sod cut and dried like bricks. Often these houses were dug into a rise of hill which offered good protection but poor ventilation.

Log cabins were built if the homesteader settled near mountains where wood was plentiful. Nelly Burger, who homesteaded near Buffalo, remembered "the houses were all of logs, chinked with chips cut from the corners and daubed with clay or dirt." Still other homesteaders, especially in later years, built homes of lumber hauled in by wagons. While the settlers built their shelters, most lived in their wagons or in a tent. One could only hope to have the building done by winter!

Improving The Land

During the next three years, the homesteader had to make other improvements aside from building a house. Many chose to plant a first crop. Because of the lack of rain, homesteaders in Wyoming dry farmed at first. This meant they planted only half their land one year, leaving the unplanted or fallow land to absorb the moisture. The following year they would use the moisture rich land and leave the other half "fallow." In addition, after each rain the land was cultivated to hold moisture and kill weeds. Finally, fewer seeds were planted per acre than in the East.

Homesteaders usually planted wheat but were warned not to risk their "all" on it. It was true that wheat brought the most money, but it also left "little margin for error." Highly favorable weather conditions were required to raise a good crop. But Wyoming weather didn't always cooperate. So wise homesteaders planted potatoes, oats, or hay—anything as a hedge against losing their wheat.

Once the first crop was in, the homesteader was free to continue improvements. Many needed more water than they had on the surface, so they dug wells. Digging was usually done with an auger, a sharp, pointed drill to which extra sections could be added as it bore deeper into the ground. A pump or windmill would then be used to draw the water out. Self-governing windmills, which made use of the Wyoming winds, sold by the thousands in the 1880s. Those who couldn't afford the $250 to buy one made their own.

Even though they were often far from the claims office, homesteaders were expected to live up to their side of the bargain. Government men, Katherine Nuttle wrote, "would come out every year to see if we were living there." These agents also checked to make sure improvements were being made regularly.

The Desert Land Act

In addition to the Homestead Act, the Desert Land Act brought many settlers into the area. This act opened dry land for settlement. To own this land, a homesteader had to spend $1 per acre for each of three years to make improvements. He had to irrigate by well what could be watered and raise a crop on at least one-eighth of the land—not always the easiest thing to do. "They had to break and farm 40 acres of ground," one homesteader wrote, "and that was pretty tough to do. How much land it takes to make a living out here! 160 acres just was nothing."

Not all settlers in Wyoming homesteaded their land. Some bought the land outright. A homesteader who wanted his land quickly could pay $1.25 per acre, the going rate for government land in the 1880s and own his land, improvements or not. Other land could be bought from the railroad. The Union Pacific had been granted alternating sections of land for twenty miles on either side of the transcontinental railroad. Selling the land was supposed to help pay the cost of the line. This land was often considered valuable because it was more expensive than government land, running $4 to $5 per acre. This land could not be homesteaded but had to be bought outright, and because of this, it was not the first choice for many.

Another way settlers got land was to buy out a homesteader who gave up. When a homesteader did not live on his or her land or when improvements were not made, the homesteader "relinquished" or was forced to give the land back to the government. The land office would then offer it to other homesteaders. Or, a homesteader who wanted to move back east—or was forced to because of circumstances—could sell off his land. The requirements of living on the place and improving it would then pass to the new owner. Usually, the price was just enough for a ticket home.

Why would a homesteader give up his land? Some homesteaders brought nothing with them with which to begin a farm or ranch. A homesteader needed about $1,000 in cash, equipment, or supplies to really succeed. Many of the people homesteaded because they had nothing back east. When they arrived in Wyoming, they had a rough, if not impossible go of it. They used up their small savings quickly, and when the flour and bacon ran out, so did they.

No Easy Life

But even if a homesteader did bring good equipment and a tidy sum of cash to see him through hard times, fate could deal a crushing blow. Prairie fires had plagued early pioneers crossing the state. Now these lightning-started blazes could destroy a homestead, especially in the fall when the dry air turned the wheat golden. Wise homesteaders dug a fire ditch around their homes to protect their goods and families. But nothing could be done to save a crop if the wind shot the flames the wrong way.

Homesteaders, Albany Co., 1904 (Wyoming State Archives)

Cow Creek Ranch (Wyoming State Archives)

At times glistening black clouds of grasshoppers or locusts descended on homesteads, eating everything in sight. Some farmers protected their gardens by using ashes or garlic water on leaves to ward off hungry pests. But nothing could be done to save a whole crop of wheat or barley.

At other times, the ruthless Wyoming winds could strip a crop in an hour, just as they could drive a lonely homesteader to despair. Nothing, however, tried the spirit of a homesteader like winter. As the temperatures fell and the snow piled up, every weakness of man and beast became painfully obvious.

Normally homesteaders stored provisions to last a winter, including a thousand pounds of flour, seventy-five pounds of coffee, and at least three hundred pounds of bacon. Outside, a mountain of firewood or chips would ensure fuel for the long months ahead. Animals, however, had to fend for themselves in severe cold. Martha Waln remembered that "it was blowing a blizzard and the cattle were banked up around the house where they had broken every window" during the winter of 1886. Later Mrs. Waln's husband took her out to the barn to see the cattle eating the horse blankets she had just woven. All that was left, she said, "were two little patches where the quilts had been riveted to the two straps that held them in place."

Winter travel proved especially dangerous to the homesteader. More than one settler froze to death going to or coming from town because a beautiful day had dawned but brought an unexpected blizzard. Elinore Pruitt Stewart remembered how a young soldier had tried to return home to his mother's homestead near Green River as a Christmas surprise. Weeks later his wolf-gnawed body was found frozen beneath a tree. Hanging from a branch was a message warning his finder not to tell his mother how he had died. Mrs. Stewart and other neighbors faithfully kept the secret.

With few doctors in the territory, homesteaders faced serious medical hazards in the winter. Childbirth was perhaps the most difficult and dangerous of all inevitabilities women had to face. And even if a child survived birth, the chances of living beyond a year were much lower than they are today. Both Martha Waln and Elinore Pruitt Stewart joined thousands of pioneering women who buried children on their homesteads as the harsh life took its toll.

The Expansion of Homesteading

Despite the problems, success came, especially as the twentieth century dawned. By then homesteads had grown and become more profitable. By

1909 a homesteader could settle 320 acres and by 1916, double that, 640 acres. In 1914 alone over four hundred homesteads were filed for in Goshen County. It is estimated that one-eighth of Wyoming's territory was homesteaded from 1880 to 1930 when homesteading dwindled dramatically. This is a vast amount of land when one considers that fifty-five percent of the state is still in governmemt hands and much of the mountainous terrain is unusable for agriculture or livestock production and thus unavailable for homesteading.

As homesteads succeeded, more people settled, particularly in river valleys. The face of Wyoming had now changed from the barren, buffalo scattered plains bucking up against huge mountains to a tamed land speckled with wooden homesites. As one Buffalo homesteader wrote, "Gradually the country took on a new atmosphere. School houses began to appear and women began to discuss the possibilities of a centralized church. Bad places in the roads were fixed . . . door knobs replaced the buckskin stringed latch. Some of the women had dainty curtains and sewing machines."

These changes set the stage for statehood.

Lawlessness Plagues the Frontier

One of the great problems facing the new territory was the establishment of law and order. After thousands had used the Oregon Trail in the 1840s and 1850s and after the completion of the transcontinental railroad in the 1860s, Wyoming became more than just a place to pass through on the way to somewhere else. People began to settle in Wyoming. With the railroads came towns and many different types of people.

Unfortunately, some of these people were undesireables, and Wyoming was a perfect place for them. Other than the few towns along the rail line, Wyoming was thousands of square miles of high mountains, narrow passages, and wide plains. Since it was an unorganized territory there were not nearly enough lawmen to handle the problems in this new, wide-open land. To complicate matters, most early lawbreakers were constantly on the move, never staying longer than a few weeks in the same vicinity.

Outlaws committed crimes frequently in the Old West, and Wyoming outlaws were no different than those found in other western states. Of all crimes investigated in the West, one in forty was a murder. This figure could mean that there were many murders committed or that lawmen did not often investigate other crimes. Fighting, disturbing the peace, and destruction of property were common crimes.

An 1875 territorial law forbade the wearing of firearms within the limits of Wyoming's towns and cities, but it was never enforced. A drunken cowboy with a Colt .45 in his hand caused the other crime for which the old west is famous, the gunfight. The killer's plea was usually self-defense, and few were ever prosecuted or punished. As the *Cheyenne Daily Leader* stated, "In Cheyenne, it's gettin' easier to kill a man than to steal his horse."

The West and Its Crimes

Most crimes committed in territorial Wyoming had a connection with the railroad or with stagecoaches.

Wyoming's most famous outlaws, Robert LeRoy Parker, alias Butch Cassidy, and Harry Longabaugh, alias the Sundance Kid, were notorious for their train holdups. Operating during the last decade of the nineteenth century, the Wild Bunch, as Cassidy's gang was called, ranged across Wyoming and into Utah and Colorado, holding up trains for the money carried in baggage car safes. Considered by most as a "gentleman outlaw," Cassidy claimed never to have killed a man in any of his holdups. His companions, including the Sundance Kid, could not make the same claim.

Harry Logan, alias Kid Curry, and "Flat Nose" George Currie, along with Bob Lee and Lonie Logan, were frequent members of the "Wild Bunch" who would "hit" a train and then make good their escape to one of the many places in Wyoming that provided more than adequate protection from the law. "Hole in the Wall," near present-day Kaycee,

The Wild Bunch with Butch Cassidy (front row, right) and the Sundance Kid (front row, left) (University of Wyoming)

"Brown's Hole" covering the borders of Utah, Idaho, and Wyoming territories, and "Jackson's Hole" in the Tetons were favorite hideouts.

Most historians believe that Cassidy, the Sundance Kid, and the Kid's girlfriend, Etta Place, fled the United States in 1901 and traveled to South America where they continued to rob banks and trains. Bolivian troops apparently killed them in a shoot-out. Legend has it, though, that Cassidy escaped and returned to the United States, where he lived until 1937. No one knows for sure, however, the fate of Wyoming's most famous outlaw, Butch Cassidy.

The most notorious and possibly most written about of the West's outlaws were the James boys, Jesse and Frank. Some historians believe that in 1878 it was Frank James who met up with a Wyoming outlaw, "Big Nose" George Parrott. Parrott had built his reputation as a road agent (thief) on the Cheyenne-Deadwood stage route. Together he and James planned to rob a train. They picked a Union Pacific western express at a site near Carbon, between Medicine Bow and Rawlins. The plan was to wreck the train, open the express car, and steal the loot. An alert handcar operator, however, spotted the dislodged rail and reported the danger to the approaching train. A posse searched the area. Near Elk Mountain they discovered footprints, and two deputies felt they had the outlaws. But James and Parrott killed them and escaped.

After 1879 Frank James met up with Jesse in southwestern Wyoming and survived a severe winter there. Jesse was later killed by Bob Ford, and Frank went to California where he died of natural causes as an old man. A "vigilante" committee eventually lynched Parrott in Rawlins in 1881 for his part in killing the two deputies.

Another famous train robber in Wyoming was Bill Carlisle, who robbed trains from 1916 through 1919. In February 1916, armed with a fake pistol, Carlisle boarded the eastern "Portland Limited" near Green River, covered his face with a scarf, and robbed the sleeping passengers. Twice more he eluded railroad detectives and pulled off surprise robberies. But he was finally captured and sent to the state prison at Rawlins for life. The sentence was later reduced to fifty years. Bill could not stomach the idea of fifty years in prison, so in November 1919 he broke out of prison. On November 21 he again tried to rob a train. He accidentally shot himself in the escape attempt and was captured. He ended up serving twenty years as a model prisoner.

Bill Carlisle was the last of the Wyoming train robbers. By the time of his final robbery, money was more securely kept, and trains moved too fast under greater protection for an old-fashioned hold-up to take place ever again in Wyoming.

Road Agents Rob Stages

The stagecoach robbery is a classic of western novels and movies, and it is entirely based in fact. From 1860 to 1900 in Wyoming, The Overland Stage Line, the Central-Overland California, and the Pikes Peak Express all fell victim to the armed "road agent" who stopped the stagecoach, relieved the passengers of their money and valuables, and took the express box from under the driver's seat.

Most Wyoming stage robberies took place along the Cheyenne-Deadwood stage line, which connected the Union Pacific Railroad in Cheyenne with the gold mining region in the Black Hills of Dakota Territory. Such stagecoaches were inviting targets for a road agent because they carried gold bullion to Cheyenne and returned with cash for the miners. Typical stations along the line were "Eagle's Nest" and "Robber's Roost," named for obvious reasons. Two notorious outlaws along the line were "Persimmon Bill," who killed a sergeant at Fort Laramie in a fight at the "hog ranch," and "Big Nose" George Parrott. Parrott was among the most difficult to apprehend. He successfully robbed so many stagecoaches that many feel there is still loot from his robberies hidden in the Black Hills area.

Rustling Cattle on the Open Range

Because Wyoming was big and open in the years between 1865 and 1900, it was natural for cattlemen to also see the value in Wyoming's open range. With huge herds in the area, it was also only natural that there would be cattle "rustlers" or thieves. Rustlers could take calves that had

Stagecoach (Wyoming State Archives)

not yet been branded or steal branded cattle and alter the brand with a tool they carried called a "running iron." They would then either begin their own herds or sell the cattle for profit. Much cattle rustling took place from 1870 through 1910, and some erupted into open warfare as seen later in the Johnson County War. Often rustlers or would-be rustlers were caught, given a hasty trial, and lynched on the nearest tree. Indeed, cattle rustling, horse stealing, and associated murders were the most serious crimes during the late 1800s.

Famous among Wyoming cattle rustlers and horse thieves was Harvey Gleason, alias "Teton Jackson." Jackson teamed up with an ugly gang known as the "Destroying Angels" that raided ranches and homesteads along the border of western Wyoming for cattle and horses. Having murdered two United States deputy marshals, Jackson had a handsome price on his head. In 1885 Sheriff Frank Canton of Johnson County arrested Gleason, and after considerable difficulty, "Teton Jackson" was brought to trial and sent to prison.

Tom Horn—Detective Turned Outlaw

Many crimes in early Wyoming had to do with land and the right to use it. Conflicts developed between those large ranchers who profited greatly from the "open range" and those who wanted to put up fences. Cattlemen could not tolerate sheepmen or people who built homes (called "squatters" or "settlers") in the middle of fine grazing land. These situations all led to quarrels, gunfights, and eventually many deaths.

Tom Horn, Wyoming's most infamous hired gun, made his name as a result of conflict over the right to use land. Horn worked both sides of the law. He worked as a Pinkerton detective in the 1890s on the Union Pacific Railroad. He then went to work for the Wyoming ranchers as a stock detective, running down rustlers. He had been an army scout and liked life on the open range trailing rustlers. Gradually Tom Horn became an "exterminator." He saw that killing a rustler was quicker and more effective as a warning to other thieves than any courtroom trial. Eventually he earned over $300 for each rustler he killed.

His reputation grew rapidly as fear of his name spread throughout Wyoming. Horn also took credit for many killings he didn't even commit, and few would argue with him and his deadly gun. His bragging eventually caused his undoing. In the summer of 1901, Horn was accused of ambushing and killing a fourteen year old boy, Willie Nickell. Tricked into a liquor-induced confession by U.S. Marshal Joe LeFors of Cheyenne, Horn was

Tom Horn awaits execution
(University of Wyoming)

convicted and sentenced to be hanged. In November of 1903, Horn was hanged in the Laramie County Jail in Cheyenne after legal maneuvers and an escape attempt failed.

The death of Tom Horn essentially marks the end of the "Outlaw West" in Wyoming. Crimes were committed after that time, and some were certainly more serious than those of the "Old West," but the era of the gunfighter, road agent, and rustler in Wyoming had ended forever.

Media Reporting Spins Legends

Most of the information we have regarding Wyoming's outlaw element has come to us as the result of tireless and fearless work done by news reporters who served the West and informed the public. Newspapers sprang up in Wyoming's new towns and later cities. One traveling newspaper followed the growth of the railroad as it crossed Wyoming in 1868. Legh and Fred Freeman were the editors of Freeman's *Frontier Index*, a virtual "newspaper on wheels." It was printed wherever the construction crews stopped long enough for the presses to be set up. The "end of track" towns were the scene of nearly every kind of frontier "debauchery" imaginable, and the Freemans reported what they saw.

Unfortunately the *Frontier Index* took the side of the vigilance committee in Bear River City when it printed a notice to all "garroters" to "vacate the city or hang within sixty hours from this noon." On November 20, 1868, after the lynching of three undesireables, a riot broke out and the *Index* office was burned and the press was destroyed. Apparently enough was enough, and the editors left town in a hurry.

Probably the most famous of the early newspapers was the *Cheyenne Daily Leader*. Begun in 1867 with the founding of Cheyenne, the *Daily Leader* reported incidents of territory-wide significance. The Leader reported on the condition of the end of track town of Benton, saying, "there is more whiskey walking about in that community than in any the same size in the world." Other leading newspapers of early Wyoming were the *Cheyenne Star*, the *Laramie Sentinel*, the *Laramie Boomerang*, and the *Wyoming Tribune*, begun in 1869.

Occasionally the news as it happened was not quite spectacular enough for readers in the "civilized" East. Much money was made in the late nineteenth century by "dime novelists" who embellished outlaw activities taking place in Wyoming. Common criminals became heroes, a shot fired under cover of darkness from behind a tree became a terrific shoot-out, and a cowardly hold-up by a common road agent became a "Robin Hood" drama.

Probably the most dramatized event on the frontier was the classic Hollywood-style gunfight where two men approached each other from opposite ends of a dry, dust-blown street at high noon. The outlaw always drew on the sheriff or marshal, who was faster on the draw. Those on the law's side always won. This classic of Hollywood almost never happened in Wyoming. According to the *Daily Leader*, the only true "code duel" ever fought in Wyoming ended with one of the participants being only wounded and the two "gunfighters" reconciling their differences. In the real world of territorial Wyoming, deaths were not nearly so glamorous and romantic as portrayed in the "cowboys shows" of movie fame.

Vigilantes Bring Justice—of a Kind

Before the coming of the lawman, the outlaw had things pretty much his own way. That was, of course, until enough good people got fed up with his behavior and lynched him. From 1868 through the first decade of the twentieth century, outlaws were "taken care of" by groups of "good, upstanding citizens" who were fed up with the slow and sometimes ineffective legal processes. These citizen groups, which formed for the

"Big Nose" George Parrott
(Wyoming State Archives)

purpose of ridding their communities of undesireables, were called
"vigilance committees." Vigilance committees operated in areas where
legal authority had not yet been established or had not gained strength.
They generally were very willing to disband when the lawman appeared.

Wyoming vigilance committees were common in the new railroad towns
along the transcontinental line. Wyoming's first vigilance activity occurred
in January 1868 in Cheyenne when three thieves were tied together and
a sign hung on them warning that the next time they were caught they
would "go up a tree." The day following the warning, the vigilantes of
Cheyenne hanged three outlaws at Sherman Hill to show they meant
business.

As the railroad moved over the Laramie Mountains to Laramie, so did
the undesireable track followers. A city government was organized at
Laramie in May 1868 but soon forced to resign because it could not cope
with the lawlessness of the community. Leading the outlaws were Con
Wager, Asa Moore, and a character known as "Big Ned." A large,
well-organized vigilance committee was formed, and the three leaders
were hanged.

The citizens of Rawlins also took matters into their own hands in 1881
when they dragged "Big Nose" George Parrott from jail and hanged him
from a telegraph pole. "Big Nose" was then skinned, and a section was

The Lynching of Big Nose George at Rawlins Wyo. in the Year of 1881 This Drawing is From a Description of the Lynching, by a Witness.

Hanging of "Big Nose" George Parrott by vigilantes at Rawlins (Wyoming State Archives)

removed from the top of his skull as a souvenir. Dr. John D. Osborne, who later became Governor of Wyoming, made a pair of shoes from Parrott's skin.

Vigilance activity was indeed accepted by the solid, well-respected members of the community and was deemed necessary.

Lawmen Ride the Range

Fortunately, as time went on, law and order came to Wyoming's settlements. When the sheriff or marshal showed up and took control, the vigilante groups were no longer needed and so dissolved. Wyoming had many early "peace makers," and several have become legends in the history of law enforcement.

Thomas Jefferson Carr was elected sheriff of Cheyenne in the fall of 1870 and immediately began to clean up the town. In an attempt to jail Charley Stanley, who ran a house of prostitution and harbored known criminals, Sheriff Carr was shot in the ear with a secretly-drawn derringer. Carr forced the pistol away from his captive and smashed him on the head with it. Charley Stanley quickly realized that T.J. Carr was not to be "messed with."

Later that year Sheriff Carr assisted in the first legal execution in Wyoming Territory when John Boyer, a convicted two-time killer, was hanged. It did not take the criminals of Cheyenne long to realize that T.J. Carr meant to clean up Cheyenne, and shortly the railroad town began to show a semblance of law and order.

Many early lawmen earned their reputations on the wrong side of the law. When an opportunity presented itself for them to become respectable, some outlaws saw law enforcement as an escape. Such a person was Frank Canton, who, after a lawless life in Texas, served as sheriff of Johnson County from 1882 to 1888. His term as sheriff was very respectable and culminated in the arrest and confinement of the notorious outlaw, "Teton Jackson."

In 1888 Canton worked as a detective for the Wyoming Stock Growers Association and began to gather evidence of rustling. Many thieves were arrested and tried, but "it was almost impossible to convict a rustler." Canton then took charge of criminal warrants for several rustlers and was one of the leaders of the vigilante Johnson County Invaders in 1892. After being freed, Canton gathered more fame as a gunfighting sheriff in Oklahoma and Alaska.

Marshall Thomas Jefferson Carr (Wyoming State Archives)

Sheriff Frank Canton (Wyoming State Archives)

Mangled baggage car blown up by the Wild Bunch in Wilcox train robbery, 1899 (Wyoming State Archives)

In the 1890s when Butch Cassidy's Wild Bunch robbed more and more trains, the Union Pacific decided to get help in dealing with the desperados by hiring a professional detective agency. It hired the Pinkerton Agency, which had gained fame by guarding President Lincoln during the dangerous time of the Civil War. The successful record of the Pinkerton Agency instilled fear in the minds of criminals everywhere.

Probably the most famous of the Pinkerton detectives in Wyoming was Charles Angelo Siringo. Siringo managed to infiltrate the Wild Bunch and foil many a train robbery by tipping off local officials. When Cassidy found out, Siringo vanished, only to reappear as a lawman hunting for the outlaw and his gang. For four years, Siringo followed Cassidy around the country, giving up only when the outlaw's gang was whipped in a gunfight, forcing the leaders to flee to safer territory in South America.

Other peace officers gained prominence because of their dealings with famous cases. Sheriff Joe LeFors of Cheyenne became famous when he tricked a confession from Tom Horn, which eventually led to Horn's conviction and execution.

Boswell—The Toughest of the Lot

Undoubtedly the most famous Wyoming lawman was Nathanial K. Boswell, Sheriff of Laramie and Albany Counties. Nicknamed "Old Boz,"

Sheriff Nathaniel K. Boswell
(Wyoming State Archives)

he was considered to be the most successful lawman ever produced in the
Rocky Mountain region. "Old Boz" came to Cheyenne in 1867 and quickly
moved to Laramie in the spring of 1868. He got his first taste of law
enforcement by leading the Laramie vigilante committee in the lynchings
of Con Wagner, Asa Moore, "Big Ned," and "Long" Steve Young, local
thugs who operated out of the "Bucket of Blood Saloon."

Boswell soon became the first sheriff of Albany County, appointed by
the territorial governor John A. Campbell in May 1869. "Old Boz" thus
became responsible for over 16,000 square miles of outlaw territory.
Outlaws soon realized that this was not the country to operate in as Boswell
always seemed to "get his man."

Once when Boswell was visiting Cheyenne, a local thug named Jack
Watkins had begun to "shoot up the town." Boswell was deputized and
sent to arrest him. After mistakenly disarming a deputy who was also
trying for the arrest, Boswell confronted Watkins. Watkins threatened
to shoot Boswell. "Old Boz" said that was fine, but there were many

citizens outside who would fill him with lead if necessary.

Watkins said, "Who the hell are you?"

"I'm Boswell," was the reply.

"Well," said Watkins, "that's something else. I ain't afraid of that crowd, but I'm not ashamed to be arrested by Boswell."

Boswell's reputation also came in handy while escorting Watkins through the crowd to jail. The mob had lynching on its mind, but when Boswell gave Watkins his gun back and drew his own, the crowd lost its stomach for the match.

Boswell was appointed deputy United States marshal and served for years. He also served as chief of detectives of the Wyoming Stock Growers Association, beginning in 1883, and held the same office in the Union Pacific Railroad's Wyoming division.

Boswell always proceeded without personal fear in upholding the law. It is claimed that at one time Boswell arrested six stage robbers seven miles east of Rock Creek Station on the old Cheyenne to Deadwood stage line. Boswell tried to gather evidence against the six but failed to put together a case and saw the outlaws released. Only later did Boswell find out that among those he had released was the notorious outlaw, Jesse James.

Boswell also served as the first warden of the Wyoming Territorial penitentiary. Prior to 1872 those arrested by Boswell and other lawmen were sent to the Detroit House of Corrections in Michigan. After C.H. Bussard dedicated the penitentiary on October 21, 1872, Wyoming's prisoners could be kept within the territory.

Boswell closed the door on the first prisoner in June 1873. The prison stood west of the Laramie River in Laramie and served until the state prison was built in Rawlins. The first prisoners were sent to Rawlins in 1902, and only a handful were kept at Laramie after that until 1907 when the stone structure was given to the University of Wyoming.

Boswell was a "real" western hero who fearlessly worked to make territorial Wyoming a place safe enough for civilization to grow.

8
Statehood at Last

The Country Changes

As Wyoming approached the 1890s, the United States was in a time of change. The peak year for foreign immigration had been 1882. Most of these immigrants, along with many disenchanted farmers, were moving to the cities.

Cities were experiencing phenomenal growth due to the rise of industrial giants like Andrew Carnegie, Cornelius Vanderbuilt, John D. Rockerfeller, and Jay Gould, who made dramatic advances in everything from oil development and production, to railroads, shipping lines, steel production, and business management.

The growing industries created many jobs that were not available prior to the late nineteenth century, and this drew millions to the cities. By 1900, for example, Denver's population was approaching 100,000. The YMCA had been organized as well as the Salvation Army, and cities were trying to get their rapid growth under control.

Electricity had been harnessed and was in general use, lighting city streets as well as powering factories. Women were going to college, and people were better informed all across the country. *McCall's, Popular Science, Cosmopolitan, Ladies Home Journal*, and *Harper's* had already begun publication, and magazine distribution soared. Education was stressed, and the illiteracy rate began a sharp decline in the early 1880s. America's most famous humorist, Mark Twain, had already published his most famous works, *Tom Sawyer* and *Huckleberry Finn*.

Yet these changes did not touch Wyoming quickly. While industry was booming, agriculture was not. Farm prices were falling (wheat sold for

$1.25 per bushel in 1881 and was heading toward $.70 by 1890), and mortgage rates for agricultural loans in the West were above ten percent and in some places approaching fifteen percent. Away from the settled areas near Wyoming's young cities, the "code of the West" was still the law. Disputes were often settled with guns regardless of how civilized the West appeared to be.

Obstacles to Statehood

As more and more people began to talk about statehood for Wyoming Territory, more and more people began to talk against it. Those opposing statehood for Wyoming felt that there were two big problems that could not be overcome before the twentieth century.

One was population. According to the Northwest Ordinance of 1787, a territory could write its constitution and take other steps necessary to become a state when its population reached 60,000 people. Most critics of Wyoming statehood believed, and rightly so, that Wyoming's population was, at most, about 50,000. Territorial governors, though, had estimated the population more optimistically at various times during their terms of office. The governor's estimates were:

F. E. Warren, 1885 65,000
F. E. Warren, 1886 75,000
T. Moonlight, 1887 85,000
T. Moonlight, 1888 85,000

Thus, because of the inflated population figures, political "big-whigs" in Congress had no way of knowing the true count until an official census was taken after statehood in 1890. According to these inflated estimates, Wyoming qualified as a state.

The other problem that could possibly have kept Wyoming from statehood was that it was the only territory in the United States allowing women the right to vote. "Giving women the right to vote goes against the very core of Republican government," an eastern newspaper editorialized. Former Territorial Governor John W. Hoyt countered by saying, "No man has ever dared to say in the territory of Wyoming that women's suffrage is a failure." The debate raged. It was even proposed at the constitutional convention that women's suffrage not be included in the final document. Cooler heads prevailed, and Governor Hoyt's sentiments were apparently shared by the state and nation.

Lesser problems involved with statehood emerged as 1890 approached.

The honor of being a state carries with it higher costs of operation and much greater government responsibility. It was feared that the additional cost of $95,000 per year would be impossible to raise. It was also feared in Washington that a state run by a bunch of "cowboys, railroad workers, and a few miners" could not function on an even plane with the forty-three previously admitted states.

The Benefits of Statehood

The benefits of statehood far outweighed the problems posed by small population, women's suffrage, and increased cost. The most significant benefit would be "self-determination." The people of Wyoming, since 1868, had been subject to territorial officers appointed by presidents. Most of these officials had never even seen Wyoming Territory, and knew little of its needs. Most appointments came as rewards for political favors. Governors, marshals, and judges were naturally more loyal to the president who appointed them than to the territorial citizens. Wyoming's interests would be much better served by people elected from within the territory than appointed from without.

Another benefit would be that a state controls the use of water, land, and minerals within its borders. Wyoming, having an abundance of all three, had much at stake here. During the drafting of the state constitution, Melville C. Brown, the president of the convention, advanced a proposal that would attach a tonnage tax to coal. At the time, coal was thought to be Wyoming's most valuable resource. Brown's plan was to collect $100,000 from the tax, which would more than pay the additional cost of state government. The federal government regulated the sale of coal in the territory, and the people of Wyoming realized little benefit from it.

People of influence in the late 1800s felt that a state would draw settlers more readily than a territory. Better law enforcement, local control, and the benefit of state services were more inviting to an emigrant than the conditions in a territory.

Moves Toward Statehood

Beginning in February 1868, various attempts were made to pass an "enabling act" that would allow the citizens of Wyoming Territory to write their constitution and take other steps toward becoming a state. Following the guidelines of one of the bills that had been introduced (the Teller Bill), Governor Warren split the territory into ten voting and congressional districts. He then called for the writing of a constitution by a convention consisting of fifty-five delegates elected by the people of the ten districts. The constitutional conventional opened in September 1889 and worked through the month. Melville C. Brown, elected president of the convention, commented later that "the convention represented all the business interests of the state."

The Constitutional Convention

As the convention began it was obvious that the forty-nine men present had no experience in writing state constitutions. Fortunately, requests had been made for the constitutions of states previously admitted. The final constitution contains phrases and sections from the constitutions of Colorado, Kansas, Illinois, Missouri, Nebraska, Pennsylvania, Texas, and Washington. But the Wyoming constitution borrowed most heavily from North Dakota, South Dakota, Idaho, and Montana. This practice of borrowing when writing a state constitution was very common, going back to the original thirteen. Writing one from scratch was unnecessary and would have taken much longer. As Dr. T.A. Larson of the University of Wyoming states in his *History of Wyoming*, "How else could the constitution have been produced in twenty-five working days, except by the scissors and paste method?"

The part of Wyoming's constitution showing the most originality is Article VIII (8), which deals with water rights. The elected delegates made Wyoming's water the property of the state. The people could then receive water rights from the state. For many years after, Wyoming led the way for the western states in the formation of laws regarding use and distribution on water, thanks to the farsightedness of the authors of the state's constitution.

After working for twenty-five days, the constitution was officially accepted by a unanimous vote of the delegates. On November 5, 1889, the people of Wyoming Territory approved the constitution by a wide margin, even though very few citizens, less than ten thousand, voted.

Wyoming's constitution is nearly five times as long as the United States constitution. It contains provisions for women's suffrage, fair and equal taxation, and a listing of the basic rights for all Wyoming citizens in the "Declaration of Rights." The framers of the constitution set up an executive branch, a legislative branch, and a judicial branch. Within the executive branch are the governor, the secretary of state, the state treasurer, the state auditor, and the state superintendent of public instruction. No lieutenant governor was provided for.

The two house (bicameral) legislature consists of a senate and a house of representatives. Counties are considered to be the governmental units represented. A state supreme court was created, with lower courts to be provided for by the counties. The Australian ballot form of voting was chosen by the framers of the constitution, thus protecting the right of secret ballot in all elections. The framers also included a section for amending the constitution, making any change extremely difficult.

Statehood at Last

On December 16, 1889, Senator Platt of Connecticut introduced a bill proposing Wyoming as a state. Two days later, Joseph Carey of Cheyenne, representing Wyoming in the House of Representatives, introduced a bill asking for the same thing. House Bill No. 982 was to become very important in Wyoming's development.

Carey's speech to the House was "remarkable in both content and in length," containing at least 10,000 words. Carey, seeing that statehood was good for the people of Wyoming, stretched the truth somewhat in order to embellish Wyoming's appeal. In answer to a direct question by another congressman, Carey estimated that there were between 110,000 and 125,000 people in Wyoming at the time of his speech. The figures actually represented about twice the number found in the 1890 census, which showed just over 62,000 people, including 1,800 Indians. Carey also estimated that there were ten to twelve million acres of timber, and a "great storehouse of minerals."

Despite some minor objections and questions mainly dealing with population, the bill passed the House of Representatives on March 26, 1890. On June 27 the Senate passed the bill, and President Benjamin Harrison signed it into law on July 10, 1890.

All across Wyoming there were great celebrations. In Cheyenne on July 24, the official state celebration drew many visitors. Governor Warren gave an inspiring address, after which Esther Morris presented a flag to the governor. The constitution was presented by Convention President Melville C. Brown, and the party began. That evening fireworks exploded around the capitol building, and three bands played at the "Statehood Ball."

Early State Organization

Francis E. Warren was the state's first governor, but he served for only two months. He and Joseph Carey won United States Senate seats

Francis E. Warren (Wyoming
State Archives)

in the election of 1890. Secretary of State Amos Barber then served as
governor until he was replaced in the election of 1892 by John E. Osborne.
When the census of 1890 came out, it showed Wyoming with a population
of 62,555, which included nearly 2,000 Indians on reservations. Senator
Carey, having doubled that figure in his speech to Congress, received
little criticism for his exaggeration. The people of Wyoming were thankful
for statehood and proudly called Carey "the architect of statehood."

With 11,690 people, Cheyenne was the state's largest city in 1890.
Laramie was second with just half of Cheyenne's population, and Rock
Springs was third with 3,400. Casper, yet to grow, had only 544 people
within its limits at the time of the first census.

The mere fact of statehood did not change much of anything for the
average person across the state. Laborers and cowboys could earn from
$35 to $45 per month, a carpenter or bricklayer could make $4 to $6 per
day, and a working woman took home about $25 per month. A person
could expect to pay $8 per week for room and board. Board only ran about
$6 per week.

Joseph M. Carey (Wyoming
State Archives)

THE WESTERN UNION TELEGRAPH COMPANY.

This Company TRANSMITS and DELIVERS messages only on conditions limiting its liability, which have been assented to by the sender of the following message.
Errors can be guarded against only by repeating a message back to the sending station for comparison, and the company will not hold itself liable for errors or delays
in transmission or delivery of Unrepeated Messages, beyond the amount of tolls paid thereon, nor in any case where the claim is not presented in writing within sixty days
after sending the message.
This is an UNREPEATED MESSAGE, and is delivered by request of the sender, under the conditions named above.
    THOS. T. ECKERT, General Manager.   NORVIN GREEN, President.

| NUMBER | SENT BY | REC'D BY | CHECK |

Telegram from Senator Carey announcing statehod (Wyoming State Archives)

State Capitol Buildings

Wyoming's state capitol had its beginnings in an act signed by Territorial Governor Warren in March of 1886, which approved the building at a cost of $150,000. The same bill established the University of Wyoming at a cost not to exceed $50,000. The $150,000 was for construction of the central part of the capitol that stands today. There were no east or west wings on the original building. In 1888 the legislature authorized $125,000 for the construction of these wings. Finally, in 1915, the structure we see today was authorized and the Senate and the House of Representatives chambers were built.

Wyoming State Flag and Seal Adopted

The fourteenth legislature in January 1917, adopted the state flag designed by Miss Verna Keays of Buffalo. It has a red border with white stripe surrounding a blue field. Within the blue field stands a buffalo with the state seal across its ribs.

The first act providing for a state seal was passed by the first state legislature on January 10, 1891. Twelve designs were submitted. The one chosen was submitted by a Mr. Buechner, a representative from Laramie County. The seal never reached the governor for his approval. Somehow a different seal was struck and turned over to the secretary of state on March 1, 1891. It was then discovered that the figure in the wrong seal was, as a newspaper of the day shuddered, "shamefully nude." The territorial seal was used until 1893.

The second state legislature passed an act of February 8, 1893, providing for a new state seal. Today's seal remains the same as the original, only somewhat smaller at one-and-one half inches in diameter. The central figure on the seal is a draped figure of a woman with broken chains on her wrists, symbolizing the freedom that women achieved in Wyoming. She is holding a staff with a banner proclaiming "Equal Rights."

Cattle Problems Continue

Unfortunately, once the excitement of achieving statehood had died down, old problems surfaced again. The most serious was the intensifying range conflict between large ranchers on one side and settlers, homesteaders, and small-time ranchers on the other.

In order to better control ownership of strays and unbranded calves, the "Maverick Law" was passed. This law organized government-run roundups in the spring with the cattle being sold and the proceeds going to support the roundup. Since the territorial, and later state, officials were all cattlemen, the law protected them. To nearly everybody else, it appeared that the law benefitted the big ranchers and hurt the settlers with small herds.

The Wyoming Stock Growers Association, founded in 1879, grew so powerful that it gained control over who could sell cattle and where they could be sold. Certain settlers and small ranchers were "blackballed" by the association because of their alleged rustling. They were then prevented from selling and buying livestock. Eventually, many were driven from the territory. Honest citizens along with the occasional rustler began to feel the pressure.

With more and more settlers moving to the young state, more fences were put up to hold small herds. These fences hindered the easy movement of the large herds. Ranchers would therefore cut the settlers' fences, and their livestock would be included in the roundup and sold as part of the large herd. As such activity increased, so did retaliation by the settlers. Violence seemed to be inevitable.

The Hangings of Cattle Kate and Jim Averell

Sadly, the first open attack against the settlers came on the eve of statehood, igniting a series of bloody confrontations that would mar the new state's history.

It began on a hot July day in 1889, about seventy miles west of Casper, along the shallow, winding Sweetwater River. Ella Watson, a hundred-and-sixty-pound farm girl originally from Kansas, homesteaded about three miles east of Independence Rock. She had been invited to settle on the Sweetwater by a quick-talking, well-educated homesteader named Jim Averell, whose place lay a mile from Ella's. Unfortunately, they both settled on land claimed as open range by several local cattle barons.

From the start, Averell was a thorn in their sides, speaking loudly against the cattlemen's taking all the land as their own. "Is it not enough to excite one's prejudice to see the Sweetwater River owned or claimed for a distance of 75 miles from its mouth by three or four men?" he wrote in an April 1889 letter to the *Casper Weekly Mail*.

Averell led the small ranchers and homesteaders along the Sweetwater against the cattle barons. He owned a saloon and post office on his place where these "nesters" met.

Ella "Cattle Kate" Watson
(Wyoming State Archives)

Though evidence was skimpy, the cattlemen thought Averell rustled cattle to keep himself and Kate rich. But neither of them had ever registered a brand, and most say Averell owned only a milk cow or two. Ella's corrals however, were usually well-stocked with cattle. These were believed to be mavericks given her by cowboys as payment for her services as a prostitute. The cattlemen didn't see it this way. They insisted her cattle were their rustled stock, but no legal action was ever taken against Watson or Averell.

Whatever the truth, on July 29 a group of cattlemen headed out to Ella Watson's to scare her and Averell into "leaving the country." The group passed Ella and her hired man, John DeCory, who were riding out to buy beadwork at an Indian camp nearby. When Ella returned to her small cabin, she found the ranchers running cattle from her corrals.

She dashed to the cabin, but two ranchers blocked her way. They ordered her into their buckboard.

"Where are we goin'?"

"You're going to Rawlins," one man told her.

Gene Crowder, a fourteen-year-old boy who worked for Ella, was forced into the wagon with DeCory. "She got in, then," the boy said a few days later, "and we all started for Jim's."

When they arrived at Averell's, the cattlemen caught him at his second gate with a team and wagon ready to head to Casper.

At gunpoint they forced him into the buckboard while they tossed Crowder and DeCory out. Crowder recalled when he tried to follow the wagon, one of the men "pointed his gun at me and called me a bad name and told me to go in the house and not show up that day."

Not taking the situation seriously, Averell and Watson, "laughed and joked and taunted" the ranchers as they rode west toward the Rock.

Near the mouth of a small canyon, the buckboard halted. The pair was ordered down and was then marshalled over the "boulder-strewn" canyon ridge to a split cottonwood which hung out over a small cliff that dropped to the Sweetwater River.

Meanwhile, John DeCory and Gene Crowder had told the settlers gathered at Averell's what had happened. Only one cowboy, Frank Buchanan, jumped on his horse with his six-shooter in his holster to pursue and possibly stop the ranchers from bloodshed.

When he slid from his horse near the buckboard, he could hear shouts coming from the ridge. He "crawled over rocks, keeping behind the brush," to get within range. The ranchers were ordering Averell out of the country. The homesteader laughed. The men then threatened to throw Ella into the river.

Laughing, she was reported to have answered, "There ain't enough water in there to give you hogbacks a bath!"

By now the angered ranchers knotted two lariats into nooses, tossing them over a branch of the tree hanging over the water. Frank Buchanan remembered one of the ranchers "had a rope around Jim's neck and had it tied to a limb." He told Jim to be game and "jump off." Another man "was trying to put the rope around Ella's neck, but she was dodging her head so that he did not succeed at that time."

Buchanan opened fire suddenly. He emptied his gun as the hangmen took cover. But quickly their rifles returned the fire across the boulders. As bullets screamed around him, Buchanan desperately retreated.

Now terrified, the men turned to Watson and Averell. After what one reporter later called "a fight for their lives until the last," a noose tightened around Ella's neck.

Suddenly someone pushed Averell off the boulder. He fell two feet to the end of the rope as Ella was also "helped to eternity." Their hands and feet not tied, the "kicking and writhing of those people was awful to witness." At last, though, they swung motionless, side by side.

Covering the Crime

By the time the bodies were cut down on Monday, the Wyoming newspapers had spread the story of the hanging of the only woman in the territory's (and state's) history. In a well-orchestrated campaign to protect the killers, writers dubbed Ella "Cattle Kate" while Averell was called "a desperado." The Cheyenne papers said the hangings were the result of "a case of life and death between honest men and cutthroat thieves." Lies and half-truths spread like brushfire across the whole country, destroying much of the truth forever.

Meanwhile, four witnesses—including Crowder, DeCory, and Buchanan—told the sheriff their stories. The coroner's jury declared it was "death by hanging at the hands of persons unknown." But six ranchers were arrested and identified by the witnesses: Albert Bothwell, R. B. Conner, John Durbin, R. M. Galbraith, Ernest McLain, and Tom Sun.

With four witnesses, it was thought a solid case could be built. But by the time the grand jury met in Rawlins to indict the men, not one witness showed up to testify.

Gene Crowder died supposedly from "Bright's Disease," which does not usually attack children. Some say he was poisoned by the killers. John DeCory was last seen in Steamboat Springs, Colorado, but then vanished. Ralph Cole disappeared, one source saying he was murdered and his body burned to ashes. Strangest of all, after his lone attack on the killers the day of the hangings, Frank Buchanan vanished from the face of the earth.

With no witnesses, the six accused were released for lack of evidence. Applauded for their stand against the homesteaders, nesters, and settlers of all kinds, the men rode home triumphant. Perhaps they thought the rustling problem was over. But the bitterness caused by the hangings grew and festered. A feeling of hopelessness gripped rural Wyoming. To many on both sides of the question, the law had failed. What was left but for the settlers and ranchers to settle the score their own way?

More Killings Set the Stage for War

After getting away with the "executions" of Averell and Watson, the cattlemen became bolder in their attempts to stifle homesteading and settling.

On June 4, 1891, Tom Waggoner was hanged a few miles outside Newcastle. Rumor pointed to certain guilty parties, but "they had pull" and no action was taken. Waggoner was a small-time rancher who had fences for his horse herd in the middle of prime open range grazing land.

In November twenty-three year old Orley Jones was ambushed and shot three times while driving his buckboard home from Buffalo, the county seat of Johnson County. Like Waggoner, Jones was a settler suspected of swelling his herd with rustled cattle. An eyewitness, and other evidence, pointed to Frank Canton, past Sheriff of Johnson County, as the killer. After a preliminary hearing, Canton fled the state, only to return as one of the leaders of an armed invasionary force the next year.

By early 1892 it was obvious that people "in high places" were becoming more and more sympathetic to the plight of the cattle barons.

In January 1891 the state legislature had created a "Board of Livestock Commissioners of Wyoming" to support the livestock industry in Wyoming. The board consisted of three members: J. W. Hammond, W. C. Irvine, and Charles Hecht. H. B. Ijams was employed as secretary. Secretly and without written records, this group began to explore means of eliminating the rustlers and settlers from the open range of Wyoming.

Plotting the Invasion

The commissioners found support in the executive branch of the young state government. Governor Amos Barber and former Territorial Governor and Senator Francis E. Warren and Senator Joseph Carey were party to discussion and possible solutions being proposed by the commissioners. Some people suggested that the President of the United States was involved in the invasion later executed by the commissioners. The President, Benjamin Harrison, did order the transfer of forty U.S.

Johnson County Invaders, 1892 (Wyoming State Archives)

marshals from Texas to Wyoming for the purpose of helping to round up rustlers but probably had no idea what they were actually going to do.

With nearly everyone in a position of power willing to support them or at least look the other way, the emboldened cattlemen hit upon the idea of invading the northern part of the state with hired guns and influential cattlemen. The plan would cost approximately $200,000, so it was decided that each of approximately 200 cattlemen would donate $1,000. Although Senator Joseph Carey denied contributing to the fund, A. S. Mercer writes in his book, *Banditti of the Plains*, that Carey "was a willing contributor."

With enough money, the commissioners proceeded with their plans. They would first hire forty gunmen from Texas, who would be met in Cheyenne by forty to fifty representative cattlemen, supplied and armed. Thus prepared, the group would continue by train to Casper where they would mount horses and ride to Buffalo to kill as many rustlers as possible and issue warnings to others about the consequences of their rustling.

Governor Barber had forbidden all Wyoming National Guard commanders to take any action without his direct order. This cleared the way for the invaders by leaving only local police and sheriff departments to deal with the powerful invasionary force.

The Invaders Move North

The Texas gunmen arrived in Denver on April 1, 1892, and in Cheyenne on April 5. Fewer representative cattlemen were on hand in Cheyenne to join the group than had been expected, but enough were present to continue. Approximately thirty hired gunmen and twenty-five cattlemen left Cheyenne by rail for Casper and arrived shortly after midnight.

Major Frank Wolcott of Glenrock commanded the invasion. Captain of the Texas men was Tom Smith, and captain of the cattlemen from Wyoming was the accused murderer, Frank Canton.

The group proceeded toward Buffalo, where most of the alleged rustlers were located, according to their information. Some historians also believe that information necessary for the prosecution of Frank Canton was stored in the Johnson County Courthouse, and the invaders planned to destroy it.

Death at the K. C. Ranch

Before traveling very far, the gunmen were informed by Mike Shonsey that a group of rustlers were at the nearby K. C. Ranch. It was decided to postpone the trip to Buffalo long enough to kill the alleged rustlers at the ranch. Because they were waiting for the arrival of a supply train, they were unable to reach the ranch house until the next morning, April 9. By the time the invaders surrounded the ranch house, most of the rustlers had escaped.

The four remaining men were unaware of the peril they were to face. Two were captured when they ventured out to get water. From them the invaders learned that two "known rustlers" they had planned to kill were still in the house. The two men were Nate Champion and Nick Ray.

Both men had faced problems with cattlemen before and were quickly aware of the danger they faced when their companions failed to return with water. Ray made an attempt to run but was shot down just outside the door of the cabin. Champion risked his life to pull the wounded Ray into the cabin.

Champion was able to hold off the invaders until late afternoon. Ray had died about 9:00 A.M. With bullets hissing about, Champion began to write a diary about his feelings while alone and under attack. As late afternoon approached, he finished his last entry: "Well, they have just got through shelling the house like hail. I heard them splitting wood. I guess they are going to fire the house tonight. I think I will make a break for it when night comes, if alive. Shooting again. I think they will fire the house this time. It's not night yet. The house is all fired. Good-bye, boys, if I never see you again."

Champion made a break and was quickly shot down. Twenty-eight bullet holes were found in his body at the inquest held later in Buffalo.

The Invasion Backfires

After killing Ray and Champion, the invaders sat down to a "hearty meal" before continuing on to Buffalo.

Fortunately, word of the coming invasion had reached Buffalo, and "Red" Angus, Sheriff of Johnson County, formed a posse of two hundred men and rode out to intercept the invaders.

Hearing of the posse, the killers retreated from their position twelve miles outside of Buffalo and took refuge at the friendly T.A. Ranch. They were quickly discovered by the posse and surrounded. Angus and his men lay siege to the house for two days, April 11 and 12.

When it became apparent that the invaders would not be successful, Governor Amos Barber interceded by wiring the President of the United States: "An insurrection exists in Johnson County, in the State of Wyoming, in the immediate vicinity of Fort McKinney, against the government of said state."

Asking that the president order federal troops stationed at Fort McKinney to the T.A. Ranch, Governor Barber stopped further bloodshed.

After sun-up on the thirteenth, Colonel J.J. VanHorn rode into the T.A. Ranch with three troops of cavalry, took custody of the invaders and escorted them to Fort McKinney.

Saving the Invaders

The invasion was now over and a total failure. From the confession of one the invaders, George Dunning, we know that the men were indeed killers. They had a list of men whom they were going to kill in Johnson County. They were to be paid $5.00 per day and would receive an extra $50.00 for each rustler killed by the group.

The invasion lasted from April 5 through April 13. During that time no action was taken by any law enforcement agency except the sheriff of Johnson County. When asked why he did not take any action, Governor Barber said: "The matter has not been brought to my attention, officially. I know only rumors." Given the time spent preparing, the people involved, and the seriousness of the act, it was simply impossible for the governor not to have known what was going on.

The invasion was a direct violation of the Wyoming State Constitution, Article XIX, Section 1, which states that no armed force shall ever be brought into the state without the approval of the legislature or of the governor, if the legislature cannot be convened.

During the next year attempts to find a jury and bring the invaders to trial failed. A change of venue from Buffalo to Cheyenne was asked for and won, making the climate of a trial much more favorable to the invaders. As time dragged on, the cost of quartering the men at Fort D.A. Russell in Cheyenne added up to over $100 per day. Finally, Johnson County, finding itself without the funds to continue the prosecution, was forced to drop the charges.

The illegal invasion of Johnson County gained nothing. Settling, homesteading, and some rustling continued at an ever-increasing rate. The "open range practices" of the ranchers were doomed. In a last ditch effort to continue their old ways, some ranchers hired "regulators" or range detectives, such as Tom Horn. But they, too, gained only temporary relief, and the fencing of the land continued.

Due to the heavy tax burden imposed on the people and businesses of Johnson County following the invasion, the Burlington Railroad, which had planned to build a line to Billings, Montana, through Buffalo, changed its plans. The line eventually went through Sheridan where the railroad did not have to pay such high taxes.

Economic Woes Follow the Range Conflict

No sooner had the range conflict reached a bloody climax than a nation-wide depression created havoc in the economy following the "Panic of 1893." Businesses around the country collapsed, and tens of thousands lost their jobs. Wyoming was affected by falling farm prices, poor livestock markets, unemployment, and business failures.

In 1893 the Union Pacific went bankrupt. This crushing blow to the state's economy was followed by Francis Warren's Livestock Company going under a year later. Nearly a quarter of the state's banks failed, and other Wyoming industries folded up as well.

Bitter labor disputes added to the troubles. Railroad workers joined a national sympathy strike against the Pullman Campany, which laid off one third of its work force. After the army broke the strike, over eight hundred Wyoming strikers lost their jobs with the Union Pacific.

But hard times caused the enterprising citizens to look forward to new industries, and during the first decade of statehood, the exploitation of Wyoming resources began in earnest.

Few of the early visitors to Wyoming realized the vast wealth that lay beneath the state. The mountain man did find wealth in beaver, and early emigrants found success in crossing South Pass easily. But as their wagons rolled over the dry prairies and through the rugged foothills, they passed over a fortune in minerals that included gold, oil, copper, iron, and a host of other resources.

Gold Discovered Early

The glitter of gold caught the eye of hard-luck pioneers as early as 1842, when a trapper working for the American Fur Company picked up chunks of gold in a mountain stream near South Pass. For a year he worked the creek but was brutally murdered just after he told some other trappers his plans to form a mining company. His killers, however, had little interest in panning for more gold and only took what he carried in a possibles sack around his neck. Once the well-publicized California gold rush got under way, few bothered to search Wyoming streams.

Yet a few returning and disappointed Forty Niners rediscovered South Pass gold and spread word of their find to Fort Laramie. By 1866

Miners in South Pass City (Wyoming State Archives)

prospectors panned the streams flowing around South Pass, and their work paid off the the Carissa Lode was discovered in 1867. Hearing the news, thousands swarmed to the area, building South Pass City as they filed claim upon claim. Though the mining camp eventually boasted such luxuries as a bowling alley and a beer garden for tired miners, correspondent John Chisolm wrote, "There are some fifty dwellings, but the greater part of them are forsaken or were never inhabited."

Of course, the miners were apt to pick up quickly and rush from South Pass City the moment they heard of a new strike within a hundred miles of the Carissa. "Every day there is a new report," said W.G. Smith, "and excitement about placers and everybody as is duty bound 'rushes.' "

Other Gold Strikes in Wyoming

But legendary amounts of gold never turned up, and when the railroad finally routed through Green River rather than the ramshackle mining town, South Pass City residents moved to more promising pastures.

A strike at Lander in 1868 brought miners into the Wind River country.

A later strike in the mountains outside Laramie brought some prospectors into the Snowy Range looking for gold. In 1877 seven Swedish prospectors working streams south of Buffalo made a lucky strike, pulling over seven thousand dollars worth of gold from the clear mountain water in three days. But their luck changed when Indians attacked, killing five of them. The two survivors fled to Fort Fetterman only to tell their tale and then disappear. Needless to say, prospectors have since searched for the Swedes' "Lost Cabin Mine" for years.

A Miner's Life in Wyoming

Most Wyoming gold was found in streams. A large deposit of gold in a stream was called a "placer" (rhymes with passer), and prospectors panned for gold or used a sluice box in which gold was separated from gravel by means of a shaking box and screen.

The life of a gold miner in Wyoming was both dangerous and lonely. One danger came from Indians. Charles Rapp, who worked the streams near South Pass City at a miserable settlement misnamed "Miner's Delight," wrote in 1876: "The Indians are getting troublesome down below us. They have killed several persons around the Black Hills and I hear General Crook is trying to kill some of them."

Another danger was the weather. Earlier that year floods washed away half the town of Lander. Still another danger was the terrible loneliness. Rapp confided to his correspondent, "I haven't got over that case of the Blues yet . . ." The "Blues" hit particularly during the dreary, never-ending spring.

But there were occasional good times for lonely miners. "We're making as high a $20.00 a day," one miner gleefully commented in an age when workers back East earned $3 to $5 per week. And there were social events. When a group of emigrants camped outside Lander in 1876, the miners and pioneers had a dance in a roofless building that was under construction. A mouth organ, cracked fiddle, and bagpipe provided the music.

Yet any real appetite for gold could never be satisfied in Wyoming, so those struck with "The Fever" eventually moved on to Montana or Colorado where true "mother lodes" awaited the lucky few.

A Wealth of Coal

But for the clever businessman there was indeed a fortune to be made by merely digging. Beneath Wyoming's sagebrush and yucca is the largest

Gold miner near Wheatland
(Wyoming State Archives)

deposit of coal in the United States, and this resource helped fuel
Wyoming's economy during the territorial and early statehood days.

As the Union Pacific snaked into Wyoming, convenient fuel sources
were needed to keep the trains running. Enterprising John Creighton saw
an opportunity to make a quick profit as the railroad approached the plains
between what became Medicine Bow and Rawlins. Here he developed a
small coal mine, which he sold to the railroad.

The town of Carbon sprouted up around his deepening mine. Miners
lived in dug-outs, caves, or crude shacks at first, but later a church, school,
dance hall, and a variety of stores signaled a full-blown town.

Though Carbon provided plenty of good fuel, it was not enough. The
Union Pacific convinced Missourian Tom Wardell to open more mines.
Forming the Wyoming Coal and Mining Company, Wardell developed
sixty mines along the U.P. route.

The Rock Springs field opened in 1869 when the railroad finally arrived
there, and another huge mine opened at Almy. Later coal was discovered
in the southwest corner of the state where a mine was opened at Spring
Valley in 1899. As the demand for coal across the country grew because

of increased industrialization, the Cumberland mine opened in 1901, and privately owned mines began operation at Hanna, Diamondville, Kemmerer, Frontier, Sheridan, Sublet, and in Gillette.

The Kilpatricks Build Cambria

What was perhaps the most famous coal mine in Wyoming opened at Cambria, outside Newcastle. Founded by the Kilpatrick Brothers in 1888, the town and mine at Cambria formed a model coal mining community. In decent, wooden bunkhouses, miners lived in comfort. Each year 375,000 to 400,000 tons of coal were pulled from the hills surrounding the narrow town and hauled along a unique elevated railroad track that ran above the city. Stores opened, an opera house provided minstrel shows, and the notorious Soapy Smith brought his medicine show up "Railroad Gulch" to con the unwary miners out of their quarters.

Cambria (Wyoming State Archives)

McDonald's Coal Mine, a one-man coal operation in Big Horn County

A Dangerous Job

Miners at the turn of the century worked deep within the earth in "dark, dank, poorly ventilated mines . . . . Light was furnished by evil-smelling kerosene lamps" worn on miners' caps. Paid by the ton, "the strongest and steadiest workers" could earn only about $3 each ten hour day.

Dangers haunted coal miners who were, by Eastern standards, fairly well paid. The mines at Almy, for example, were so filled with explosive gases that blasts killed 87 men from 1881 to 1895 and helped force the owners to shut down in 1900. On June 30, 1903, gases exploded in Mine #1 at Hanna, killing 171 men. According to Dr. T. A. Larson, 600 children lost their fathers in Wyoming's worst mine disaster. One hundred and three more lost fathers five years later when two explosions roared through the same mine shaft.

Though spared explosions, residents of Cambria faced train disasters. One time a switching error sent a salt car hurtling into the Cambria Drug Store, killing the pharmacist.

Another time a substitute engineer hauling a shipment of coal and passengers to Newcastle from the Cambria Hills let his engine go downhill too far before applying his brakes. Accelerating from ten to sixty miles an hour in only five minutes, the fifteen gondolas and a passenger car sped toward a dangerous curve. The brakeman frantically tried to apply the brakes at eighty miles and hour as the conductor tried to calm jostled passengers. He finally had to lock them in in order to keep the panic-stricken from jumping. Outside the car, the conductor struggled to cut his car loose from the gondolas. When the coupling finally snapped, he applied the brake and saved the passengers.

But the train roared on at ninety miles an hour toward the lights of Newcastle. As it hit the hardest curve, the train and gondolas flew from the track. Rescue workers later found the fireman's corpse in the mangled wreck. The brakeman was seriously injured, but the engineer was found unhurt.

Despite the dangers, the demand for coal was at an all time high at the turn of the century, and the young Wyoming industry was one of the state's strongest. Ten percent of Wyoming's workers toiled in mines in 1903, with the majority of them hauling out the rich black fuel to keep the optimistic, industrial nation moving.

Oil—the Boom Begins

Though the full importance of oil would not be realized until well into the twentieth century, oil was discovered and put to practical use early in Wyoming's history.

The Indians were said to gather oil from seeps—or leaks—in the ground. They used the oil as medicine, rubbing it on wounds to seal them from the air.

Explorers noted a petroleum spring at Hilliard in Uinta County in 1849. Emigrants often made a point of stopping there to use the black ooze as grease for their wagon wheels. By 1851 Cy Iba collected oil from Poison Spider Spring near Casper, mixed it with flour, and sold it as axle grease to emigrants. Iba later discovered seeps at Salt Creek where he filed one of the first claims.

First Wells Are Dug

In 1883 the first flowing well opened at Dallas Dome field south of Lander. Six years later the Salt Creek fields came under the control of

Early gusher, Salt Creek Fields
(Wyoming State Archives)

Phillip Shannon, a Pennsylvania oil man who drilled a thousand foot well at "Shannon Field." When it proved profitable, he had the oil hauled over rough roads in huge wooden tank wagons to Casper. It was then shipped to Chicago for refinement, since there was no market for crude in Wyoming.

Shannon finally built his own refinery in Casper in 1894. Daily the plant could produce a hundred barrels of oil, which was used as lubrication.

When automobiles began to run horses off the road and planes frighten birds from the sky, oil became important. By 1910 as "motor cars" grew in popularity, the Midwest Oil Company built a second refinery in Casper while a French company put in a pipeline from Salt Creek to the booming city. In the ten years following, Casper's population rose 333% as workers, executives, drillers, and wildcatters flooded the area seeking their fortunes in oil.

Standard Oil Company arrived in Wyoming in 1913, followed by the Continental, the Ohio, the California, and Texas oil companies.

Drilling for oil in those days was done largely by wildcatters—drillers who sank wells where oil was not known to exist. They made educated guesses as to where to drill, then hoped for a gusher—a well from which oil burst into the sky in a terrific explosion. Digging was done with nothing more than water drilling equipment. If oil was found, a wooden derrick would then be used to help pump the crude from the ground. The work was difficult, at times dangerous, and workers were forced to move frequently. But as America turned to oil, the financial benefits were worth the risks.

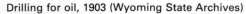

Drilling for oil, 1903 (Wyoming State Archives)

The Copper Boom—and Bust

As Wyoming entered statehood, settlers uncovered a wide variety of other minerals. Copper strikes in the Snowy Range and Sierra Madres caused a boom at the turn of the century. Ed Haggerty, a poor English sheepherder, stumbled upon "tons of red ore" high in the mountains west of Laramie. Soon copper was pulled from the huge Ferris-Haggerty mine, then processed at a smelting plant sixteen miles away at Grand Encampment. To move the copper that distance, the longest tramway in the world was constructed. The railroad built a spur to Grand Encampment to help keep the copper industry growing. Unfortunately, mismanagement, financial problems, and the difficulty of getting the ore out during the bitter winters caused the mine's premature closing in 1908.

Copper was also mined at Hartville as early as 1880. But iron ore made the Hartville-Sunrise area famous. Indians had used the red iron ore found there for ceremonial paint. By 1887 steel interests had begun mining iron at Hartville. A massive "Glory-Hole"—a huge pit gorged into the earth as ore was pulled from it—was dug at Sunrise. By 1941 the hole reached 650 feet deep in spots—a hundred feet deeper than the Washington Monument is tall! The twin towns of Hartville-Sunrise wound through a narrow canyon and were populated by miners from all over the world.

Soda mines at Green River opened in 1906, a silver mine operated briefly at Lusk, and bentonite mines boomed in Weston county. Bentonite, a clay that swells to ten or fifteen times its dry size in water, is used in oil drilling, in the cosmetics industry, and even in the manufacture of paper.

The Great Diamond Hoax

At times the prospect of making a fortune from mining led to outlandish schemes. Phillip Arnold and John Slack set up an elaborate hoax to make themselves rich. In 1871 they deposited diamonds in a San Francisco bank, stating the gems had come from a massive diamond field in Wyoming. California businessmen were taken blindfolded by way of a zig-zagging trail to the field near Rawlins where diamonds glittered on the dusty plain. Excitedly the men spread word of the find, and investors (including Baron Rothchild, Horace Greeley, and General George B. McClellan) bought stock. Arnold and Slack sold out for $300,000 each. Shortly after, a cautious government survey employee, Clarence King, uncovered the "hoax": Arnold and Slack had spread $35,000 worth of "cast-off" diamonds from South Africa as the phony investment scheme.

Though the Diamond Hoax briefly blackened Wyoming's name, progress could not be stopped. As statehood matured and demands for raw materials increased, newly discovered mineral deposits throughout the state provided profitable, if often short-lived, industries for Wyoming.

Conservation Efforts Begin

As the resources in Wyoming began to turn profits for industry, the first true conservation movements made waves in Washington that would ripple through the state during the turn of the century.

Much of Wyoming was public domain in 1890. This meant the land was "owned" by the federal government. Homesteaders, ranchers, and businessmen did own land that they either bought from the government or "proved up on," earning the cherished homesteader's patent. The Shoshone Indians did own the Wind River Reservation, but much of the state was still under government control. But Uncle Sam did not control the land carefully and allowed grazing and some industrial development to flourish without regulation.

Teddy Roosevelt (sixth from left) visiting Wyoming in 1903 with Sheriff N.K. Boswell (fourth from left) (Wyoming State Archives)

By 1890 people began to worry about how the land was used. They felt the federal government should protect the land for future generations. This became the strong conservation movement of the next twenty years.

In 1891 the world's first forest reserve was established at Yellowstone. Later reserves were established at Big Horn, Uinta, and Medicine Bow. Within the boundaries of a reserve, people could not buy land nor use the land without regulation. The forests were thus protected.

Coal deposits came under government control during the administration of President Theodore Roosevelt, and by 1910 much public land was fenced in. By that time ranchers were leasing or renting the land they used for grazing.

Indeed, by the turn of the century even big game hunting, long a sport in Wyoming, came under some control when a state game warden was hired. His job, to enforce laws on the books since 1869 but most often ignored, was a difficult one. Improved legislation (for example, making it a felony to trophy hunt elk or other big game) helped conserve wildlife.

Reclaiming the Land for Farming

It was also during the 1890s that the first true efforts to turn the dry Wyoming valleys into productive farm areas were made.

Though Wyoming has 20,000 miles of rivers and streams, this water comes mainly from snow melt and flows out of the state. The climate is so arid that for many years travelers did not think there was much chance to farm in Wyoming. Mormons did lay out and operate successful farms in the arid country west of the Rockies in the early 1850s. They irrigated the land by digging ditches that diverted water from a natural stream, but few followed their example.

Dry farming interested early homesteaders, but the fickle Wyoming weather was often too dry to provide even the minimum rain needed. During the very dry August of 1891, Cheyenne actually hired Frank Melbourne, a professional rainmaker to produce half an inch of rain. For $150 Melbourne worked his magic in secret, and on schedule two thunderstorms showered the city with half an inch of rain. From city to city he traveled on this reputation, sometimes successful, but most often not.

What Wyoming farmers needed was a carefully planned irrigation system to supplement dry farming techniques. Senator Joseph Carey knew this and wrote the Carey Act which President Cleveland signed in 1894. By this new law, the government gave the state up to one million acres of dry land for settlement provided it was "reclaimed" from the desert by

Cultivating potatoes in the Greybull Valley (Wyoming State Archives)

using irrigation. The state could control and then profit by the settlement of land.

Wyoming became a leader in irrigating dry lands. By 1897 eight projects were approved under the Carey Act. One of the most successful was at Wheatland, where water from the Laramie River irrigated fifty thousand acres. In 1906 the town of Riverton grew up around an irrigation project that saw huge canals divert water from the Wind River.

Soon it became apparent that if reservoirs were built, the water flowing from the mountains could be stored for use during the driest months of the year, July and August. With federal help, the number of reservoirs created increased dramatically after 1900.

The first major dam built in the state was begun in 1899 by Buffalo Bill Cody and Nate Salisbury. They wanted to dam up the Shoshone River west of Cody to irrigate thousands of acres. Work on the project was stop and go, but the dam was finally completed in 1910. It helped irrigate 94,000 acres and provided power for northwest residents.

Pathfinder Dam, southwest of Casper, and Whalen Dam, west of Fort Laramie, helped reclaim thousands of acres along the North Platte by 1911. Later dams, such as Alcova and Seminoe, would continue the work of reclaiming dry land. By 1913, less than ten years after the Carey Act took effect, over 531,000 acres of Wyoming were being farmed through irrigation.

Wyoming's First Taste of Foreign War

As the twentieth century approached, a movement begun by the Eastern newpapers favoring Cuban independence from Spain was well received in Wyoming. The independent life, where a man could do as he pleased, was an ideal typical of Wyoming. Most Wyoming citizens believed, as the newspapers told them, that the Cubans needed liberating. After the destruction of the American battleship *Maine* anchored in Havana harbor, desire to help free the Cubans reached fever pitch. Before long the battle cry "Remember the *Maine*" was seen in Wyoming newspapers and heard in general conversation.

On April 25, 1898, at President McKinley's request, Congress declared war on Spain. Each state was assigned a quota of soldiers. Wyoming's quota was 231 infantrymen to serve for two years. In order to reach the quota, most of Wyoming's National Guard was called up. Nearly 340 Wyoming soldiers under Colonel F.M. Foote of Evanston left for the Philippines. One week after arriving in the South Pacific, they fought in the battle for Manila on August 13, 1898—one day after the armistice was signed ending the war. The Wyoming Battalion is credited with raising the first United States flag in Manila.

Two other Wyoming groups fought in the war. One group of 125 Cheyenne men composed an artillery battalion. They served in the Philippines—not against the Spanish, but against the Philippine rebels they thought they were coming to liberate.

The most glamorous of Wyoming units was the group known as "Torrey's Rough Riders," patterned after the famous Rough Riders commanded by Teddy Roosevelt. But after preparing for war and suffering a delaying accident in Tupelo, Mississippi, which claimed the lives of five Wyoming soldiers, the Rough Riders never saw action.

There were only sixteen Wyoming casualties in the Spanish-American war, and none was battle-inflicted. Disease and accidents claimed sixteen lives out of the approximately one thousand total Wyoming servicemen in the war. Nearly one percent of Wyoming's population served in the war, a much higher percentage than can be claimed by any other state.

Home front activities were alive in Wyoming as women's groups of all kinds worked together to produce sewing kits, underwear, and "care

Wyoming Light Artillery, Battery A, 1898 (Wyoming State Archives)

packages." They also wrote letters to servicemen who had no families.

In August 1899, there were homecoming celebrations around the state for the returning servicemen. Most had come home by spring of 1899, but the official celebrations were held off until all the soldiers had returned.

The Spanish-American War revived the "frontier spirit" in Wyoming, which had suffered during the first decade of statehood. It also brought prosperity back to Wyoming. When the new year rang out in 1900, citizens all across a chilly Wyoming felt more optimistic about the upcoming second decade of statehood. And they had good reason to feel that way. The average lifespan in 1900 was now 47.3 years. The illiteracy rate across the country had dropped to 10.7 percent, and already 8,000 "horseless carriages" puttered across nearly 150 miles of paved roads. There was even one telephone for every seventeen people.

In Wyoming things looked bright. Miners were unlocking the mineral wealth of the state. New dams and irrigation projects were reclaiming thousands of acres of land for farming. And the government was beginning to preserve the beauty of the state for future generations.

The Railroads Revive

Though the Union Pacific had gone bankrupt in 1893, by 1900 the railroad industry boomed once again. In fact, in the first fourteen years of the new century, "the state's railway mileage almost doubled."

The Burlington managed to complete its line through Sheridan in 1894, before the depression halted all construction. But once prosperity returned, a number of new lines opened: the Burlington built a line from Alliance, Nebraska, to Guernsey in 1900; a line from Montana to Cody opened in 1901; and by 1914 Lander, Riverton, Shoshone, and Cody were connected to Denver by way of Casper and Cheyenne.

Rail travel was no longer hot, dusty, and uncomfortable. Depending on your pocketbook, you could ride in luxury, sleeping in Pullman cars where attendants made up your bed, ride in an observation car to catch the scenery, or feast in a lavish dining car. On the menu you might encounter such delicacies as "saddle-rock oysters on shell," "mutton kidneys," "loin of antelope," and "fried eggplant."

J.C. Penney Opens His Doors

An enterprising Wyoming merchant took advantage of the optimism sweeping the state. J.C. Penney opened the doors of his new department store in Kemmerer in 1902, selling a wide variety of good merchandise at reasonable prices. Allowing no credit—in a town where mining company stores charged on the next paycheck—Penney chalked up $466.59 in sales the first day. After cash registers had rung up $29,000 in the first year, Penney opened other stores across the state. By 1920 he had 312 stores throughout the nation and by 1929, nearly 1,400 and a booming catalog business.

More Range Conflicts

Ironically, one state industry that took a violent foothold on the range was the sheep industry. It grew tremendously during the first two decades after statehood, despite many setbacks.

Sheep had been introduced into Wyoming during the early exploration of the state. Marcus Whitman brought sheep and cattle as well as his bride on his second trek through Wyoming. By 1857 Judge William Carter, a sutler at Fort Bridger, owned a herd of merino sheep, "a Spanish breed with fine, silky wool." The enterprising probate judge (for whom the original Carter county was named) recognized Wyoming's potential for raising sheep. The cool climate helped the wool grow long and fine, and the sheep could graze easily at both high altitudes and on arid plains.

Huge flocks of bleating sheep could be seen trailing across Wyoming's open ranges by the turn of the century. The sheepherders followed their

Interior of sheep wagon (Hemry Collection, University of Wyoming)

Sheepherder on Duck Creek (Wyoming State Archives)

flocks living in sheep wagons—light, efficient, yet complete houses for one or two. Resembling a modern camper, the wagons held a small stove, table, benches that converted to bunks and storage space for the herder's equipment. Herding sheep was a lonely life, but it was profitable since it brought two cash crops a year: wool in the spring for clothing, and lambs in the fall for eating.

Unfortunately, problems developed early. The cattlemen, whose herds grazed the open range, claimed the sheep cropped the grass too short for the cattle, leaving nothing for them to eat. Futher, they said the sheep poisoned the water. "They're ruining the range!" angry ranchers cried. By 1902 nearly six million sheep—six times the number of cattle—were feeding on Wyoming grasslands.

The cattlemen tried to scare the sheepherders out. They "rimrocked" herds of sheep by running them off cliffs. They burned sheepherder's wagons, poisoned flocks, turned dogs loose on the sheep, and even murdered sheepherders. The sheepmen were especially easy prey since they were usually alone with their defenseless and unwitting flocks.

The conflict came to a head in April 1909.

The Ten Sleep Raid

A sort of compromise between herders and cattlemen had been reached early in 1909. "Deadman's Lines" were drawn. These were boundaries over which sheep or herders could not step. If "Deadman's Lines" were not crossed, herders would not be harassed.

On a clear April 3, 1909, a cattleman-turned-sheepman, Joseph Emge, and his partner, Joe Allemand, trailed their sheep over a deadman's line near No Water Creek at Ten Sleep. They wanted a shortcut to their camp, and since it was dark, they relaxed after their quick trip through cattlemen's territory.

Suddenly a group of cattlemen wearing gunny sack masks rode up to their camp. Because Allemand was well-liked, the angered invaders decided only to burn his wagon in warning. But a fearful Emge and his herder, Joe Lazier, refused to come out of their hiding place inside the wagon. To Allemand's horror, the raiders set the vehicle ablaze, burning the two sheepmen alive.

A "cold-blooded killer" named Herb Brink leveled his gun at Allemand as the fire crackled in the distance. Allemand begged, "Why, Herb, you wouldn't shoot me, would you?"

Brink fired, killing Allemand instantly.

Wildly, the raiders slaughtered sheep, destroyed the camp, then cut telephone wires before disappearing into the night.

But the noose tightened around these "vigilantes." A grand jury investigated what became the "Ten Sleep Raid," and the National Wool Growers Association backed the prosecution. Fearing he would have to incriminate himself before the grand jury, one witness, William Garrison, "blew his brains out in the prairie" behind his house.

Racing to his study, the sheriff found three letters incriminating various raiders. By May seven men were arrested. When two agreed to confess, the case was clinched. Four of the men received long prison terms, while Brinks was sentenced to die.

Though his sentence was later commuted to life in prison, the law had finally done its job. No more killings were reported, even if bad feelings existed for years and years to come. New and respected compromises and better control of the range gradually allowed both the sheep and cattle industries to thrive free from violence.

New Inventions Delight Wyomingites

The first decade of the twentieth century saw Wyoming moving cautiously into the mainstream of American life. The frontier, despite lingering problems, was giving way to civilization, and isolation was gradually disappearing as exciting inventions and ideas linked Wyoming to the rest of the country.

The airplane—that startling invention of two bicycle shop owners from Dayton, Ohio—first flew over Wyoming during the Fourth of July celebration at Gillette in 1911. A Denver pilot awed the crowds as his biplane puttered several hundred feet overhead. Yet the real impact of aviation in Wyoming would not come until the 1920s.

Alexander Bell's telephone, however, was now commonplace in Wyoming towns, so news about neighbors could travel faster than ever before. Of course, the operators—who had to put calls through—had an ear to many a conversation.

By the turn of the century, Wyoming cities glowed with electric light. Cheyenne was one of the first cities in the country to be converted from gas to electric lighting, and the W.C. Irvine mansion is supposed to have been the first American home wired for electricity. On August 19, 1908, an electric railway, commonly called a trolley, opened for service in downtown Cheyenne, providing transportation. A later electric train operated in Sheridan, where the two-car trolley ran from downtown to the coal mining town of Monarch several miles away.

Bell Telephone board "Hello Girls" (Wyoming State Archives)

Modernization became commonplace even in the kitchen. A convenient wooden icebox could now keep food fresher than ever for a modest $8.92. A cherry stoner made pie-making a breeze for $.70. And an "electric toaster" could greatly ease breakfast cooking chores.

A World of Entertainment

While rollerskating had been the rage in the 1880s, Wyomingites enjoyed new sports as a state. Football, introduced to America from England in 1869, began to spark interest in the 1890s as a "rough and tumble" alternative to the summertime favorite baseball, which as always attracted many players on town teams. Basketball, invented in 1892, was first played in Wyoming ten years later and became the winter favorite of sports fans. Golf and tennis provided "healthful exercise" for city-dwellers, while rodeo caught on wherever cattle was king. In 1893 Lander

Evanston High basketball team (Wyoming State Archives)

hosted the world's first commercial rodeo, which included "bronco bucking and roping."

More sedate entertainment could be found in card playing, reading the latest Victorian novel—Owen Wister's *The Virginian*, all about Wyoming, was popular—or attending a play. Cheyenne, Laramie, Casper, and other cities had community theatres in which local actors presented comedies and melodramas. Professional troupes toured the state as well. At Cambria one of the most popular productions at the Opera House was a version of "Faust," the heavy German opera—except that the miners liked it read, not sung. And at Evanston in 1898 a popular troupe called the Spooner Dramatic Company brought in not only a new play each night for a week, but "astonished audiences" with "the latest improved motion picture machine . . . the Cinneograph giving life like news of scenes in and about Cuba." The infant movie industry made quite an impression on the young cowboy state!

Buffalo Bill's Wild West Show

Probably the most spectacular entertainment of the era was Buffalo Bill Cody's Wild West Show. Cody had gained renown when he rode the

Wild West Show with "Buffalo Bill" Cody center front, 1906 (Wyoming State Archives)

longest ride in Pony Express history. He went on to kill Chief Yellow
Hand in hand-to-hand combat. And he clinched his fame and name by
killing thousands of buffalo to feed the railroad workers.

In 1882 as the "wild west" began to settle down and Cody aged, he
conceived the idea of his "Wild West Extravaganza." He assembled a huge
company of cowboys, actors, Indians, and variety performers to produce
a lavishly exciting reenactment of the West people wanted to see.
Audiences in the grandstands the world over thrilled to the open air
spectacle.

The Grand Processional, a parade of the entire troupe, featured Buffalo
Bill himself on his white charger. The show then opened with horse races
and a Pony Express demonstration. Then actors staged the duel between
Buffalo Bill and Yellow Hand, followed by a full-fledged Indian fight.
Next, Annie Oakley, the famous markswoman, thrilled crowds with her
trick shots. One of her most famous seems impossible: she placed her rifle
on the ground, threw three glass balls into the air, picked up her rifle,
and shot each ball before it could hit the ground! Cowboys then rode
"bucking ponies" which starred the greatest bucker of all time, "Dynamite." Cody himself performed sharpshooting tricks just before the climax

William F. "Buffalo Bill" Cody
(Wyoming State Archives)

of the show. Audiences held their breath as the Cheyenne-Deadwood stage was chased and robbed by road agents. Finally, a pioneer family was attacked and held hostage as their log cabin burned to the ground.

Audiences around the country loved the Wild West Show. Its combination of circus and history, fact and fiction, helped build the myth of the American West.

Dances as Popular as Ever

Certainly the most common form of community amusement in the new state was still dancing. For miles around, Wyomingites would gather for any special occasion and dance to a fiddle, mouth organ, or piano. "Turkey in the Straw" was a favorite dance, as was a waltz to the sentimental strains of "A Bird in a Gilded Cage," "Meet Me in St. Louis," or other songs of the era. Even politicians depended on dances. They hosted such entertainment and passed out cigars to help voters make up their minds. Frank Mondell, Wyoming congressman for twenty-six years, commented in his autobiography, "I enjoyed those campaign dances, though one had to be careful not to confine his attention to the younger and better dancers."

Picnics, camping trips, fishing, and hunting all provided relaxation for Wyoming families, though there was not much time for vacations, and transportation to the mountains from Wyoming towns was difficult.

A Novelty Turned Necessity

One invention, certainly the most important of the first two decades after statehood, changed Wyoming and the rest of the nation. It enabled people to get from town to town and from city to mountains quickly and effortlessly (almost!). That invention was the automobile.

Though actually invented in 1893, the "horseless carriage" first puttered about Wyoming in 1898. Elmer Lovejoy of Laramie is said to have built the first auto in the state that year in his workshop. Slowly but surely automobiles began appearing in Wyoming cities, though in rural areas farmers and ranchers remained skeptical. It seemed all the noisy gas-powered buggies could do was scare cattle and horses.

By 1908 many people realized that like it or not, the automobile was no mere fad. Though not many Oldsmobiles, Columbias, or Baker Electric cars motored along Wyoming's dirt roads, Wyomingites were treated to a spectacular auto event when the New York to Paris auto racers (later popularized in the film, "The Great Race") roared through the state in March.

New York to Paris automobile race (Wyoming State Archives)

On Sunday, March 8, Cheyenne patriotically welcomed the lead car with a banquet at the Industrial Club. It was an American Thomas Flyer, a sixty horsepower monster. The driver, Montague Roberts, who had driven the car from New York, delighted Cheyenne. "All roads lead to Cheyenne," he beamed as he turned the keys over to the new driver. During the next week, the Americans plowed into heavy snow west of Laramie, were feted at Rawlins with a breakfast and flag-waving crowds, found muddy roads and a quick lunch at Rock Springs, and then continued into snowy Utah.

The Italian car, some two days behind, arrived in Cheyenne to a warm welcome. The two French and a German car pulled up the rear and caused excitement days afterwards throughout the state.

As if struck by auto-fever, Wyomingites also thrilled to a new Denver-to-Cheyenne record on March 11, 1908, when H.G. Colburn piloted his Colburn Roadster the 116 miles in four hours, seven minutes. A few days before a red Pennsylvania "45-50" drove up to the Inter-Ocean Hotel in Cheyenne holding four frozen men and two chilly ladies who had just made the same daring run. "We had an exciting race with a loose horse," one rider commented. "That horse was some runner!"

Especially alongside an auto setting a speed record of thirty miles per hour!

A New Era

By 1913 there were enough "horseless carriages" scaring livestock on Wyoming roads that the legislature decided to license and regulate cars.

That same year a new trail through Wyoming helped link East with West as the Oregon Trail had done eighty years before. The Lincoln Highway opened across Wyoming: a narrow dirt road following the U.P. Railroad trail through the southern half of the state. Running from Jersey City, New Jersey, to San Francisco, California, this "Main Street of the U.S.A." was supported by President Taft. He hoped it would "wipe out sectionalism" and bring about "a national unity of thought and sentiment." As bonfires flickered along the 450 mile stretch of road during Wyoming's opening celebration, the state looked forward to a bright future.

But as quickly as old problems such as range conflicts settled, new troubles loomed on the horizon.

9
Wyoming During World War I

As 1914 dawned life had never been better in the United States. Wounds from the Civil War had healed. Modern inventions provided instant light, music in the home, and motion picture entertainment. Shiny black Model Ts puttered along a growing network of highways. Problems of poverty and corruption in business and government were being weeded out.

Wyoming citizens shared this good feeling. The young state was healthy, with the mineral industry and agriculture booming. Beef prices were stable, and the latest inventions had brought Wyoming into the twentieth century.

Yet events taking place half a world away would soon sweep Wyoming into a whirlpool of world tragedy.

The War Begins

Since the 1870 Franco-Prussian War, France and Germany had hated and feared one another. They each formed alliances (or partnerships) with other countries for defense. France formed the Triple Entente with England and Russia. Germany formed the Triple Alliance with Italy and Austria. As fear of war grew, preparations for war intensified. Countries trained soldiers, built ships, and manufactured weapons

Little of this news impressed Wyoming citizens. Only tiny articles appeared in newspapers describing the growing tension. Homesteaders were busy filing claims, cowboys were herding cattle for the spring roundups, and Wyoming seemed peacefully isolated from the rest of the world.

But on June 28, l914, Gavrilo Prinzip, a Serbian student, shot the Austrian Prince Franz Ferdinand and his wife Sophie as they rode in an open car through Sarajevo, a city in Serbia (now in Yugoslavia). By midnight, Austria had declared war on Serbia, a country Russia had promised to defend. Like a chain reaction, one country after another fell to war.

Food show and 100% American parade, Cheyenne, 1918 (Wyoming State Archives)

Early Effects of the War

Remote as it all might have seemed to many in Wyoming, newspaper editors suddenly saw the coming storm. The *Goshen County Journal* noted on its front page "the commencement of the greatest war in the world's history."

While the United States did not enter the war until 1917, the conflict affected Wyoming quickly. In early fall, a Goodyear advertisement told Wyoming drivers they could still get tires at the pre-war price of $11.50 for a short time. But soon, the ad guaranteed, prices would soar since rubber was being closely regulated.

Another immediate effect of the war was that farmers and ranchers were notified to step up food production.

Officially the United States remained neutral. Having no hatred for either side—and many immigrants from both—the U.S. had no reason to fight. Besides, both sides eagerly bought American goods. But as the war dragged on, Germany blockaded England, sinking ships attempting to deliver goods to the British Isles.

Wyoming Supports Allies

Wyomingites supported President Wilson's warning that America would not tolerate neutrals being killed on the high seas. In March 1917 when three American ships were torpedoed near the English coast with loss of American lives, the *Wyoming Tribune* screamed in bold headlines: "U.S. READY TO GO TO WAR!" Urging Americans to unite for the approaching fight, the state newspapers called for patriotic meetings in every town and city.

The Cheyenne paper commanded "all patriotic Americans to assemble at the school gymnasium on Wednesday, April 4, 8:00 P.M., to repledge their allegiance to America the free!" Rallies, patriotic speeches, and American music filled that starry April night across the state.

U.S. Declares War

By Friday, April 6, three-inch headlines announced that the United States was at war. The state immediately erupted in a show of patriotism.

The Germans now became the dreaded "Hun" in Wyoming newspaper headlines. Editors warned that "every German or Austrian . . . unless known by years of association to be absolutely loyal, should be treated as a potential spy." "Be on the alert," the warning continued, "whenever any suspicious act or disloyal word comes to your notice, communicate at once with the police." As a precaution against enemy attack, fifty armed guards patroled the city water supply in Cheyenne.

It must have been difficult to have been one of the only 2,500 German-born immigrants in the state, which had sided with the Allies from the start. Patriotic groups and 100% American Leagues sprang up around the state. Like "Wild West" vigilante committees, these clubs watched aliens (foreign-born residents) and promoted patriotism.

By November 14, 1917, German aliens had to be registered by the police. In some Wyoming communities, those suspected of being disloyal were forced to kiss the American flag or kneel in front of it.

A German Lutheran church near Burns came under suspicion because sermons were delivered in German every other week. Schools also quickly dropped German classes.

Wyoming Buys Bonds

An almost immediate effect of the war was the sale of Liberty Bonds and Loans. War is expensive. To pay for it, the government borrowed

Female laborers in the Union Pacific freight yards, Cheyenne, 1918 (Wyoming State Archives)

money from citizens by selling bonds. A bond could then be redeemed after the war for its original value plus interest.

Within two days of the declaration of war, Cheyenne and Laramie alone pledged $250,000, "making the counties extremely unpopular in Potsdam!" (meaning Germany).

Ads for bonds appeared everywhere. Many Wyoming merchants plugged bonds patriotically in their own sale bills. One Cheyenne piano and music store suggested "Buy Liberty Bonds and pianos—but bonds surely."

By the war's end, Wyoming citizens had bought an astounding $32,810,600 worth of bonds and loans. Of course, there was some incentive to help the reluctant buyer. Those who did not "subscribe" to a library loan had their names published as "slackers." As the *Cheyenne Tribune* leered, slackers would "suffer scorn and ostracism, humiliation and disgrace" in the eyes of their "patriotic neighbors."

Cowboys to Doughboys

The Wyoming National Guard had been mobilized in late March as Washington anticipated war. But more soldiers were needed quickly. Many Wyoming men heeded the famous poster of Uncle Sam pointing his finger at the reader and commanding, "Your Country Needs You!" Over 4,920 Wyoming men enlisted to "fight the Hun" and "make the world safe for democracy," all for $14.00 a month pay.

Still more soldiers were needed, however. By May President Wilson signed the first draft bill, and in June formal induction of men began. An additional 8,279 men were drafted from Wyoming. Interestingly, Wyoming men were considered the healthiest in the nation with nearly 80% of the draftees passing their physical exams. In all, about 13,500 Wyoming men donned uniforms and marched off to the war to cheers and tears of patriotic rallies that bid farewell to troop trains across the state.

The excited Wyoming soldiers adopted "Powder River!" as their battle slogan because the cowboys of the Powder River were "the hardiest, toughest, most reckless, most belligerent, most devil-may-care, and hardest drinking specimens that ever rode the range."

Soldiers in Wyoming, though, were not a common sight since most Wyoming men went through basic training in Washington or California. Officers, however, were trained at the University of Wyoming. As male enrollment dwindled, one student wrote, "Across the campus there comes the grind of marching feet in the gravel of the driveway. A long column swings across the lawn and the brown sward muffles the beat of their steps to a softer cadence. There comes a barked command and the column swings in line. For a minute the men stand at ease and silent . . . then the men snap to attention and out of the twilight comes the notes of the band. It is the national anthem."

To the Trenches!

But no anthem greeted the Wyoming men who served in the trenches of France. Events so remote at first now seemed to be happening at the next ranch or homestead. The war dominated the news, and reports of Wyoming men killed, injured, or missing in action dominated the headlines. A grim reality set in as the war took its toll. Four hundred and sixty-eight Wyoming men died in action, and more than 880 were wounded.

Yet Wyoming men faced the enemy with courage, and at times, defiance. "No thought of gas or schrapnel and bombs" crossed the minds of Wyoming's doughboys (soldiers) heading to France on crowded troop ships, wrote Paul Dusapin of Laramie. "Death? It was a thing of the future."

"Don't worry about me," Arthur Kincaid wrote to his mother shortly after he landed in France for combat duty. "I am all right and will be if I get killed. They haven't scared me the least little bit yet!"

Cheyenne High School cadet officers (Wyoming State Archives)

War Spawns Heroes

And heroes were made. Morgan Spicer, a University of Wyoming student and graduate of the officers' training corps, was seriously wounded by machine gun fire during the Battle of the Argonne Forest. He lay on the battlefield twenty-four hours before getting help.

Edward B. Center also fought in the Argonne Forest battle. Wounded on October, 7, 1917, after schrapnel shells exploded near his trench, he was sent to Base Hospital #61. After doctors removed the metal fragments, infection set in. Center struggled to live, but finally died on November 16. Ironically, he was tended at the hospital by Red Cross nurse Virginia Helms—of Casper.

A group of Wyoming soldiers was part of the "Rainbow" Division that suffered heavily at the Battle of Chateau Thierry. Two hundred and fifty Wyoming men along with six officers went into battle, but only twenty-six men and one officer escaped unhurt.

Paul Dusapin, a member of the "Rainbow" Division, earned the Distinguished Service Cross of the United States and the croix de guerre (War Cross) from Belgium for bravery at Chateau Thierry. Realizing the men in his trench were out of ammunition, he crawled on his hands and knees under heavy German fire to reach a bunker and more ammunition for his men.

Captain Matteson, a University of Wyoming student, was wounded seventeen times at Chateau Thierry but survived. Gilbert Smith was not so lucky. He was killed in the same battle on July 16.

Another croix de guerre winner was popular University of Wyoming student Louis Irwin. While fighting in France, Irwin saw a wounded American lying in "no man's land"—an open area between the trenches. As bullets flew overhead, Irwin crawled from his trench, reached his comrade, and dragged the soldier back to safety. He was later wounded himself in another battle before returning to a hero's welcome in Wyoming at war's end.

Corporal Ralph Robinson, "although suffering from the effects of gas" (poisoned gas was one of the weapons used in the war), "voluntarily left his dugout during a heavy gas and shell attack and without assistance repaired important telephone lines. As a result of his devotion, Corporal Robinson suffered further severe burns from gas."

First Lieutenant Robert Anderson, another university student, discovered the "Lost Battalion" and made a report that led to its rescue. An early air pilot, he "practically destroyed" a German convoy, killing sixty men.

Wyoming Red Cross workers, Liberty Loan exhibit, Cheyenne, 1891 (Wyoming State Archives)

Women in the War

Wyoming women served overseas as nurses.

When Edith Francis' sweetheart was "blown to pieces near Ypres," she "went to work to get over there." After contacting former Governor Francis Warren, she joined the Red Cross. She found herself being fitted for a uniform in New York. With her "gray whip cord uniform, overseas cap and hat, rain coat and top coat," she and 350 fellow nurses traveled to Quebec before embarking on a South African steamship to sail the chilly North Atlantic where "icebergs bobbed about."

Francis found war-time England "dreary, dark, and cold"—and expensive. Apples cost seventy-five cents apiece! A long Channel ride brought the nurses to France where Red Cross headquarters had been set up in Paris. There Nurse Francis served at a hospital to the end of the war and during the occupation afterwards.

A large room in the building called "The Hut" became her home away from home. A pot-bellied stove dominated the barn-like structure. A piano and "Victrola" provided musical entertainment for the convalescing men who turned to the Red Cross volunteers for comfort.

The War at Home

Although only six percent of Wyoming's total population served in the armed forces (this was above the national average), the "War Effort" demanded participation from everyone in the state. Because of this, Wyoming life changed dramatically during 1917 and 1918.

One major change was the regulation of key industries. The federal government regulated mining, agriculture, and livestock production in Wyoming. Public consumption of fuel was controlled, and the production of coal was greatly increased in the state.

"Lightless nights" began December 15, 1917, in an attempt to save energy. But Wyoming cities were so small that any savings in the national fuel consumption was considered insignificant. As a token gesture, only some sections of Wyoming cities were darkened.

But the full effect of the war showed up in the home. No one could escape the Liberty Loan ads or soldiers selling products from posters or in the newspapers. Even "Lydia Pinkham's Vegetable Compound," a cure-all medicine, ordered: "Attention sick Women! To do your duty during these trying times, your health should be your consideration!" Stores closed regularly to allow customers and employees time to attend Liberty Rallies and buy bonds.

U.S.S. *Wyoming*, 1916 (Wyoming State Archives)

Food Turns the Tide

The War Food Administration (WFA), headed by future president Herbert Hoover, controlled all food. In general farms and ranches were at full production. Shredded by war, Europe was starving by the end of 1916. Wheat itself became a war weapon. As long as the United States could produce food for England and France, the Allies stayed one step ahead of a hungry Germany. Feeding so many was a huge task. By May 1918, half of all food produced in America was being shipped to Europe.

Because of this, Wyoming homemakers joined the nation in cutting back. "This is everybody's war," Katherine Bennett wrote in *Wyoming Roundup Of Wartime Recipes*. "This is your war. What are you doing to win it? Every man, woman, and child must help win the war!"

While farmers raised more wheat than ever, Wyomingites heeded Bennett's words and cut back. The fifty-fifty rule ordered consumers to buy a pound of cereal such as rice or corn for every pound of white flour. As the songs "Over There!" and "Tipperary" played on the Victrola, housewives baked loaves of "Victory Bread." This very plain staple was made from wheat substitutes with far less fats and sugar than regular bread.

Uncle Sam also ordered consumers to cut back on meat and substitute eggs, poultry, cheese, milk, nuts, fish, or beans. Although the WFA ordered "Wheatless Mondays" and "Meatless Tuesdays," they were abondoned quickly in favor of voluntary reduction. Foods closely associated with Germany either disappeared entirely or changed names during the war. Sauerkraut, for example, became "victory cabbage."

Birth of the Sugar Industry

While Wyoming homemakers tightened belts, ranchers and farmers across the state enjoyed good prices and eager markets for their goods. Sugar beets, first grown at experimental farms in the state at the turn of the century, became a major crop in Wyoming because of a worldwide sugar shortage. Refineries at Sheridan, Worland, and Lovell sprang up as a result. The Torrington plant followed the crest of the sugar boom in the twenties.

Wyoming Supports the War

Producing food and belt-tightening were not the only ways Wyoming citizens helped during the war. Clubs and organizations across the state contributed to the war effort. The Worland Women's Club, for example, made "comfort kits" for soldiers. These kits contained scarves, hats, or other knitted items, toilet articles, writing paper, envelopes, and postcards. Made "with a cheering smile and a stiff upper lip," they were sent to soldiers in the trenches of France. The champion knitter, by the way, produced ninety-two pairs of socks, twenty-six refugee stockings, six scarves, six shawls, and three sweaters!

Other organizations made surgical dressings, while many groups joined in the nationwide effort to gather peach pits. These were ground up and used as material in gas mask filters. Gas masks protected soldiers from mustard gas—a blinding and often fatal poison used as a terrible weapon of the war.

Most organizations at one time or another had War Fund Drives to raise money for relief agencies such as the Red Cross. At one Worland auction, a single cake went to a generous bidder for $450! Book drives were popular as well, with clubs collecting new and old titles to send to the lonely, bored soldiers at home and abroad. In June 1918 Wyoming set a record by sending 130 boxes containing 8,000 volumes for the U.S. soldiers in France.

Flu Strikes Wyoming

As the United States turned the tide of war against Germany, a new enemy surfaced. This enemy knew no allies—it killed globally. The enemy was influenza.

Even with today's antibiotic medicines, "flu" can be a killer. In 1918, before modern medicines, it was devastating. The Spanish Flu, as it was called, emerged in April 1918. Some say it originated in prisoner of war camps in Austria and Italy. But no matter where it started, it spread around the war-weakened globe, invading Wyoming in the late summer of 1918.

Reports of flu deaths spattered the front pages of local papers. The *Cheyenne Leader* reported, "Victims of the dread Spanish influenza epidemic: "The bodies of little Mrs. Eva M. Sullins 19 years of age who died Tuesday night, and her tiny year old baby who breathed its last on Saturday were yesterday shipped back to their old home . . . for burial in the family plot."

Because the disease was so contagious, face masks were sold, meetings cancelled, schools were shut down, and Wyomingites were urged to avoid even talking to other people. At Hanna and Medicine Bow, the disease killed seven people in twenty-four hours. Since schools were closed, teachers were asked to "render what assistance they can in cases where the regular nurses are not available and to allow the use of their school houses as temporary hospitals for influenza cases."

By October, the disease had infested every community in the state, but by Christmas it had mercifully run its course. Around the world 21,640,000 people died in the epidemic. Seven hundred and eighty of those were in Wyoming, and more than 600 others died here of flu and pneumonia combined.

Armistice!

As bad as the flu was, though, it could not overshadow the growing joy of watching Germany's defeat. By early November 1918, the "Huns" had had enough, newspapers reported. On November 11 word finally came from Washington: Germany had surrendered.

Celebrations burst out across the state.

"Torrington celebrated right," the *Goshen County Journal* reported. "A bunch of men about town started out to arrange for a parade. People decorated their cars. It was a glorious sight!" The mile-long parade was led by a truck carrying an orchestra playing "patriotic airs." Into the chilly night, speeches from prominent citizens praised the doughboys from Wyoming and the United States for making the world safe for democracy.

Effects of World War I

World War I affected Wyoming in many ways. It was an economic boom providing state industries such as mining and agriculture with profitable, expanding years. It opened sugar production as a major industry in the state. It united the state against a common enemy on the other side of the world. It saw Wyoming produce some of the toughest recruits in the hastily mobilized U.S. Army. It saw heroes made as 468 Wyoming men who had lost their lives were buried on the battlefields of France.

Most importantly, it brought Wyoming into the mainstream of global affairs. Until the first World War, Wyoming was so remote a territory that it was often isolated from Washington, not to mention the rest of the world. But by 1918, this had changed. The "Wild West," independent, isolated Wyoming was gone. Like it or not, from now on world events would help shape Wyoming's destiny.

Bucking horse emblem on Wyoming artillery unit equipment, 1918 (Wyoming State Archives)

10
Hard Times

Once the guns fell silent and the doughboys returned home to Wyoming following World War I, people wanted to get back to "normal." They wanted to leave behind the savagery of war and the rigors of life at the front. As a result, Warren G. Harding swept Wyoming in the 1920 presidential election by preaching a return to what he called "normalcy." Yet the two decades separating the world wars saw no real return to life as Wyomingites knew it before the war. The twenties and thirties were troubled decades filled with growth and failure, laws and lawlessness, hope and despair.

Farmers—First to Lose

One of the most important effects of the return to "normal" following the war was an unfortunate one for Wyoming farmers and ranchers. Their markets collapsed.

As the government war machinery ground to a halt, food production regulations were quickly dropped. Remember that during the war, farms were at peak production. Markets demanded as much food as could be grown. So farmers and stockmen in Wyoming, like food producers across the nation, eagerly expanded their operations. More acres were cleared and seeded. Herds increased, and new equipment dotted the rolling farmlands. To pay for all this, farmers and ranchers went into debt, believing the markets would stay hungry. And with good reason: just after the war ended, U.S. farm income was $16.9 billion, and the future looked bright.

But suddenly the European food market dried up. Farmers in France,

Mrs. Harnsberger at her Sunrise farm, 1932 (Wyoming State Archives)

Belgium, and Germany reseeded battlefields to feed their own. The U.S. Army sent millions of soldiers home, cutting out a huge market for farm products, and the Wyoming farmer found too much food was being produced to keep prices high. As a result, total U.S. farm income dropped nearly fifty percent by 1921 to $8.9 billion. And yet because of their debts, farmers and stockmen could not cut back on their production.

This drop in farm income lasted for nearly two decades and made life miserable for many Wyoming farmers and ranchers. How bad was it? One agricultural expert gave an example: a $10,000 loan to buy farm machinery could be paid off in 1920 with less than 6,700 bushels of wheat. By 1933,

Thrashing wheat (Wyoming State Archives)

the price of wheat was so low that it would take over 33,000 bushels to pay off the same loan!

Towns that depended mainly on farming and ranching felt the effects of these hard times. Fewer automobiles were sold, fewer houses were built, and luxuries hardly sold at all. Banks failed in Wyoming. Largely because they couldn't collect money on their farm loans, 101 out of 132 banks closed during the 1920s. With no federal deposit insurance yet, investors lost everything they had.

Oil Enjoys a Heyday

While farmers and ranchers struggled through the twenties and thirties, other Wyoming businesses rode a rollercoaster of highs and lows.

During the twenties, most of the nation enjoyed a good deal of prosperity. Wyoming provided some of the resources necessary for enjoying that prosperity—oil, coal, and other minerals. These industries formed the backbone of the state's postwar economy, and they peaked in the twenties but plunged to terrible lows in the thirties.

The oil industry had enjoyed a tremendous boom during World War I as Uncle Sam eagerly bought up barrel upon barrel to fuel tanks, planes, and warships. During the years right after the war, production skyrocketed, especially in the Salt Creek area north of Casper. By 1923, 45 million barrels of oil were being pumped annually. Casper enjoyed the boom as its population swelled to 25,000 by 1925. The entire town of Parco (later dubbed Sinclair) was built in 1923 as a model town for oil company employees who worked there at a new refinery. The oil was shipped from Salt Creek by a new pipeline.

Yet problems developed to dramatically slow the oil industry in the state. The most important was the Teapot Dome Scandal that thrust Wyoming into the national spotlight.

Wheeling and Dealing at Salt Creek

One historian wrote: "The Teapot Dome Scandal was the first scandal in the United States that led to a criminal conviction of a high cabinet official (Interior Secretary Albert B. Fall). Along with Watergate, it ranks as a flagrant government scandal of the Twentieth Century." The story of Teapot Dome goes back to the turn of the century.

During the administration of Theodore Roosevelt, the nation became highly interested in conservation. As a result, many national parks,

Teapot Dome Oil Field (Wyoming State Archives)

monuments, and reserves were established. Locations of vast mineral wealth were also put under control of the federal government reserves.

In 1904 the Naval Oil Reserve Law was passed in order to provide necessary fuel for the navy which had converted from coal to oil near the turn of the century. In 1915 President Wilson selected Teapot Dome—9,841 acres located about thirty miles north of Casper and just a few miles from Salt Creek field—as one of these Naval Reserves.

In order to insure that the oil in these reserves would be there when needed, several plans were proposed. Buying up surrounding lands, preventing drilling around the reserves, and drilling and pumping the oil out of the reserves and storing it in huge tanks were all considered.

With the election of Warren Harding in 1920 and his return to "normalcy," policies toward conservation loosened. Harding's secretary of the interior, Albert B. Fall, believed that reserves were unnecessary and should be turned over to private development as soon as possible. He managed to have all the Naval Reserves transferred from the Department of the Navy to his Interior Department by 1921.

In April 1922 Secretary Fall secretly, without competitive bidding, leased the Teapot Dome reserve to oil tycoon Harry F. Sinclair's Mammoth Oil Company for rapid development.

When the lease was awarded, there were companies already in the field drilling. President Harding, pressured by Secretary Fall, sent Marines to Wyoming to evict the unauthorized drillers. An officer and four soldiers arrived in August 1922 and halted all drilling without incident. Wyoming

Governor Joseph Carey objected, but President Harding felt the action was necessary and had been carried out with great success.

Soon independent drillers and developers complained to government officials that they were not allowed to gain leases to drill on the reserves. Wyoming Senator John Kendrick began to believe the rumors that competitive bidding was not being allowed. He brought the matter up in the United States Senate and forced the disclosure that indeed Harry Sinclair's oil company had the sole lease for Teapot Dome.

Hearings on the controversial issue began in October 1923. The Senate discovered that Secretary Fall had received over $400,000 in loans from Sinclair. He had also received "gifts" of livestock from Sinclair to stock his ranch in Arizona.

In 1925 a civil suit was filed against the Mammoth Oil Company by the United States government. The trial was held in Cheyenne in the court of Judge T. Blake Kennedy. He found the company and leasing practices legal, but the U.S. Supreme Court upheld a later government appeal that reversed Kennedy's decision.

As a result of the suit, the government regained control of the reserves. Sinclair was ordered to pay $12 million to the United States for the oil that had been pumped from Teapot Dome.

Secretary Fall was convicted of defrauding the U.S. government. In addition, he was found guilty of bribery in 1929, fined $10,000, and sentenced to a year in prison. Sinclair also ended up serving seven months for contempt and jury tampering.

Other Problems Force Oil Production to Decline

The question of control and ownership of Wyoming's minerals continued to slow production. Other factors contributed to oil's decline as well.

For one thing, transporting oil out of Wyoming was expensive. Refined or unrefined, it was cheaper for oil companies doing most of their business in the East to order from an Eastern refinery. For another thing, taxes were levied on oil. The Oil and Gas Leasing Act of 1920 gave Wyoming 37.5% of the royalties tax on oil taken from the state. This money was—and is—used to support schools and build and maintain roads. Oil companies became suspicious, though, when a "severence tax" was proposed by the legislature. This additional tax was payment to the state because some day the oil would run out, leaving Wyoming "high and dry." Though the proposal didn't pass, it scared oil producers. A final reason for the gradual decline in production was that by 1930 demand for oil had dropped tremendously. Though more Americans had cars, they were using them less in the early thirties because of the national depression, which will be discussed later.

In all, then, the oil industry rose to a tremendous peak in 1923, then gradually declined to a low in 1933 at the depth of the Great Depression. The slump would end as the nation pulled out of the depression and into World War II.

Coal Rides a Rollercoaster

The coal industry followed the same pattern as the oil business. In 1920 coal was the country's major fuel. It supplied power not only for railroads, but also for electrical plants and most major industries such as steel.

Coal also heated most homes. In Wyoming towns, cement driveways were built so a coal wagon could be driven up to a basement window. Coal would then be dumped into a coal room for storage. The homeowner shoveled the coal into the furnace, which most often heated hot water for radiators upstairs. Some lucky homeowners had automatic stokers which fed coal into the furnace continuously.

Automatic coal shovel, Gillette (Wyoming State Archives)

To provide fuel for the country's needs, the ninety-eight Wyoming mines operating in 1920 employed over nine thousand men. Coal production peaked in 1919, and once again, as with farmers, the future looked bright.

But problems arose. In 1922 the government, which controlled wages in the industry, wanted to cut back on miners' pay. So miners across the country struck. In Wyoming mines closed down for several weeks.

Though mine safety had improved after the Hanna mine disasters in the first decade of the century, two similar tragedies in 1923 and 1924 blackened the history of coal production in the twenties.

On August 13, 1923, a foreman in Hole 15 of the Frontier Mine in southwestern Wyoming, tried to relight his lantern with a match. The spark ignited a build-up of dangerous gases, causing an explosion to rip through a shaft where 137 miners were chipping coal from the rich walls. As "a thick black cloud of smoke rolled over the stunned workers," they scrambled for safety. But only thirty-seven made it out. One hundred men suffocated a mile underground.

New safety legislation was proposed, but a year later, not fifty miles away (at Sublet), a second mine explosion claimed thirty-one more men.

Despite these disasters, miners would rather have worked than been laid off, but few were given the choice. As the demand for coal gradually dwindled from wartime production, layoffs overwhelmed the industry in Wyoming. In 1928 coal miners took a pay cut from $7.90 a day to $6.72. But even this could not save jobs. By 1931 only 4,675 men worked in Wyoming mines. Some of the biggest mines had been forced to close. The Cambria, probably the most famous of Wyoming's mines, was shut down in 1928, leaving a ghost town in its wake.

Tourists Discover Wyoming

Several industries did enjoy a true heyday in the twenties, though. One was tourism. Because of beautiful mountain ranges, an abundance of wild game, and isolation from urban life, Wyoming has long been a magnet for tourists. But it wasn't until after World War I that Wyoming became accessible to all travelers.

It might be said that the earliest visitors were really the first tourists. Perhaps John Colter coined the phrase, "It's a nice place to visit, but I wouldn't want to live there" after his run from the Blackfeet Indians. The first true "motels" could arguably have been Fort Laramie and Fort Bridger, where travelers could rest for a night in relative comfort.

Tourism wasn't really launched, though, until the creation of Yellowstone National Park in 1872. The "Sheepeaters," a mixture of Shoshone and Bannock Indians, were among the first inhabitants of Yellowstone. Because they had no guns or horses, they stayed in the rugged region of geysers and paint pots largely for protection. They lived poorly, but few of their enemies would dare enter the mysterious land of steaming earth.

But during the 1830s and 1840s, word filtered back to Washington of the incredible beauties and wonders of the area. After Yellowstone was officially explored in 1870 by Washburn, Langford, and Doane—who had mountains named after them—Congress set aside a sixty-two by fifty-four mile area as the world's first national park. The hope was to preserve the area for the enjoyment of the American people.

Early Tourists Face Dangers

Little was done to bring tourists into the area or make them comfortable. In fact, a trip to Yellowstone could often be dangerous. In 1877, during their retreat to Canada, Chief Joseph's Nez Perce Indians encountered some early tourists on horseback and killed several of them.

By 1914 tourists rode stagecoaches through the park, and since they weren't allowed to carry firearms, they made tempting targets for thieves. "An outrageous character" named Ed Trafton, a local outlaw from Jackson Hole, and his partner robbed sixteen coaches in an hour one sleepy July morning. Warning each driver he would be shot if he proceeded, Trafton eventually had sixteen coaches halted just outside Old Faithful. While he did get about $1,000 in money and goods, the passengers were more entertained than frightened by a bit of Wild West excitement.

The Development of Yellowstone National Park

Territorial Governor John W. Hoyt took an early interest in developing the park. After visiting Yellowstone in 1881 on horseback with an army escort, Hoyt commented that the park "was destined to attract a constantly increasing number of visitors from all parts of the world." He urged that roads be built from the Union Pacific rail lines to the park.

Tourists in the late 1800s generally took the train to Rawlins, then traveled north to the park by stagecoach. Inside the park, every one to five minutes they could catch touring stages which took them to Yellowstone Falls, Old Faithful, and the Paint Pots. By 1900 the park was attracting over 18,000 visitors annually. Improved roads and the advent of the automobile would boost that figure to an astounding 300,000 by the end of 1930.

Yellowstone Park tour bus near Old Faithful (Wyoming State Archives)

Luxury in the Wilderness

Before World War I travel was limited to the wealthy, for going across country for a visit was very expensive. In order to attract wealthy clients and to provide them with comfort, some of the state's most impressive hotels were built.

The Sheridan Inn opened on July 1, 1893. Buffalo Bill was only one of many famous—and infamous—guests. Cody interviewed prospective performers for his Wild West Show on the long porch of the Inn. Now a historical landmark, the Inn boasted the first telephone and hotel bathtub in the area. In 1902 Buffalo Bill himself built the Irma Hotel in Cody, a city named after him. This luxurious inn at the gateway to Yellowstone Park was named for Cody's daughter.

One of the most beautiful hotels in the world, Old Faithful Inn, inside Yellowstone Park, was constructed between 1903 and 1904. Its lobby, graced by soaring timbers and huge sloping roof, bespoke luxury in the wilderness for tired visitors. From a second story balcony just off a lounge, guests could view the hourly eruptions of the most famous geyser in the world.

Traveling the Early Highways

By the end of World War I, the automobile was becoming commonplace. Thanks to the economical Model T, Americans could take to the highways

Lincoln Highway tourist camp near Rawlins, 1930 (Wyoming State Archives)

on their vacations. The Lincoln Highway (U.S. 30) stretched across the continent, and promoters boasted it was the most beautiful route west. Since the well-traveled road cut across Wyoming, the state's economy was boosted by both those traveling straight through or stopping for side trips to Yellowstone or elsewhere.

Wyoming's towns built campgrounds for visitors, and enterprising individuals created "cottage camps" and "cabin parks"—the first real motels. Some campgrounds had police protection, electric lights, and hot and cold water. In the "cabin parks," tourists stayed in tiny cottages usually equipped with a minimum of conveniences.

Traveling in the twenties and thirties was very different from travel now. A ride in a Model T was one bump after another. With no air-conditioning, the cramped ride was hot and windy. Dust-coated travelers were a common sight in remote Wyoming towns where cafes served lunches for a quarter a plate.

The biggest difference was that there were no paved highways in Wyoming at the time. The state highway department, created in 1917, graveled a good-sized network of highways across the state. By 1929, though, only eighty-seven miles had been oiled. Due to government programs in the thirties, most main roads were oiled ten years later, but travel was still dusty in the summer and muddy and often impossible in the winter.

Frontier Days Highlights Special Events

Yet visitors came, and towns held special events to attract tourists. Frontier Days began in 1897 as an annual "Old West Show." The first celebration, held on September 23, involved the whole city. Bells rang, the railroad whistles blew, and rifles fired throughout the city at noon. Soldiers from Fort Russell marched to the fairgrounds where Sioux Indians were encamped, now in peace. Horses roamed freely between the "wild horse race and bucking contests."

Edith Johnson visited Frontier Days in 1909. She recalled, "We were so wild with excitement (at the rodeo) that we screamed at the antics of the clowns, gloated over the handsome riders, and cried over a steer that broke a leg and had to be shot."

By the thirties, tourism was a multimillion dollar industry in the state. George Houser, executive director of the Wyoming Department of Commerce and Industry, said that Wyoming hosted five times its own population in guests in 1938 and predicted that 1939 would be the best year ever. Highway maps showed a vast network of roads and included information on many places to stay. Cabins cost $1.00 to $1.50 per night, and popular attractions aside from Yellowstone were the hot springs of Thermopolis, the history of Sheridan and Buffalo, and the adventure of dude ranching in the northwest.

Opening day festivities, Cheyenne Frontier Days, 1930s (Wyoming State Archives)

Industries Open

Other industries prospered in the twenties. The large Sheridan Flouring Mills opened in 1927; the huge refinery and town of what is now Sinclair was completed near Rawlins in 1923; the Homestake Gold Mine of Lead, South Dakota, opened Moskee, a sawmill and lumber company near Newcastle; and sugar refineries in the North Platte Valley prompted a first page ad in the *Torrington Telegram* asking for 1,600 workers to turn beets into sugar in 1922.

Wyoming Takes to the Air

One industry that boomed like a cannon during the twenties and thirties was aviation. Though the first plane landed in Wyoming in Gillette in 1911—only nine years after the Wright Brother's first flight—few planes were seen in Wyoming skies until World War I proved that the airplane was more than just a novelty. New designs to turn planes into fighters improved the entire industry. And since Americans had built so many planes for the war, the surplus aircraft sold cheaply after the fighting stopped.

Horse pulling plane following Cheyenne accident, 1912 (Wyoming State Archives)

Many Wyomingites saw their first plane at barnstorming shows. Trick fliers in their brightly colored biplanes (with two wings) enthralled spectators by walking on the wings, flying upside down, zooming through open barn doors (hence the name "barnstormers"), and giving rides to the bravest members of the crowd. So many people wanted to ride a single engine, two passenger plane in Cheyenne in 1920 that a lottery had to be held to determine who would go first. The winner, Mrs. Elizabeth Brown, loved her flight.

Post Office Initiates Coast to Coast Mail Delivery

In 1920 the Post Office saw an opportunity to put aviation to practical, profitable use. It announced plans to begin a New York to San Francisco air mail run. Ironically because planes could only fly at nine to ten thousand feet and needed to follow landmarks, the Union Pacific Trail through Wyoming was selected as the best route. The trail, which was a major force in turning the frontier into a territory, would now launch Wyoming into the air age.

Notified that it would be one of two Wyoming stations where planes would refuel, deliver, and pick up mail, Cheyenne leaders scrambled to build an air field. The air strip was to be located at Fort D.A. Russell, but a month before the first scheduled flight, the War Department refused to give the city the land.

A plot of prairie a mile north of town, barren land owned by the city, became an alternative site. Workers prepared the landing field by simply filling in holes and ditches. They then began work on a hangar.

On September 8, 1920, the first mail planes carrying 400 pounds of letters took off from Cheyenne. The next day planes arrived from both Salt Lake City and Omaha. At Cheyenne mail was put on the train to head north and south. This new air mail system cut two days off the five-day train run from New York to San Francisco, so the post office was delighted, and the citizens of Cheyenne were justly proud.

U.S. Mail planes loading parcels at Cheyenne airport (Wyoming State Archives)

A Dangerous Job

But flying in those early days was dangerous. In late September mail had to be held up because so many accidents had occurred that there were not enough planes to fly out of Cheyenne. Engine trouble was the biggest cause of crashes, but treacherous Wyoming weather also took its toll. In an October snowstorm, James Murray crashed near Arlington. He survived but his airplane was destroyed. On November 6, 1920, pilot John P. Woodward wasn't as lucky. He was killed when his plane slammed into Red Buttes in heavy fog. He had been trying to follow the U.P. tracks, which at times were only slightly visible from the air.

By 1923 beacon lights guided pilots at Pine Bluffs, Burns, and Laramie. These lights were on top of fifty foot towers placed every twenty-five to thirty-five miles. A single postal employee was on hand to keep the generator going since there was no rural electricity at the time. These early lights allowed night flying which, while doubly dangerous, cut the cross-country trip to about three days.

Passenger Service Begins

By 1927 regular passenger service to Denver began, with ticket holders able to take up any space not filled by mail. Sometimes passengers were left behind if there was too much mail. At other times they had to sit on mail bags or hold mail sacks on their laps.

By 1930 the situation for passengers had improved since United Airlines and Boeing had located in Cheyenne. Bigger and faster planes now flew coast to coast in twenty-seven hours. Passengers sat comfortably in a special compartment away from freight. But there was still no pressure control in the cabins, so planes could not go much over 10,000 feet or the passengers and crew would become dizzy and ill. Because of this, Cheyenne became a hub of western aviation. Planes traveling from east and west stopped and refueled in the capital since there was no lower route through the mountains.

Even during the thirties, while the Great Depression ravaged most industries, Cheyenne was fortunate to have the growing United Airlines. The airline kept adding the latest equipment and expanded its operation in Cheyenne.

Unfortunately for the state, as World War II broke out, airplanes had become so advanced that they could fly at altitudes over 30,000 feet. This meant shorter, more direct routes over the Colorado Rockies to San

Francisco and Los Angeles. And that meant an end to the aviation boom in Wyoming.

Radio Stations Begin Transmitting

Regular radio broadcasts also began in the twenties in Wyoming, as they did across the country. KFBU in Laramie was one of the pioneer radio stations to regularly broadcast in the state, beginning in 1923. While on a trip east, Nathaniel Thomas, Episcopal Bishop of Wyoming, saw the potential of using radio to reach the remote areas of his flock. With private funding, he managed to set up his radio station in the basement of his Laramie church, and the station "From the Top of the World," as it became known, was born.

Soon after stations began transmitting across the state. The first commercial station was KDFN, begun in 1930. In the evenings, it was not unusual, even in rural Wyoming, to see a family gathered in the living room listening to a few hours of radio. At first, news, musical programs, and talk shows helped connect Wyoming to the world. Later, shows like "Amos 'n Andy," "Dr. Q.," and "Quiz Kids" amused and entertained audiences.

Prohibition Closes Saloons

The twenties have been called "The Jazz Age" and "The Roaring Twenties." Indeed, the twenties was a decade of recklessness and sensationalism. Spectacular crimes splashed across the headlines, dresses rose above the knee, and the "Charleston," a wild dance that embarrassed many matrons, was the symbol of rebelliousness in young people

Moonshine stills confiscated during raid near Salt Creek Oil Field, 1924 (Wyoming State Archives)

everywhere. It was an age when people felt disillusioned and lost since the world they felt safe in had been destroyed by World War I.

In contrast to this recklessness—or perhaps one cause of it—was one of the most unusual events in American history: prohibition. Under prohibition, people could not buy, sell, or make any liquor in the country. The 18th Amendment, ratified in 1920, closed bars, distilleries, and breweries across the country. It also opened an age of lawlessness and crime.

By 1915 the wild-west, hard-drinking and gambling saloon image of Wyoming was largely a thing of the past. Like the rest of the country, conservative Wyoming now favored prohibition, which was advocated by powerful temperance (anti-drinking) groups across the nation. A Cheyenne editor wrote in 1917 that "liquor is doomed." He warned saloon owners to obey the coming laws and begin to liquidate since he saw prohibition on the horizon. "There's no such thing as stemming the tide," he said.

Indeed, the state overwhelmingly ratified the 18th Amendment to the constitution in the November 1918 election.

A Lost Cause

But problems were quick to develop when the law went into effect in January 1920. Some people refused to get rid of all their liquor. According to T. A. Larson in Thermopolis, Sheriff Henry Holdridge and his deputies raided "saloons, resorts, trains . . . confiscating 1,500 gallons of whiskey and 500 gallons of beer and wine" on the first morning of prohibition. As the sheriff explained, unlike saloon keepers who got rid of their supplies before the "fatal hour," some Hot Springs County saloon keepers had planned "to hold out for a while."

If anyone in Wyoming wanted a drink, prohibition or not, he or she could get it. In March 1923 Elizabeth Phillips described an annual dance in Cody. "The Trapper's Ball was the typical booze party predicted," she told a correspondent in New York. Some people had liquor hidden away. There was also plenty of "moonshine" being made in the stills dotting the countryside. And there were always "perfumes, hair tonic, flavoring extracts, and patent medicines" for the desperate.

Speakeasies—hidden bars usually located behind or beneath legal-businesses—sprang up in many Wyoming cities. A patron gave a password to get in. If police or federal agents raided the speakeasy, patrons flooded out a back door while the liquor was dumped down the drain before it could be taken as evidence.

Evanston had nine speakeasies. Owners paid a fine once a month for running an illegal business, a fine which was really nothing more than a license to operate. But this was not unusual. As one resident said, "They were that way around the state. Evanston was no different than any other town in Wyoming."

"Bootlegged" whiskey that was brought into the state illegally, sold for three to five dollars a gallon. But when things "tightened up" and it became hard to get, the price soared to eight or ten dollars per gallon. Drinkers developed unusual ways of hiding their "hooch." Thin pint flasks were strapped to thighs, hollow canes could hold a cup of liquor, and fashionable racoon coats could conceal a forbidden bottle.

While many law officers looked the other way or treated prohibition violations lightly, enforcing the law sometimes turned tragically violent. On a cool June night in 1923, county officers "lay in sagebrush near a moonshine cache" at Cody. Out of the darkness, two men approached. Before any questions were asked, the agents fired. Scotty Shirran of Greybull was killed in the blast, and his companion's leg was shattered.

As more and more violations were reported, stiffer prison terms were recommended, but convictions became harder to get. In the Wyoming House, Milward Simpson said that juries would not convict if it meant a jail term.

By the late 1920s, embarrassed prohibitionists had turned against the 18th Amendment because of the lawlessness it had created. Even top officials were not immune to breaking the law. In 1929 William C. Irvine—an instigator of the Johnson County War and a former state law enforcement commissioner—was convicted of taking pay-offs from Rawlins speakeasies and for other violations. He spent eighteen months in prison. And he was not alone. City officials in Thermopolis, Rock Springs, and elsewhere were charged with violations.

Wyoming had had enough. In 1932, nearly seventy-two percent of the state voted for repeal, which finally took effect in Wyoming on April 1, 1935, ending a decade during which many a common man broke the law with regularity.

Strengthening Women's Equality

Remember that in 1869 Wyoming became the first government in the world to extend full rights to women. By 1920 the nation had finally followed Wyoming's example, and women could vote and hold office throughout the country. In 1924 further ground was broken for women's equality when Wyoming elected the first woman governor.

Nellie Tayloe Ross (Wyoming State Archives)

Governor William Ross, who had been in office two years, suddenly fell sick with accute appendicitis on September 23 after speaking in Laramie. Though doctors operated, complications set in. On October 2 he died, only six weeks before the general election.

The Democrats met to nominate someone to fill the last two years of his term, since Wyoming has no lieutenant governor. As has become tradition, the delegates nominated the late governor's wife, Nellie Tayloe Ross. Mrs. Ross accepted the nomination but refused to campaign. Her opponent, Eugene Sullivan, a former speaker of the house, campaigned actively, but in the end, "chivalry and sympathy reigned." Mrs. Ross won the election by 8,000 votes and, as T.A. Larson notes, "was a good governor who gave the state a respectable, dignified, and economical administration."

Though not elected to a second term, Mrs. Ross went on to become the first woman to direct the U.S. Mint in Washington, D.C.

County Map Completed

Another important political event of the twenties was the addition of the last two counties in the state. Wyoming began as a territory with only five counties (Laramie, Albany, Sweetwater, Uinta, and Carbon). By 1911 the number had swelled to twenty-one, increasing the size of the state house and senate. In 1923 Sublette and Teton Counties were organized, completing the Wyoming political map that we have today.

Economic Disaster of 1929

As the twenties came to an end, there was hope that the prosperity sweeping the nation would finally extend to Wyoming. President Hoover, who took office in January 1929 was preparing to help farmers by pushing legislation designed to provide relief. So the future looked brighter than it had. In fact, "few economists foresaw . . . or even dimly realized . . . that the country was headed for hard times."

On the surface the national picture looked rosy. Yet underneath, key industries were sick. Agriculture was a good example. Farmers and ranchers across Wyoming and the nation had suffered for a decade already. The coal and oil industies were also going through an economic low period, again affecting Wyoming. Elsewhere, the textile industry in the South and East was experiencing hard times. Though there was a good deal of prosperity for some people, too much of the money being made was actually going into the pockets of the already rich. Business income increased sixty-five percent in the twenties, but worker income increased only eleven percent. The wealthy began to invest their money carelessly, boosting sales at the stock market to all time highs.

Suddenly the bottom fell out.

A chain reaction took place that shook the world. Gradually the demand for goods had slowed. This resulted in workers being laid off their jobs. With no unemployment insurance or social programs to keep spending up, demand fell further, and more layoffs occurred. The businesses the wealthy had invested in began to collapse. Hoping to save the money they had invested, speculators on Wall Street tried to sell everything they owned. In a single, disasterous day—Black Thursday, October 24, 1929—over 16,000,000 shares changed hands "amid the wildest confusion the stock exchange had ever known." Financial panic spread as many investors lost everything they had.

Problems Hit Wyoming

At first, people did not believe things were going to be too bad. The *Wyoming State Tribune* cautioned the "slump not to hurt business,"

Wyoming man and his possessions, 1930s (Wyoming State Archives)

Wyoming drug store, 1930s (Wyoming State Archives)

according to official Washington press releases. The stock market, the paper assured Wyoming readers, was "recovering strength."

But all too soon it became apparent the slump would be huge and devastating. During the thirties, the years of the Great Depression, poverty became a way of life for millions of Americans, most of whom had known a decent life before 1929. Wyoming, while not as affected as highly industrialized states, nevertheless suffered along with the rest of the nation.

Agriculture and livestock industries continued to decline in the thirties and were devastated from 1934 to 1936 by terrible drought. The coal and oil industries, as we have seen, faltered and almost came to a standstill. Other mining followed as demand for raw materials dwindled to a trickle.

Governor Ed Herschler recalled, "It was a terrible time." He remembered foreclosures and soup lines as prices fell to all time lows. "We were selling beautiful cows for $100 and working for fifty cents to one dollar a day."

At home in the 1930s (Wyoming State Archives)

By 1932 newspapers in Casper ran daily front page ads urging employers "no conscientious objectors in the War Against Depression! Work Means Wages . . . Join in United Action for Employment."

Employment offices across the state had far more applicants than jobs. Burt Wagner, for example, who was an agent in the state employment office in Cheyenne, had three hundred registered for jobs, but could only place seventy-five. Most people, he recalled, would take anything.

The Laramie Police Department allowed transients—jobless people passing through while looking for work—to take overnight refuge in the city jail. After sleeping in unlocked cells, the jobless were fed a meagre breakfast, and then most continued on their way, looking for work that wasn't there. So many "rode the rails" recalled one U.P. agent, that most railroad workers "blinked at the rules."

At Salvation Army headquarters, the jobless could find a free meal and other assistance. In fact, "shabby, bearded transients" who "tramped through city hall" at Laramie were referred to the Salvation Army because few federal or state programs assisted the poor.

Help From Uncle Sam

At first, little was done by the federal government to help the country pull out of depression. Republican President Hoover, who had carried Wyoming in the 1928 election, felt business could put itself back on its own feet. But as breadlines at soup kitchens from New York to Casper grew, the public became bitter. In 1932 Wyoming joined the nation in turning its back on the Republicans who had led the country during the twenties. By a state margin of 14,787 votes, Democrat Franklin Roosevelt carried Wyoming and the nation.

Roosevelt felt the government held the only key to recovery. He wanted to put people back to work to get them spending again. And he was willing to use federal money to do this. His famous relief programs began almost as soon as he took office in 1933.

Immediately, Democratic Governor Leslie Miller applied for federal relief for Wyoming, much to the dismay of some conservatives in the state. Social programs in Wyoming were not well accepted, Governor Herschler remembered. They were viewed as "give-away programs." In fact, he said, some conservatives thought it "was a play to dictatorship." Longtime Torrington resident Hattie Cook recalled the new social programs were "tolerated, but never liked."

But in 1933, a low point of the Depression, 20,000 people in Wyoming were out of work (the state's population was under 250,000), and, once aid was available, one in every five Wyoming residents was receiving some kind of federal or state help. Governor Miller even turned the governor's mansion into a headquarters for federal relief programs and lived quietly at his own home.

The Works Progress Administration was a popular program in Wyoming, pumping $19 million into state projects over the decade. Over 120 public buildings were constructed as well as 113 miles of new roads. Bridges, athletic fields, playgrounds, swimming pools, and even three state golf courses were built under this employment program and earlier programs like it.

Boys Join the Famous CCC

The most memorable recovery program in Wyoming was the CCC—Civilian Conservation Corps. This training program was not only for "the delinquent and destitute" but for the average boy "who could learn a trade while doing a useful job and living decently." The boys lived in camps, usually outside urban areas. Nineteen camps were located in the state from Guernsey to Cody.

Often the boys stayed in tents until wooden barracks could be built, and they had plenty of work and play. Each boy was given a scrapbook in which he could record his CCC experience. At the end of the book, he could list his favorite "enrollees"—most popular, handsomest, smartest, and even "best ladies' man."

The volunteers in the CCC program cleared thousands of acres of burned forest lands, improved campsites, built monuments, established parks, and improved forest roads throughout the state.

One of the most hazardous duties of the CCC was firefighting. The Corps saved millions of acres of forest lands that could have been destroyed. This dangerous job, though, could end in tragedy.

Tragedy at Blackwater Creek

On Friday, August 20, 1937, pilot Bill Munday discovered a fire burning near Blackwater Creek outside Cody. The Cody CCC enrollees helped fight the blaze, but by Saturday, it was out of control. Reserves from the surrounding area were called in, with Forest Ranger Alfred Clayton placed in charge.

Cautiously Clayton split his men up. He led a group of about fifty into a ravine to dig a fire break. The ever-changing Wyoming wind suddenly came up in a deadly fury and trapped Clayton's crew. Like a blast furnace, the fire seared the ravine. One man recalled, "when the wind came up, I ran from the heat!" CCC enrollees scrambled to rimrocks where they were trapped.

As flames roared over Sam Van Arsdale, he thought "of how they would find us up there on that hill and we would be all crisp and burned so badly they couldn't do anything for us."

When relief squads could finally get through, they found fourteen charred bodies, including that of Ranger Clayton who had helped save many of the thirty-six young men who survived.

The work and dedication of the CCC enrollees and directors is still evident in the state today. Many parks and monuments bear the three "C's" as a rememberance of one of the programs that put people back to work during the Great Depression.

The Last of the Outlaws

One of the results of the disillusionment of the thirties was that Wyoming's suicide rate went up. Some people could not face the prospect of losing the material wealth they had accumulated. Another result was that people turned to crime. Petty theft and robberies were commonplace as some residents tried to "supplement their incomes" by taking what they could from the more fortunate. Though the age of the Wild West outlaw was gone, one last "bad man" is worth noting in a decade that produced such names as Bonnie and Clyde, John Dillinger, Baby Face Nelson, and Machine Gun Kelly.

Earl Durrand, the "long-haired, raw meat-eating Tarzan of the Tetons" had terrorized the northwest part of the state for several years. In March 1939 he was arrested in Cody, but broke out after taking two hostages. He killed Sheriff Lewis and Deputy Baker in his escape to the mountains.

Several days later as a posse was "scouring the rocky hillside for the bad man," he shot two more officers. Shortly after, Bill Munday took off in a plane armed with dynamite in hopes of bombing Durand's "lair." But the mission was unsuccessful since Durand had already fled. He turned up in Powell, where he kidnapped three people and dragged them to the First National Bank. There, surrounded, he was ordered to give himself up. Officers wounded him in a gun battle, which stopped when Durand turned the gun on himself.

Earl Durand (University of
Wyoming)

Across the Seas

By 1939 the people in Wyoming knew they were pulling out of the Great
Depression. Hopes had been revived, and the future for farmers,
stockmen, miners, and businessmen looked much brighter than at any
time in the previous twenty years. Yet those who read the front page
carefully knew the reasons why. Across the globe, a small, mustached
dictator of Germany had already violated the World War I treaties. At
the same time, the Japanese were dangerously expanding their "empire"
in the Far East. Prosperity was indeed just around the corner for
Wyoming, but so was another world war.

11
Wyoming During World War II

Pearl Harbor Attack

Only a few sailors and pilots were on duty at the naval base of Pearl Harbor at 7:55 a.m. on December 7, 1941. It promised to be a beautiful Sunday—still misty, but the warm Pacific sun would soon burn the fog from the coast of Oahu. For Harold Bordman, this morning was a far cry from the cold, snowy Decembers he had known in his hometown of Lingle, Wyoming. Around him flowers speckled the lush Hawaiian hillsides that enclosed the U.S. Navy's largest base.

Suddenly the drone of 140 planes drowned out the gentle slap of waves along the beaches. As anxious sailors looked up, bombs fell, and explosions shattered the morning air. Japanese high-altitude, torpedo, and dive bombers attacked the core of the nation's battlefleet—the *Arizona*, *California*, and others—unleashing pounds of whistling bombs and silent torpedoes into the sleeping ships. Fireballs mushroomed over the base, orders were frantically screamed, and men ran hopelessly for cover.

Two waves of Japanese attackers and 110 minutes later, the U.S. Pacific fleet lay crippled—six battleships sunk or sinking, two more plus three cruisers and three destroyers damaged, 188 planes destroyed on the ground, and 2,400 men killed. Harold Bordman died that morning along with fellow Wyomingites Richard Wallenstein of Rawlins and Harvey Schmidt of Sheridan. Other Wyoming men on routine duty were injured.

The next day President Roosevelt asked Congress to declare war on Japan. The *Wyoming State Tribune* put it as simply as possible once

Congress had granted Roosevelt's request: "We no longer have to hunt a name for the conflict which whelped in eastern Europe just over two years ago. It's the second World War at last."

Backgrounds Of The War

Many view World War II as the second part of World War I. The seeds had been sewn in the same field, Germany, and grew in the bitterness left as a result of the vengeful Treaty of Versailles signed in 1919. The problems of Germany—loss of prestige, severe inflation followed by disasterous depression, lack of leadership—opened the way for dictatorship. Adolph Hitler took brutal advantage of the weakened German people. At a time when they needed a new identity, he convinced them they were the "master race," destined to rule the world. Mussolini of Italy joined in his plan to take over the world, and Japan under Prime Minister Tojo had its own plans for conquest in Asia.

Terrorizing Europe with his vicious persecutions of the Jews and other minorities, Hitler marched into Austria and then Czechoslovakia. Fearfully, England and France backed off both times, naively thinking Hitler would stop with only two conquests. But in September 1939 the German army swept into Poland, crushing the brave but antiquated Polish army. Having agreed to defend Poland, France and England finally declared war on Germany.

Neutrality at All Costs

The events of September 1939 held clear meaning for Wyomingites. Wyoming writer Caroline Lockheart scribbled in her diary on the third: "The most momentous day in history, this fine September morn England and France have just declared war on Germany and soon all hell will break loose."

Fearing all hell would sweep Wyoming along with the rest of the nation into the conflict, Wyoming women launched a peace movement to "build a strong statewide block to keep the U.S. out of any European conflict." Mrs. Charles Green and Mrs. Ruby Miller, "both mothers of boys old enough to fight if there is a war," convinced Wyoming Senator Joseph O'Mahoney to declare, "I will do everything possible to keep the U.S. out of any war in Europe." The women claimed ninety percent of the state was behind the movement.

Most Wyomingites did take heart in President Roosevelt's assurances that "I believe I can" stay out of the new conflict in Europe. Yet even as early as 1939, Wyoming editors saw a need for preparedness. The *Wyoming State Tribune* applauded the early build-up of the U.S. Merchant Marine, saying, "We're prepared on the seas." The editorial concluded with the ominous sentence, "This is one more conclusive case in which forewarned is forearmed!"

From the start, the state supported the Allies, and anti-German feeling increased as Hitler's forces swept over France, Belgium, and Scandanavia. Across the Pacific, the Japanese struck at China with a particular vengance. Slowly the whirlpool of war widened, threatening the tenuous neutrality the United States tried to maintain.

By mid-1940 national defense became a major concern. Though one Wyoming paper declared "no desperate urgency" to prepare for war, the *Wyoming Eagle* saw the state's role in the upcoming conflict. In Wyoming, "tremendous coal reserves, pools of petrol, forests, water power, minerals, and metals . . . can play an important role in the national defense." By 1940 aliens were registered within the state for security reasons, but no acts of sabotage occurred in Wyoming. As weeks passed, Wyoming residents came to expect war.

War Hits the West

Once the bombs fell on Pearl Harbor, neutrality blew away with the smoke from the burning battleships. Senator O'Mahoney did vote for war as the state periodically rallied to fight back. "America must be unified," the *State Leader* commanded the day after the attack, "From this moment let there be no peace until the wrongs against America . . . have been avenged." The paper also warned citizens that the war would be devastating: "Let Americans dedicate themselves . . . to whatever sacrifices no matter how severe or bitter as are necessary to the vindication of American ideas."

Almost immediately the fear of further attacks caused a strengthening of defenses throughout the west. Though "the average person in Wyoming did not share the panic common on the Pacific Coast," public facilities such as water works and power plants within the state received twenty-four hour guard.

As in World War I, Wyoming men quickly answered their country's call to duty. When Pearl Harbor was attacked, 5,560 Wyoming men and women were already in uniform. By noon on Monday, December 8, 1941, hundreds

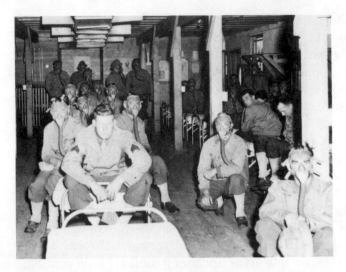

Wyoming soldiers in Fort Warren barracks, 1942 (University of Wyoming)

more had enlisted. By war's end, nearly 30,000— well over ten percent of the state's population—had served in uniform. And once again, Wyoming was far ahead of the national average in the number of soldiers enlisting and the health of the men and women signing up.

Several Wyoming families saw many sons go off to war. The Lewis family of Kemmerer, for example, said goodbye to six boys. The Mike Ruskins of Thermopolis had five children—four boys and a girl—who served in uniform.

Although the Reserve Officers' Training corps was based at the University of Wyoming, most state enlistees trained elsewhere, such as the "reception center" at Ft. Logan, Colorado, or Ft. Lewis, Washington. As they left on troop trains or busses, local organizations like the American Legion auxiliaries hosted farewell parties. Laden with packages containing candy, cigarettes, cards, stationery, and other gifts, soldiers marched off already heroes to those they left behind. Newspapers recorded every enlistee, and along the route to the crowded troop ships, lonely soldiers could find some comfort in U.S.O. (United States Organization) stations. Here volunteers served coffee and conversation, and at canteens such as a huge one at Sheridan, food could be had at any hour.

Heroes from the War

As the war progressed, bad news inched out the good on Wyoming's front pages: Corporal Frank L. Dupes of Laramie was killed in 1942; boatswain's mate Jesse Clark of Mountainview was injured; Robert Cooper from Cody, Jay Groshart of Laramie, and Charles Robertson of Manderson were all imprisoned by the Japanese at Shanghai; Waldo Sutherland was killed in the South Pacific; Tech Sergeant Jesse Stewart of Green River was captured by the Japanese on Wake Island. A complete list would fill volumes.

Yet from that list came Wyoming's heroes.

Among many decorated men, William Eder was awarded the Distinguished Flying Cross. Sergeant William Wood of Cheyenne won the Silver Star for helping to sink the Japanese battlecruiser *Hiei* in 1942. Ted Tanner of Thermopolis was cited for gallantry and bravery during the Pearl Harbor attack. He was decorated for keeping vital telephone lines open during the bombing.

Future Governor Ed Herschler rescued a "wounded fellow" as his battalion met tremendous resistance landing on a Japanese-held island in the South Pacific. Shot while dragging the soldier to safety, Herschler was later decorated for bravery.

The most decorated Wyoming soldier was Charles Carey of Cheyenne. In fighting at Remling, France, he destroyed a German tank, single-handedly captured sixteen Germans in a house, rescuing two "doughboy squads" before he was killed. He won the Congressional Medal of Honor posthumously.

In all, 1,095 Wyoming men died during World War II.

Prisoners of War in Wyoming

Unlike World War I, which remained far from the state, World War II found its way directly to Wyoming soil. Two types of "detention camps" were constructed in remote areas and brought the conflict directly to Wyoming citizens.

Because Wyoming is so inaccessible compared to other areas of the country prisoners of war (POWs) were imprisoned here from 1943 to 1945. The largest camp was built at Douglas. There, the Corps of Engineers threw up $1,000,000 worth of barracks surrounded by a high wall to house 3,500 prisoners from the European conflict. Four hundred and twelve Italian POWs arrived on August 17, 1943, to open the camp. By October over 1,900 men wandered within the compound.

Other prisoners were held at Fort Warren in Cheyenne and at side camps in Riverton, Pine Bluffs, Dubois, Wheatland, Veteran, and Worland.

The prisoners ranged in age from 14 to 80, and most worked in beet fields, lumber camps, or helped operate businesses within the compound.

At the Douglas camp, you would find tailor shops, barber shops, a bakery, and carpenter shops. Prisoners routinely received eighty-nine cents a day for their work. They were able to take classes, play sports, and pursue their hobbies. One German violin maker even used Wyoming cedar to make violins that the enterprising POW sold for over two hundred dollars each.

Occasionally, problems developed. Two prisoners, for example, escaped from Douglas in September of 1944 but were later captured near Salina, Kansas. At times the local area residents grew resentful of the prisoners. But on a whole, the POWs seemed pleased that they were so far from the dangers of war. Some liked Wyoming so much that they returned to settle here after the war. One prisoner told his camp newspaper: "My enthusiasm for this magnificent Rocky Mountain landscape will accompany me for my whole life."

Heart Mountain Detention Center

The other type of detention center camp in Wyoming did not inspire such favorable comments. Heart Mountain Relocation Center between Powell and Cody was built to house Japanese Americans during the war.

Following the attack on Pearl Harbor, "Hate the Jap" sentiment swept the nation. Out of an unfounded fear that the 110,000 west coast Japanese Americans would remain loyal to Japan and deal in sabotage and spying for the Emperor, the U.S. government ordered them to "relocation centers." This meant entire families, many of whom owned businesses and property were forced to sell or give up most of their possessions.

Nine camps in seven Western states were built in remote areas. One isolated spot was in northwestern Wyoming. Here in the summer of 1942 workers enclosed a 740 acre tract of land with barbed wire and constructed 450 oblong barracks. Each 120-foot building could be put up in fifty minutes and contained six single-room apartments. Each unit had a coal stove, two blankets, a bucket, and broom. Luxuries such as finished walls and ceilings, interior plumbing, and closets were dispensed with.

The first "Nisei" (American-born Japanese) and "Issei" (foreign-born Japanese) arrived with their meagre belongings on August 10, 1942. By September the first death, birth, fire, and wedding had occurred in the tar-roofed city. By October the population at Heart Mountain had swelled to a staggering 10,000. That same month, humiliated at their treatment as virtual prisoners, citizens of Heart Mountain protested the barbed wire fence and machine gun carrying guards who patrolled the camp. Little

Japanese Relocation Center, Heart Mountain (University of Wyoming)

sympathy could be found in Wyoming, however, and the prison treatment continued through the three years of operation.

Life at Heart Mountain was, as Wyoming Governor Lester C. Hunt said after a trip to the camp, "rather disgraceful." Families were crammed into the single room apartments and shared community bathroom, eating, and recreational facilities. Three dry goods stores, a school, churches, radio repair shop, a newspaper, and even a Montgomery Wards department store gave the appearance of a town. Yet leisure time was kept to a minimum so evacuees could not organize or agitate. For their labor on irrigation canals and in fields growing crops, Heart Mountain residents earned about ten cents an hour—less than prisoners of war. Possibly the lowest insult occurred when twenty-two children, the oldest of whom was eleven, were arrested for sledding just outside the camp.

Despite their treatment, many evacuees remained loyal to the United States. In fact over nine hundred men from Heart Mountain either enlisted or were drafted, and twenty were killed in action. Some, however, resented their treatment tremendously. During the three years of operation, over eighty Heart Mountain men served prison terms for refusing to be inducted into the army.

While Wyoming residents grew to tolerate the camp, the Nisei and Issei never earned an invitation to stay in the Cowboy State. The 1943 legislature passed a law forbidding any evacuees from owning property in Wyoming.

Paying for the War

Life on the home front was very similar to life during World War I. The main difference was that the length of the war, over three years, brought more government regulation into people's lives.

World War II cost about $250 million a day. To pay for it, the government once again sold Liberty Bonds everywhere, and Wyomingites bought over $155 million worth. School children had stamp "treasure hunts" going from door to door collecting "war stamps" so they could fill books that bought bonds. Wyoming theaters alone pledged $300,000 worth of bonds, while the Shoshone Indian tribe at Wind River Indian Reservation gave nearly a half million dollars for bonds. Everywhere the waving American flag prompted people to buy bonds.

Purse ad (University of Wyoming)

Agriculture was crucial to the war effort and remained Wyoming's major industry. As in World War I, crops and livestock saw a staggering rise in production. The "cash receipts" from Wyoming crops rose from $8,259,000 in 1939 to over $21,000,000 in 1945; the oil and coal industries prospered as well.

Wyoming schools changed their curriculums to suit the war needs. Courses like "pre-flight training," "radio communications," and added math and science appeared on high school class lists. Welding became popular, as did agricultural classes such as "farm shop" and "production of commercial vegetables."

Two problems faced schools during the "war emergency." One was decreased budgets, but some money came from national programs like the "Victory Corps" which trained students for war service after they graduated. The other problem was a severe teacher shortage. To combat this, "temporary" certificates were issued to non-professional teachers. Many retired and former teachers returned to the classroom, as regular teachers took up guns instead of gradebooks.

SUBSCRIBER

HONOR EMBLEM

4<u>th</u> LIBERTY LOAN

Fourth Liberty Loan ad
(University of Wyoming)

Women Boost the War Effort

Women "helped win the war!" proclaimed Mrs. W. B. Gray, the chairman of the Women's Division of the State Council of National Defense. And she had good reason to speak so highly of Wyoming's women. As they did all across the country, women slipped into state jobs previously done largely by men. Many women worked on the railroad, in industrial plants, on farms and ranches, and as nurses.

Women also won the war in the home. A major campaign was to grow "victory gardens." Gardening in the late thirties and early forties was not a hobby or pastime for most. Convenience foods had just come on the market, and the idea of digging, planting, weeding, and harvesting had little appeal to most people, especially those in urban areas. But slogans like "Dig for Victory, Plant for Victory, Grow for Victory" prompted clubs and organizations to help individuals plant gardens. By war's end over 16,000 victory gardens across the state yielded tons of fresh food for Wyomingites who were further urged to do their own canning and preserving.

The collection of trash—everything from aluminum to waste paper—became a patriotic duty for everyone, even children. Physical fitness programs were offered, and all were cautioned against careless talk. In writing to servicemen, wives and mothers were warned by the Ladies Auxiliary of the Veterans of Foreign Wars (VFW) to write only about "personal matters." Their *American Guidebook* also gave instructions on writing to captured loved ones: letters should be typed, would receive free postage, and should simply be addressed "Prisoner of War."

Rationing Regulates Goods

When individual conservation of food and raw materials simply could not keep up with the demands of war, rationing began. Prices were controlled as early as 1942. Soon, local "rationing boards" decided if you could buy a truck, typewriter, or bicycle. Gas rationing began at the end of 1942, with four gallons allowed to each driver per week. By March 1943 a confusing system of food rationing began. Each item in the grocery store was given a number of points. Ration books filled with stamps (or coupons) were picked up at local rationing board headquarters. When you bought food, you had to give the grocer not only money for the item, but the proper number of stamps as well. When you ran out of stamps, you could no longer buy the items needed until the next time the books were issued (usually once a month). Housewives were urged to use low-point food. For example, a pound of ground beef, which could serve five, carried five points, while a pound of porterhouse steak, which could serve only three, was worth twelve points.

Homemakers were further urged to stretch food by spreading butter thin, using cheese instead of milk, or mixing milk with geletin.

Again, women's organizations knitted sweaters for soldiers, made surgical dressings, which had to be folded "just so." Even when relaxing, those at home could never forget the war. Hostesses were urged to have "victory garden suppers" to which everyone brought a different dish made from home-grown vegetables. Games like "prisoner's base" would be played. Or perhaps a basket social would be held to raise money for the Red Cross. Parties and dances almost always included some type of fund-raising activity to help the war effort. Even the 1943 Wyoming

Cowboys basketball team, which captured the NCAA crown, played a benefit game for the Red Cross.

The War Draws to an End

On June 6, 1944 (D-Day), the Allies invaded German occupied Normandy in the greatest amphibious invasion of all time. It was a carefully calculated gamble, and conditions proved right. The Germans were taken by surprise. Slowly, with morale growing, the Allies inched their way toward Germany liberating Europe from Hitler's rule on the way. In April, 1945, as his Nazi empire crumbled around him, Hitler killed himself in his underground bunker. By May 1 the European war had ended.

Citizens across Wyoming received the news with gratitude and hope. But the state remained "calm and cool." Businesses were conducted as usual on VE (Victory in Europe) Day, and there was "No evidence of hilarity." Japan still had to be defeated.

Poster boosting women's morale during the war (University of Wyoming)

The Atomic Age Ends the War

For some time, Wyomingites had been hearing about the development of a "super bomb" based on "atomic power." By summer, as the Japanese retreated from territory they had won earlier in the war, President Harry S. Truman warned the Japanese to surrender or he would be forced to use the "super bomb." When the Japanese disregarded the warning, the atomic bomb devastated Hiroshima. Over a hundred thousand people died in the single (and now relatively small) atomic blast. A second bombing at Nagasaki within the week brought Japan to its knees in surrender.

Unlike VE Day, VJ Day (Victory in Japan) was the happiest day of many a Wyomingite's life. In less than five minutes of the announcement of Japan's surrender, crowds swarmed into the streets of Cheyenne, Casper, and other cities. Downtown businesses shooed customers and tacked up signs saying "Closed Today and Tomorrow." President Truman concurred, declaring the next two days legal holidays.

"No single description could fit the crowds in Cheyenne streets this day," one ecstatic reporter wrote. "Traffic jams occurred, cars fluttering by with ribbons of colored paper and toilet tissue."

Yet the importance of VJ Day cannot be found only in the fact that World War II had ended. It is found in *how* it ended. As one Wyoming editor wrote, "the unlocking of atomic power was of great importance, if not more importance than the war." Indeed, the need to end World War II had prompted the creation of weapons capable of global destruction. The need to control these weapons would soon become part of a new chapter of Wyoming's history.

Poster inspiring Wyoming "Victory Gardens" (University of Wyoming)

"Letters from Home" (University of Wyoming)

12
Modern Wyoming

As life returned to normal after World War II, the feelings of joy so universally shared by Wyomingites faded to fear for many. Farmers and ranchers remembered all too well the economic disaster they faced when World War I ended. So throughout the state, people wanted financial security more than anything else as the nation switched from a wartime to a peacetime economy. Regulations on prices, quantity, and quality of goods were being dropped. Contracts from the War Department were cancelled, and unused weapons and materials were stockpiled. Possibly the biggest problem in changing from war to peace was finding jobs for the millions of returning soldiers.

Wyoming Prepares for Peace

Governor Lester Hunt recognized the readjustment problem as early as 1944 when a task force on postwar Wyoming printed a booklet asking the question, "When Johnny comes marching home and hangs his gun on the wall, are we going to have a job for him?" Twenty-four thousand jobs in Wyoming would be needed to handle the returning servicemen. "Postwar planning," the booklet stressed, "must start at the grass roots." Every Wyoming community was urged to identify economic problems and provide jobs for soldiers returning home.

Prophetically, Hunt's committee identified new reclamation projects agriculture, highway construction, tourism, mining and oil development, and construction as areas where veterans could find jobs.

Fortunately, retiring men and women and young people who no longer wanted to work opened many slots in the job market for veterans.

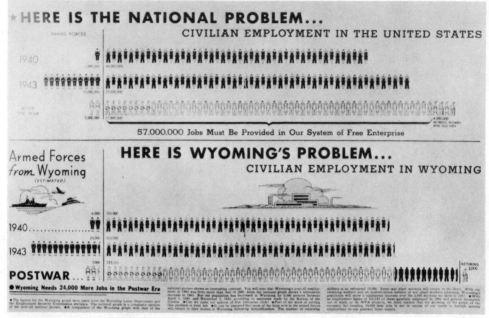

Chart showing anticipated employment problems in post-war Wyoming (Wyoming State Archives)

Staggered discharges allowed a gradual return of soldiers, easing the problem of finding jobs for the men. As a result, there was little unemployment in Wyoming following the war.

The problem of price controls was not as easy to solve, unfortunately. The Office of Price Administration (OPA) decided what goods would cost during the war. Once Japan had surrendered, many people wanted to end controls immediately. Cattlemen and meat producers, for example, wanted controls dropped because regulations had kept meat prices down during the war. Small retail businesses, however, wanted some controls, while consumers and veterans in Wyoming were in favor of continuing all price controls because they feared "ruinous inflation." When wages and prices rise too rapidly, inflation can cause serious problems.

Powerful Wyoming Senator Joseph O'Mahoney favored some controls that would help both the livestock producers and veterans of Wyoming. But the OPA was scrapped when President Truman vetoed the bill that would have extended the life of the department.

Prices soared, and labor problems quickly developed. Over 3,000 coal miners were already on strike in Rock Springs because of a wage dispute, and more problems threatened. Livestock producers did enjoy a fair price for their cattle, but it became clear there had to be some controls to keep inflation from ruining the postwar recovery. People in Wyoming shuddered at price hikes. In 1946 a sirloin steak jumped from 45¢ to 75¢ a pound. An apartment that rented for $33 a month in 1945 was suddenly worth $55. By July 1946 the OPA was back in business controlling prices—and pacifying an angry public. In spite of OPA efforts, though, food prices alone rose a staggering sixty-eight percent between 1946 and 1948.

New Pioneers in Northwest Wyoming

Despite some economic problems, most veterans settled back into civilian life quickly. Some, though chose to change their lives dramatically and return to the ideals of the pioneers by homesteading new land made available by the federal government.

One area opened for settlement was Heart Mountain. As the last remnants of the Japanese Relocation Center were dismantled, the land was offered to veterans. According to Bill Hosakawa, himself an internee

Johnny Comes Marching Home brochure cover (Wyoming State Archives)

When Johnny Comes Marching Home And HANGS HIS GUN On the Wall . . .

Are We Going to Have a Job for Him Under Our System of Free Enterprise? It is YOUR PROBLEM!

at Heart Mountain before becoming an editor of the *Denver Post*, prospective homesteaders had to have two years farm experience along with $1,000 in cash or assets such as farm equipment. The land was then divided by lottery.

The new homesteaders took up the traditional task of "proving up" in order to own the land. They were required to live on their claim three years and harvest two crops. And it wasn't any easier for these modern pioneers than for their wagon-driving predecessors. Betty Brug recalled, "Our working started at sunup and lasted as long as there was light to see. We were at it seven days a week building the house, getting the crops in." About half the new homesteaders quit before earning the land. But those who stayed found they "were never happier."

Why did these homesteaders pick up the challenge of settling new land? One postwar pioneer gave the traditional reason: "We came here because there wasn't anything where we were."

Junior Colleges Open

To help pay back the returning G.I.s and their families for sacrifices made during the war, the government passed the G.I. Bill that guaranteed benefits to veterans. One of these was free or partially paid higher education so the men could catch up on opportunities lost because of the war. As a result, thousands of new students—former colonels and privates alike—swelled classrooms at the University of Wyoming.

To help meet the needs of the eager-to-learn veterans, the 1945 legislature passed the Junior College Bill, beginning the state community college system. Casper College opened its doors in 1945 to eighty students. A year later Northwest Community College opened in Powell, followed in 1948 by Eastern Wyoming College in Torrington and Northern Wyoming College in Sheridan. Ten years later, Western Wyoming College opened in Rock Springs, and in 1966 Central Community College opened in Riverton completing the junior college system. At these two-year schools, students completed work toward their academic degrees or studied a wide range of vocational subjects.

The Blizzard of '49

Just when the livestock industry was picking up following the deregulation of prices, nature dealt a killing blow. On January 2, 1949, a blizzard roared out of Montana, blanketing southeastern Wyoming. Snow "drifted into folds from thirty to sixty feet deep." Thirty inches lay on the ground. Blowing snow stranded travelers everywhere. Motorists cut off three miles south of Lusk had to shiver for hours in freezing cars as rescue workers struggled to plow through deepening snow. Some rural residents lost their heat supplies and froze to death.

Cattle naturally sought shelter in gullies and draws. Unfortunately, the snow drifted over the huddling herds, burying many cattle. In order to save those that did stay on the range, ranchers began "Operation Haylift." Pilots flew low over the cattle and dropped baled hay for the hungry animals. While this did save many head, the losses from the Blizzard of '49 were staggering.

A New War in Asia

Almost as soon as the guns fell silent in the South Pacific, a new kind of "war" began. In the last months of the war in the drive on Germany the Soviets occupied Eastern Europe, including Czechoslovakia, Yugoslavia, and Poland. Supported by the Soviets, communist elements in each country came to power. Contact between the West and these new Russian "satellite" countries was halted as an "iron curtain" fell over Europe. This imaginary "curtain" symbolized the imprisonment of those within the new communist dictatorships. A fear of communism spread over the United States, and a new struggle between the communists and non-communist nations became known as the "Cold War."

The Cold War, which raged through the fifties and sixties, affected Wyoming as it did the rest of the nation. Wyomingites were horrified when the Russians balanced our nuclear power by exploding their own atomic bomb in 1949. The possibility of the communists using the "super bomb" was now a reality, and this spirited deep anti-communist feelings across the state.

That same year after a long battle, the communists came into power in China. In June 1950 the North Koreans, spurred on by China and Russia, attacked South Korea in an attempt to reunite the country split by the United States and Russia after World War II. For three years the Cold War burned in the undeclared Korean War as American troops—acting as a United Nations peacekeeping force—fought the North Koreans for possession of treeless knobs like "Heartbreak Ridge," "Old Baldy," and "Pork Chop Hill." Three years later, the Americans left the scarred, burned-out battlefields along the dividing line (38th parallel) where the communists had halted. In all, 33,419 Americans died. Seventy of them were from Wyoming.

At home, the war caused fear of new restrictions on goods and other controls. "Daily we are finding it necessary to practice both self-sacrifice and self-discipline," one Wyoming editor wrote in 1951. "We are continually faced with new restrictions. Copper was restricted, now cobalt. Aluminum and steel are channeled into the war emergency. Soon to be affected will be televisions and radios . . . ." Luckily for Wyomingites, the dire warnings of this editorial never materialized, and the state never felt a shortage of goods or services during the Korean conflict.

Better Dead Than Red

Yet the fear of communism was very real. A 1950 cartoon in a Wyoming newspaper showed a dike with a small boy using his finger to block a leak. The boy, of course, was the United States. The monstrously sinister sea ready to overwhelm the land was communism. For many Wyomingites, the dike had begun to leak with the Korean War, and the state valiantly supported any effort to shore up defenses.

The debate over how to defeat communism raged through the decade. Many felt a swift stockpiling of nuclear and conventional weapons would be best. Fred W. Bennison, head of the Wyoming Taxpayer's Association, was "for spending all the money that can be spent effectively to overtake them."

Yet when tax hikes were proposed to pay for the bigger defense budget, even conservative Wyoming was angered. "How high can taxes get?" the *Torrington Telegram* asked when the tax bite reached twenty-five cents out of every dollar. "Taxes," the paper warned, "may be the collapse of our way of life." The Reverend R.O. McCaslin, a Wyoming pastor and newspaper columnist, agreed that money would not stop communism: "We cannot defeat communism by increasing taxes, supplying other nations with armaments, perfecting guided missiles or atom bombs. The fight simmers down to Christianity vs. Communism."

Hunting Down the Reds

By 1953 the radical Republican Senator Joseph McCarthy of Wisconsin gained notoriety investigating communist infiltration (penetration) of our government, entertainment industry, and other phases of American life. His senate subcommittee hearings on "Unamerican activities" blackballed hundreds of Americans. In 1952 the "wooly warrior," as he was called by the *Laramie Boomerang*, visited the university city. McCarthy told the paper, "It's time to hit the traitors behind the treason" of American foreign policy. The reporter termed McCarthy an "affable, likeable character." An editorial that day went on to point out the sixteen differences between a liberal and communist. There was clear support in Wyoming for the early McCarthy movement against communism.

But in 1954 controversy over McCarthy's anti-communist activities affected Wyoming's senate race. Former Senator Joseph O'Mahoney—one of the most powerful senators in Washington before his 1952 defeat—was running against William Henry Harrison, descended from two presidents. According to T.A. Larson, when the Harrison campaign appeared to be boring itself to death, his forces injected excitement into the election by labeling O'Mahoney a "foreign agent." Apparently he had represented U.S. citizens who had invested in Cuban sugar. He had also helped one of McCarthy's key targets in his investigations (a man found innocent of being a communist). In an era of fear and suspicion these "revelations" were damaging to O'Mahoney's campaign. Nevertheless, he won re-election by a small margin.

Later that year, McCarthy himself came under fire for his ruthless and often unfounded attacks on prominent individuals. After he was censured (condemned by words) by the Senate, McCarthy's power dissolved.

But the fear of invasion from within or without persisted, as did the Cold War. Aliens (foreign-born residents) were registered amid a great deal of publicity, and county "alien" statistics were published annually. Any new political ideas were also viewed with suspicion. One writer warned: "There are many dangers to our form of government lurking around each corner. If it isn't communism, it is socialism or some other kind of 'ism."

The fears reached almost ridiculous proportions when it was thought Wyoming would "suffer a major invasion by Denver syndicates" that dealt in gambling. Apparently a grand jury investigation in Denver had closed illegal operations, and Wyoming officials were afraid the hoods would head north. "But if they should, our people are just as tough, if not tougher," one sheriff said. "If our people can't get rough enough, then we know where we can hire people who can!" Fortunately for all, the fear was unfounded as the gamblers apparently set up shop elsewhere.

A New Bonanza

The obvious way to safeguard national security, most people agreed, was to stockpile atomic bombs. This weapons build-up of the fifties affected

Uranium miners in ore car (University of Wyoming)

Inspecting uranium mine (University of Wyoming)

Dumping ore (University of Wyoming)

Living quarters, uranium mine (University of Wyoming)

Wyoming tremendously, for in order to harness atomic power, much expensive uranium was needed. With over two hundred million tons of uranium reserves, Wyoming became a prime target for prospectors seeking their fortunes in "yellowjack."

Wyoming uranium was first discovered accidently in the dump at Silver Creek mine in Lusk in 1918. Once processed, the uranium found in the yellow rocks was used in medicinal tablets and ointments. The Lusk uranium was mined and hauled to Denver for processing, but the market dried up during the hard times of the twenties and thirties. More yellowjack (uranium ore) was mined at Lusk briefly in 1952, but this find paled in the light of new discoveries at Pumpkin Buttes and Gas Hills where vast quantities of incredibly rich ore spurred a wild prospecting craze.

In 1953 "a Riverton garageman," Neil McNeice, discovered mineable quantities of uranium in the Gas Hills area of Fremont County, about eighty miles west of Casper. He opened the Lucky Mc Mine, which became a rich producer of uranium.

The Pumpkin Buttes area, south of Gillette, had been surveyed for the government by Dr. J. David Love in 1952. He reported a huge supply of mineable ore. When the government announced the find, uranium seekers flocked to the dry, dusty hills.

Hundreds swarmed over cattlemen's rangeland, tearing down fences and destroying property. No ranch was safe from the uranium prospectors holding clicking Geiger counters which screeched loudly when nearing a radioactive deposit of uranium.

When the government announced that the Pumpkin Buttes area would be "thrown open to public entry," fearful ranchers "had nightmares about their short grass range being scarred by trails, prospect holes, and bulldozer slashes." The National Guard was alerted to the possibility of violence, but by the time the prospectors arrived to stake claims, the ranchers had organized into a corporation able to control the fortune seekers legally.

The uranium prospectors came from all over the country, encouraged by national reports on how to search for the yellow ore, where to look, and what equipment to buy. Outfitters were as eager to handle the modern fortune-hunters as they were the Oregon Trail travelers a hundred years before. "The ultimate equipment," *Life* magazine stated, was now "a four-wheel drive jeep ($1,685)." The magazine then went into the essentials: "a $98 Geiger counter, canteen, ore sacks, maps, hatchet, pick, compass, tape, booklets, claim notices, and snakebite kits."

Few well or ill-equipped prospectors ever got a chance to use much more than the snakebite kit and canteen, for few struck it rich.

One who did, though, was Robert Adams, a veteran who had served time in a prisoner of war camp in Germany. He had come to Rawlins after the war to open a restaurant but heard of McNeice's success. He mortgaged his holdings and went digging in the Lost Creek area north of Rawlins. He struck pay dirt in 1955 and organized what eventually became Western Nuclear, Inc., one of the biggest uranium mining companies in the world.

Adams built the town of Jeffrey City on the site of the old town of "Home on the Range." In the vast nothingness, this "ragged knot of a town" grew up around a massive open pit mine and eventually swelled to home for 4,500 citizens. A classic boom town like the early "end of track" tent towns along the Union Pacific trail, Jeffrey City went bust in the early 1980s when the uranium mine closed down as demand for the ore disappeared.

Progress in the Fifties

As the uranium industry prospered in the fifties and sixties, Wyoming saw progress in many other areas as well.

Electricity became available in even the most remote areas of the state. The Rural Electric Association (REA) helped send lines to power ranches and farms which used either generators or even wood and kerosene. Also helping farmers and livestock producers was the promised increase in reclaiming land through irrigation. Four new dams were built in the fifties, adding thousands of acres to land that could now be farmed. The Kortes Dam was completed in 1951. In 1952 Big Sandy, Boysen, and Keyhole were all completed, while in 1958 Glendo Dam created the huge Glendo Reservoir on the North Platte River, destined to become a haven for campers, boaters and fishermen.

Modern "rainmakers" provided interesting help to farmers, too. When little snow fell in 1951, and it appeared the summer would be one of drought, the Water Resources Development Company gathered farmers and ranchers and promised to "increase or reduce rainfall and give accurate forecasts as long as one year in advance."

Unlike Frank Melbourne, who had worked in secret to "produce" half an inch of rain in Cheyenne back in 1891, these modern rainmakers openly flew over clouds, "seeding" them with chemicals to help stimulate rain and snow. Some doubted the whole scheme, but as one editor wrote, "So much like the drowning man, we say, let's give the snowpackers a trial." Seeding did work occasionally, but successes were of little value.

Despite the Cold War raging through the fifties and sixties, one battle was won in 1955. Polio, a disease which "defied the powers of the medical profession," was a dreaded fact of life in Wyoming and every other state. Though it usually struck children, it could strike at any age, leaving its victims dead, crippled, or living in an iron lung.

The March of Dimes was organized to raise money to fight the disease and help offset the expense of treatment. As progress against the disease caught the public's attention, campaigns to raise money each spring began throughout the state. Each county was assessed $10,000 or more, and Wyomingites willingly donated in a flurry of fund-raising activities.

Once an anti-polio vaccine was developed in 1955, however, Wyomingites were hesitant to get their three shots. Editors and doctors had to urge everyone to protect himself from the disease, despite the inconveniences of the early vaccinations. By 1958 state citizens had heeded the warnings, and the state was a leader in having most citizens vaccinated.

Perhaps the most revolutionary invention of all times, television, crept into Wyoming in the early fifties. Television sets could be bought as early as 1948, but regular broadcasting did not begin in the state until a Denver station transmitted programs in 1952. KFBC-TV in Cheyenne opened in 1954, followed by KTWO-TV in Casper in 1957. By then the blue glow of television sets could be seen through living room windows in most Wyoming cities each night. Though the screens were small on those early television sets, the impact was big. The remote Wyoming frontier could now view events such as national political conventions and the World Series as they happened.

The Space Age Begins

One event carefully watched in 1957 was the launching of the first space satellite by the Russians. *Sputnik* (Russian for "traveler") soared into orbit on October 4, 1957, followed later that year by a larger craft that carried a dog. Infuriated that the communists had leaped ahead in the new "space race," Washington called for changes in school curriculums to direct American youth into the new space age. Wyoming was skeptical of proposed beefing up of math and science programs at the expense of the traditional 3 R's. "Socialists, Federalists, progressives . . . whatever they want to call themselves, are using Sputnik as an excuse to ask for federal aid to speed up education!" one editor grumbled.

Despite criticism, though, an interest in space swept the state. Newspapers offered front page safety tips for amateur rocketeers, and one paper gleefully reported on the front page in 1958 "A group of high school students successfully launched a rocket . . . [that] soared well into the air . . . . It was the first known attempt locally to launch a rocket."

Wyoming's move into the space age advanced when the Department of Defense positioned missiles carrying atomic warheads inside the state. In 1957 the Russians had developed a missile launch system for delivering atomic bombs. This meant they could target anywhere in the United States without using a regular (and vulnerable) conventional airplane.

The U.S. also had a system developed, and placed twenty-four Atlas missiles and later two hundred "Minuteman" missiles in underground silos in southeastern Wyoming, western Nebraska, and northeastern Colorado. Construction began in 1959 and continued through 1965.

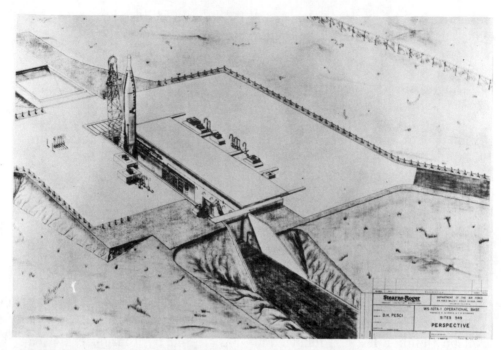

Drawing of Atlas ICBM ready for launch (Wyoming State Archives)

Launch control consoles, Atlas missile site, Warren Air Force Base (Wyoming State Archives)

Missile at Fort Warren Air Force
Base, 1964 (Wyoming State
Archives)

Because Wyoming became an important part of the strengthening U.S. position against communism, most Wyomingites applauded the missile placements. Warren Air Force Base (formerly Fort D.A. Russell outside Cheyenne) became an important Strategic Air Command Center and thus a source of pride for the state. The increased government spending in the state was also much appreciated. Only later did the missiles and the presence of nuclear weapons become controversial.

Tourism Strengthens

Undaunted by atomic bombs placed near highways, tourists flocked to Wyoming in the fifties and sixties. After the war, gas and leisure time became plentiful, so popular sites such as Yellowstone now drew millions annually. To accommodate the weary travelers, motels sprang up in every town across the state. With the help of federal money, new interstate highways speeded travel and added comfort.

Unfortunately where the interstates were placed caused problems. A town by-passed by an interstate highway would suffer greatly because tourists inevitably preferred the double-lane, limited access roads to single-lanes passing through town after town. I-80, for example, passed by Medicine Bow, so tourists did likewise. The town's economy crumbled as a result. When Governor Milward Simpson approved the building of I-90 from Gillette to Buffalo rather than to Sheridan, he lost thousands of votes in Sheridan County.

No one could complain, though, when tourists poured into the state, usually heading to see the bears and geysers in Yellowstone.

But the face of the national park was altered one night in 1959. A sudden jolt at 11:30 P.M. on August 17 woke campers who found their tents shaking "like a big bear rocking a cradle." Scurrying into the darkness, terrified vacationers found the earth shaking violently as one of the biggest North American earthquakes in history ravaged northwest Wyoming. Twenty-eight people died when a mountain slid down into the Madison River creating a wall of water that engulfed and swept them away.

Later park rangers noted many changes in the natural features of the park. Sapphire Pool, for example, had been shooting steam and hot water a measly six feet into the air. After the quake it regularly shot a spray over two hundred feet, making it one of the park's biggest geysers.

The Vietnam War

By the early 1960s, the Cold War took an anguished turn that upset one Wyoming newspaper's prediction of a "stirring" and prosperous decade ahead.

As early as 1954, unknown to most Wyoming citizens, U.S. military advisors had been sent to help stem the flow of communism in South Vietnam, like Korea, an Asian nation divided after World War II. By 1963 over 15,000 advisors (soldiers) were fighting in the steaming jungles. Two years later, the first contingent of Marines landed in the beseiged nation. By 1968 America was spending about thirty billion dollars annually and had committed 500,000 men in an increasingly unpopular war.

Unlike other states, typically conservative Wyoming naively supported U.S. involvement with enthusiasm. "What we can't quite understand," one editor wrote, "is the demonstrations going on . . . while most . . . directly affected by the war seem to have a different feeling."

As in all previous wars, Wyoming did more than its share: 2,673 Wyoming men served in Vietnam, and 135 died in combat. Wyoming was the fifth hardest hit state in the nation in terms of casualities compared to population. But this only strengthened the state's patriotism.

At the same time, the nation erupted in racial violence. With the passing of the Civil Rights Act in 1964, minorities gained further rights. Wyoming's contribution to the powerful movement was to repeal its unused 1913 law that forbad interracial marriages.

By the late 1960s, unrest on college campuses had exploded across the country. Peace marches, anti-war speeches, and Civil Rights demonstrations were common subjects on the evening news. Though the assassination of President John F. Kennedy, the growing opposition to the Vietnam War, and the demand for minority equal rights tore the country apart, Wyoming remained unaffected and aloof from the problems.

Unrest Wakes Wyoming

In Wyoming, it seemed that a different attitude toward unrest was present. As the *Riverton Ranger* put it on November 17, 1969, "Wyoming was 50 years behind the rest of the country." The 330,000 Wyoming citizens were living in a state from which everything was exported. Minerals, trees, and water all left the state. Young people also left the state to find jobs in cities to the south, west, and east. Little industry existed here—so little, in fact, that in the mid-sixties, Governor Stanley Hathaway hosted dinner parties featuring elk and buffalo to lure prospective industries to the state. The people of Wyoming appeared to believe that if too much pressure was put on developers to benefit Wyoming they would "pull up stakes and move somewhere else."

But the events of October 1969 were to force Wyoming into a national awareness from which it would never slide back.

The series of incidents began with an article in the *Wall Street Journal* on October 3, 1969. "The Lonesome Land", written by Dennis Farney, depicted Wyoming as a faltering society "dominated culturally and economically by the outer world." The article had the effect of awakening people within the state to the "look of Wyoming." Farney stated that the problems of Wyoming were "in dying towns, disappearing ranches, and a state economy that while booming in some areas is stagnating in others." He pointed out that Wyoming was one of four states to lose population since the 1960 census. Per capita income in Wyoming, he stated, "is $157 below the national average." Wyoming's citizens have "a deep seated suspicion of outsiders and a seemingly ingrained tendency to think small."

As the impact of the *Journal* article stirred up the pride of Wyoming, other events were set to explode on the scene. On October 15, 1969, a nationwide "moratorium" against the Vietnam War was planned, "A Day of Peace" where people across the country would march, make speeches, and demonstrate against the war. No one in Wyoming believed that the day would be any different than any other.

Centered mostly in the state colleges and at the University in Laramie, but not limited to them, came unexpected support for the "moratorium."

At the University of Wyoming, the moratorium was given a special name, "The Day of Propagation of Peace," and five hundred students marched without incident. They carried signs, lit candles, and held twenty-four hour vigils attended by "cowboys and hippies" alike.

To criticism of the "Peace Freaks," the *Wyoming State Journal* responded by saying that "the marchers in the Vietnam Moratorium yesterday, with the exception of a few troublemakers, love this country just as much as their fellow men; it is unfair to say otherwise . . . . They are trying, that is something."

Debate over the rights or wrongs of the moratorium might have stretched on for months had it not been for another shock to the once quiet state.

On Saturday, October 18, the University of Wyoming football team was scheduled to play Brigham Young University. This school, funded by the Mormon church, had become the focal point of concern about discrimination against blacks. Fourteen black Wyoming football players, supported by the "Black Student Alliance" at the University, wanted to protest against Brigham Young by wearing black arm bands during the game.

Coach Lloyd Eaton, saying that the football field was no place for political protest, told the players the arm bands wouldn't be allowed. After a confrontation, fourteen players were dismissed from the team.

Suddenly Wyoming, and particularly Wyoming's pride, had been brought to the forefront of national attention. Major newspapers covered the event, and national magazines presented stories and opinions.

Within a very short time, remote, untroubled Wyoming had been propelled into the national spotlight. The Cowboy State was in the midst of events dealing with racial equality and in step with the forming unity against the Vietnam War. Wyoming was suddenly a part of the "real world," not an escape from it.

Severance Tax at Last

The decade of the 1970s was destined to be one of change in Wyoming. Beginning these changes was the passing of the Mineral Severance Tax.

In 1969, after nearly fifty years of discussion, the state legislature passed a law requiring companies to pay a one percent severance tax on oil, gas, coal, uranium, trona, and other minerals destined to be used outside the state. The tax would bring needed revenue into the state and offer some compensation for the loss of valuable minerals that would some day be used up. Severance tax money was to be put into a "mineral trust fund" and could be used only if the entire state would benefit. In 1974, again in 1975, and nearly every year after 1981, the percentage rate was increased.

The severance tax money is now being used to equalize education throughout the state by giving money to counties with low property tax assessments to bring the level of education up to match that available in mineral-rich counties. It is also used to help cities and towns that suffer from population booms and for water development.

From Crunch to Cash

Realistically, though Wyoming depended on oil and gas exploration and production and on the mining of trona, coal, and other minerals, the principal lifestyle was still one of the "down home" individual involved in some way with either farming or ranching. In fact, the outlook for mineral development in the 1970s looked limited, and few experts saw the likelihood of any expansion in either the oil or gas industries. Few new discoveries had been made, and it seemed that eventually the areas already producing would dry up. By 1970 and 1971 oil and gas production had actually reached a peak and were declining.

Suddenly, in 1973 the Organization of Petroleum Exporting Countries (OPEC) halted exportation of oil from their countries, a move known as the "Arab Oil Embargo." The OPEC countries, principally in the Middle East, had been selling oil cheaply to industrial nations around the world. Stopping the flow threw the Western nations into panic.

Not surprisingly, Wyoming's oil and coal became extremely valuable to an energy-conscious nation. Wyoming's crude tripled in value immediately. Uranium leaped from $8 a pound to $40, and reserves of coal, oil, uranium, and natural gas of marginal quality had suddenly become valuable to energy developers. "The state of Wyoming is solid paydirt," heralded the *Smithsonian Magazine*.

Wyoming's citizens had mixed feelings about this unexpected "boom." Many saw problems as well as fortunes in the immediate future. The huge development would necessarily be accompanied by the greatest influx of people in the state's history. Handling these people would tax the

Wyoming oil field workers capping off gusher (University of Wyoming)

Wyo-dak open pit mine, Gillette (Wyoming State Archives)

resources of city governments as immediate housing and services would be needed. Some feared the loss of Wyoming's traditional lifestyle. The open spaces, beautiful scenery, trout streams, game animals, and the farming-ranching way of life all seemed threatened. One cartoonist saw Wyoming as one huge open pit mine by the year 2000.

Twentieth Century Boom Towns

The experience of two Wyoming cities can be used as examples of the problems of rapid growth. Gillette and Rock Springs both suffered during the first half of the 1970s due to the impact of the energy boom.

Through the 1950s Gillette had been a sleepy, dusty cowtown with a population nearing 2,000. A minor boom had occurred in the 1890s when hundreds of "roughnecks" building the Burlington & Missouri Railroad flooded the town. Shortly, though, life returned to normal when the crews moved on.

In the late 1960s an upsurge in local oil production caused unexpected impact. Furthermore, Gillette was found to be sitting on the world's largest single coal deposit—80 miles long and up to 200 feet thick. Its reserves alone total twenty billion tons. The Wyo-Dak Mine had opened by 1970, and people were flooding in.

By the time of the Arab Oil Embargo in 1973, Gillette was already in trouble. With the embargo, the population and related problems tripled. The population soared from 3,500 in 1960 to 14,000 in 1976.

Typical of boom towns, poorly built houses and hundreds of mobile homes became the standard as demand grew. City services, such as garbage collection, water, and sewers lagged behind the needs, creating health problems. The cost of living in Gillette also mushroomed. A single apartment averaged $250 per month, and in the seventies, houses could not be bought for under $50,000. Mayor Mike Enzi stated, "We're not controlling growth, we're accomodating it."

Such was the way with towns faced with swelling populations. "You cannot call an architect," Enzi said, "and say, lo, let there be a boom; and then lay it out all neat and pretty. Planning . . . takes money and you don't have your tax base until industry and the fried chicken franchises and all the rest of it have already set up shop. There is generally a three year lag between the need for a program or service and the money to support it. Unfortunately, in boom years, the cart usually goes before the horse."

Governor Ed Herschler agreed, saying the problems were "severe" because towns were "not given the opportunity to plan." The state had to take "drastic action" to help boom towns handle the crisis.

The boom in Rock Springs was also a mixed blessing. In the mid-seventies, classrooms built for thirty students were bulging with sixty. Mobile home camps, called "aluminum ghettos," sprang up as the need for housing could not be met by construction. The crime rate rose sixty percent in one year, and cases involving mental health increased nine times.

Like Gillette, Rock Springs merely accommodated the growth rather than controlled it. As Mayor Paul Wataha put it, "None of us likes to grow this fast, but you can't lock the gates of the city."

Other Wyoming cities suffered during the boom years, but to a lesser extent. Hanna, Sheridan, Green River, Casper, Douglas, Wheatland, Rawlins, Cheyenne, and Buffalo all dealt with "impact" problems.

Wright, a town built exclusively for miners working at a new coal mine, did not even exist until the demand for coal grew, necessitating housing for the many miners. Located approximately forty miles south of Gillette, Wright had the fortune to be a planned town, and problems were anticipated, making the impact less severe.

Crimes Compound Problems

As with boom towns of the past, probably the most unsolvable problem caused by rapid growth was the influx of undesireables hoping to make easy money. Towns found it difficult to deal effectively with them because of the rapid growth and the constant movement of the people.

A prime example of the undercurrent of violence and inability to handle it during boom times is the case of Mark Hopkinson. According to the evidence that convicted him, Hopkinson didn't want to pay for a sewer hook-up in a new trailer park in Evanston. So he ordered the bombing of Vincent Vehar's house. Vehar, a lawyer for the city of Evanston, had attempted to force Hopkinson to pay. In the bombing, Vehar and his wife and son were killed. Through alleged bribery and coercion, Hopkinson attempted to cover up the crime, going so far as ordering the torture, murder and mutilation of the man who did the bombing, Jeffrey Greene of Mountainview.

After many problems over jurisdiction between local law enforcement agencies, the case was finally brought to trial. Gerry Spence, a Jackson lawyer famous for defending seemingly hopeless cases, acted as the prosecutor, in part because Vincent Vehar had been his friend. In a long, hotly fought trial, punctuated with death threats to witnesses and lawyers alike, Hopkinson was found guilty of the murders and sentenced to life imprisonment for the bombing and to death for the Jeffrey Greene killing.

Hopkinson was referred to by many, including Wyoming's eminent historian, Dr. T.A. Larson, as the state's most notorious person, even worse than Tom Horn, who, as a hired gun, killed an estimated twenty people.

Television Implicates Rock Springs

The problems of Rock Springs were vividly brought to national attention when the CBS television news show "60 Minutes," narrated by Dan Rather, focused on the city. The effects were far from positive, though. Rather accused Rock Springs of being a wide-open town, run by a handful of men, where vice and corruption were rampant. The show also insinuated knowledge and complicity in the corruption by local and state officials, going so far as to implicate Governor Ed Herschler.

The show stirred up a hornet's nest. A special grand jury was called to hear evidence of corruption. Special government agents and the FBI interviewed hundreds searching for proof of organized crime and involvement by public officials.

In the midst of the confusion, Ed Cantrell, Rock Springs Public Safety Director, shot Michael Rosa, an undercover police officer. Cantrell claimed it was self-defense. Evidence pointed to the fact that Rosa was about to testify before the grand jury where he would implicate "no less than fifty state and county officials" in one kind of criminal activity or another.

As evidence in the trial later brought out, Cantrell had acted in self defense and was freed. As to any information linking public officials to crime, none was ever found.

Fortunately, most towns had less serious violence and criminal activity. The insinuations and accusations that dirtied the town names and implied corruption in the highest levels of state government, though never proved, caused anxious moments for Wyomingites.

Former Rock Springs Mayor Paul Wataha did eventually sue CBS for libel in regards to the "60 Minutes" segment about Rock Springs while he was in office. Though libel was never proven, Wataha dropped the suit only after "a series of out of court settlements with some of the defendants."

The Dust Settles

With the improved development of natural resources, mainly energy fuels, within Wyoming and other states, the demand for foreign oil decreased. Increased nationwide availability of fuel and lower prices caused Wyoming's energy production to decline in the late seventies and early eighties. As the dust settled some Wyoming boom towns even noticed a slight drop in population. Yet when one considers that the populations of Gillette and Rock Springs doubled and tripled in ten years, turning them from small towns "with a sense of community" into cities whose growth was out of control, it is apparent that it will be some time before things are considered "normal" again in Wyoming's affected cities.

Yet Wyoming citizens responded to the same challenge when the transcontinental railroad left "end of track" towns in its wake. Problems led to inventive solutions, and there is no doubt this tradition will continue.

The First Hundred Years . . . and Beyond

As Wyoming approaches its centennial as a state, its story has really come full circle.

Wyoming first offered trails to emigrants passing through on their way to better life. The trails they followed remain. The Overland Stage Trail became the U.P. route in 1868 and the Lincoln Highway later, and the transcontinental air mail planes followed its path. Today millions of travelers use the same trail as they drive along Interstate 80. The Oregon Trail, which guided so many pioneers to farms in Oregon, is today Wyoming's richest and most productive farmland.

The earliest Wyoming cities were "end of track" boom towns. Their populations swelled as railroad workers poured in, then dwindled as the track moved on. A hundred years later, the discovery of uranium, coal, and oil created new boom towns saddled with old problems demanding new solutions.

Wyoming's lifestyle has come full circle as well. The earliest visitors had to sleep under the stars, hunt and fish for food, cook over an open fire, and pass through unmarked trails as they civilized a vast frontier. Today's visitors escape civilization by seeking the very discomforts the early pioneers were forced to bear.

The earliest settlers found in Wyoming a land of opportunity. Wyoming is still a land of opportunity with vast mineral resources, the resulting financial security, and the talents of energetic and educated citizens. Unlike many states, Wyoming has the opportunity to prepare for an exciting future that reflects its pioneer heritage.

BIBLIOGRAPHY

We have divided the bibliography into two sections. In the first, the reader will find works that have been useful in preparing many of the chapters included. In the second, the reader will find a chapter-by-chapter list of works dealing with specific periods or events in Wyoming's history. The newspaper articles listed are only representative of the hundreds which were helpful in preparing this text. The Wyoming State Archives, Museum, and Historical Department will be referred to as "Wyoming State Archives" throughout the bibliography. The University of Wyoming Archives American Heritage Center will be abbreviated "University of Wyoming," and material from the Harold McCracken Library at the Buffalo Bill Historical Center in Cody, Wyoming, will be listed "Buffalo Bill Historical Center."

General Works

Boyer, David S. "Wyoming: High, Wide, and Windy," *National Geographic Magazine*, Vol. 129, No. 4, April 1966.

Bragg, Bill. *Wyoming's Wealth: A History Of Wyoming*. Basin, Wyoming: Big Horn Book Co., 1976.

Dunham, Dick and Vivian. *Flaming Gorge Country*. Denver: Eastwood Printing and Publishing, 1977.

Fanzwa, Gregory M. *The Oregon Trail Revisited*. New York: Patrice Press, 1972.

Hebard, Dr. Grace Raymond. Material appearing in many collections including letters, manuscripts, and notes. University of Wyoming.

Hendrickson, Gordon O., and Arnold L. Willems. *Living Wyoming's Past*. Boulder: Pruett Publishing Co., 1983.

Homsher, Lola. *Guide To Wyoming Newspapers*, 1867-1967. Cheyenne: Wyoming State Library, 1971.

Howard, Robert West. *This Is The West*. New York: Rand McNally & Co., 1957

Larson, T.A. *History Of Wyoming*. Lincoln: University of Nebraska Press, 1965.

A Look At Wyoming Government, Published by the League of Women Voters of Wyoming, 1979.

Linford, Velma. *Wyoming, Frontier State*. Denver: Old West Publishing Co., 1947.

Roberts, Phil. *Inventory Of The Oral History Collection*. Wyoming State Archives, Cheyenne, 1980.

Stone, Irving. *Men To Match My Mountains: The Opening Of The Far West*, 1840-1890. Garden City, N.Y.: Doubleday, 1956.

Story Of The Great American West. Pleasantville, N.Y.: The Reader's Digest Association, Inc., 1977.

Thompson, Thyra. *1980 Wyoming Official Directory*. Published by the Secretary of State, Cheyenne, Wyoming.

Trenholm, Virginia Cole. *Wyoming Blue Book*, Volumes 1 & 2. Cheyenne: Wyoming State Archives and Historical Research Department, 1974.

Trenholm, Virginia Cole, and Maurine Carley. *Wyoming Pageant*. Casper, Wyoming: Prairie Publishing Co., 1946.

Wallace, Eunice Ewer. *They Made Wyoming Their Own*. Published by the author, 1971.

Wheeler, Eva Floy. *A History Of Wyoming Writers*. Published by the author, 1981.

Whittenburg, Clarice. *Wyoming, Prelude To Statehood*. Cheyenne: Wyoming Travel Commission and State Department of Education.

Wilson, D. Ray. *Wyoming Historical Tour Guide*. Carpentersville, Illinois: Crossroads Communications, 1984.

Wyoming Data Handbook, 6th Edition, 1983. Cheyenne: Department of Administration and Fiscal Control, Division of Research and Statistics.

Wyoming Historical Institute. *The Historical Encyclopedia Of Wyoming*, Volumes 1 & 2. Dallas: Taylor Publishing Co., 1970.

Wyoming: A Guide To Historic Sites. Edited by Wyoming Recreation Commission. Casper: Big Horn Book Co., 1966.

Chapter One

Gallagher, John S., and Alan H. Patera. *Wyoming Post Offices*, 1850-1980. Burtonsville, Md.: The Depot, 1980.

Lerner, William. *Pocket Data Book, USA 1971*. Washington, D.C.: U.S. Department of Commerce, U.S. Government Printing Office, 1971.

Mattison, Ray H. *History Of Devil's Tower*. Pamphlet published by Devil's Tower Natural History Museum, March, 1973.

Paterson, J.H. *North America: Geography Of The United States And Canada*. New York: Oxford University Press, 1965.

Richardson, James. *Yellowstone National Park*. New York: Scribner, Armstrong, 1873.

Thompson, Thyra. *Wyoming Official Directory*, 1984. Published by Secretary of State, Capitol Building, Cheyenne, 1984.

Webb, Harold V. *Wise Use Of Wyoming Resources*. Cheyenne: Wyoming Soil Conservation Committee, 1957.

Wyoming: A Guide To Its History, Highways, And People. Works Projects Administration. New York: Oxford University Press, 1941.

Wyoming: Named Localities, Railroad Sidings, Discontinued Post Offices. Cheyenne: Wyoming State Archives, 1962.

Wyoming Geographic News, Vol. 1 & 2. Reston, Virginia: U.S.G.S. Topographic Division National Center, 1980.

Chapter Two

American Indians And Christian Missions. Chicago: University of Chicago Press, 1981.

Barnes, Hazel F., "The Medicine Wheel." Unpublished manuscript, Sheridan, 1927. Wyoming State Archives.

Bloom, Jo Tice. "Cumberland Gap vs. South Pass—The East or West in Frontier History," *Western Historical Quarterly*, Vol. III, No. 2, April, 1972.

Chapin, L.A. Article in *Denver Post*. November 24, 1932.

The Cheyenne: Profile In Primitive Culture. New York: Harper Brothers, 1958.

Eddy, John A. "Probing the Mystery of the Medicine Wheels," *National Geographic Magazine*, January 1977.

Edgar, Bob, and Jack Turney, *Brand Of A Legend*. Cody, Wyoming: Stockade Publishing, 1978.

Frison, George C. *Prehistoric Hunters Of The High Plains*. New York: New York Academic Press, 1978.

Grinnell, George Bird. *The Cheyenne Indians*. New Haven: Yale University Press, 1923.

Irwin, Cynthia and Henry. "Wyoming Muck Tells of Battle: Ice Age Man vs. Mammoth," *National Geographic Magazine*, June, 1962.

Lowie, Robert H. "Social Patterns of Shoshone," *Anthropological Papers Of The American Museum Of Natural History*, Vol. II, Part II. New York, 1909.

McPherson, Ida. "A Prehistoric Relic." Unpublished manuscript, WPA 1466. Wyoming State Archives.

Moss, John H. *Early Man In The Eden Valley*. Philadelphia: University of Pennsylvania Press, 1951.

"Prehistoric Pygmies," Unpublished manuscript, WPA 226. Wyoming State Archives.

Robbins, Cora. "Explorations of the Spanish." Papers relating to the history of Wyoming, WPA 7.787. Wyoming State Archives.

Smith, Marian, Editor. "The Cheyenne in Plains Indian Trade Relations, 1795-1840." *Monographs Of The American Ethnological Society, No. XIX*. New York: J.J. Augustin.

Van Derveer, Nellie H. "Prehistoric Rock Circles." Unpublished manuscript, WPA 1321. Wyoming State Archives.

Wedel, Waldo Rudolph. *Prehistoric Man On The Great Plains*. Norman: University of Oklahoma Press, 1961.

Chapter Three

Bakeless, John. *The Journals Of Lewis And Clark*. New York: New American Library of World Literature, 1964.

Billington, Ray Allen. *The Far Western Frontier 1830-1860*. New York: Harper & Row, 1956.

Bradbury, John. *Bradbury's Travels In The Interior Of America*, 1809-1811. Including an interview with John Colter. Cleveland: A.H. Clark Co., 1904.

Chittenden, Hiram M. *The American Fur Trade Of The Far West*. New York: Kelly Publishing Co., 1935.

Dick, Everett. *Vanguards Of The Frontier*. Lincoln: University of Nebraska Press, 1967.

Dominick, Dr. DeWitt. "The Colter Pageant." Manuscript of address presented at Cody, Wyoming, September 28, 1958. Wyoming State Archives.

Fetter, Richard. *Mountain Men Of Wyoming*. Boulder: Johnson Books, 1982.

Ghent, William J. "John Colter." Unpublished manuscript, July 1, 1933. Wyoming State Archives.

Gilbert, Bill. *The Trailblazers*. New York: Time-Life Books, 1973.

Goodnough, Thomas. "John Colter First Entered Yellowstone National Park," *Riverton Rocket*, March 30, 1935.

Gowans, Fred R. *Rocky Mountain Rendezvous: A History Of The Fur Trade Rendez-*

vous, 1825-1840. Salt Lake City: Brigham Young University Press, 1976.

Hafen, Leroy, R., and W.J. Ghent, *Brokenhand: The Life Story of Thomas Fitzpatrick, Chief of the Mountain Men.* Denver: Old West, 1931.

Hafen, Leroy R. *Mountain Men and the Fur Trade.* Glendale: Arthur H. Clark Co., 1971.

Heib, David L. *Ft. Laramie National Monument, Wyoming.* Washington, D.C.: National Park Service Historic Handbook Series No. 20, 1954.

Irving, Washington. *Astoria.* Philadelphia: Carey, Lee, and Blanchard, 1836.

LaVerendrye, Francois de. *Journal,* 1738-1739. Translated by Douglas Brymner for the *Report On Canadian Archives,* Ottawa, 1889.

Morgan, Dale L. *Jedediah Smith and the Opening of the West.* Lincoln: University of Nebraska Press, 1964.

Preuss, Charles. *Exploring With Fremont.* Norman: University of Oklahoma Press, 1959.

Ruxton, George F. *Life In The Far West.* Norman: University of Oklahoma Press, 1959.

Stagner, Howard R. "The Colter Stone." Unpublished manuscript. Wyoming State Archives.

Sunder, John E. *Bill Sublette, Mountain Man.* Norman: University of Oklahoma Press, 1959.

Thompson, Edith M. "Colter Ran Naked for His Life," *Casper Star-Tribune,* March 30, 1975.

Victor, Frank F. *The River Of The West.* Hartford: Hartford Publishing Co, 1970.

Waldo, Anna Lee. *Sacajawea.* New York: Avon Books, 1978.

Warner, Robert C. *The Fort Laramie of Alfred Jacob Miller.* Laramie: University of Wyoming Press, 1979.

Chapter Four

Arrington, Leonard J. *Great Basin Kingdom, 1830-1890.* Lincoln: University of Nebraska Press, 1966.

Bishop, L.C. Speech at annual meeting of Wyoming Pioneer Association, September 4, 1959. Manuscript at Wyoming State Archives.

Burton, Henry. Diary. Wyoming State Archives.

_____. "Oregon Trail Immigrant, 1864." Manuscript at Wyoming State Archives.

Carter, Kate. *Riders Of The Pony Express.* Salt Lake City: Daughters of the Utah Pioneers, 1947.

_____. *Utah And The Pony Express.* Salt Lake City: Utah Pony Express Centennial Commission, 1960.

Dinwiddie, David. "Overland from Indiana to Oregon," *The Frontier: A Magazine of the Northwest, Vol. VIII,* No. 2. State University of Montana, Missoula, 1928.

Drury, Clifford. *Marcus Whitman.* Boise, Idaho: Caxton Printers, Ltd., 1937.

Farnham, Thomas J. *Travels in the Great American Prairies, an 1839 Wagon Train Journal.* New York: Greeley and McElrath Tribune Building, 1843.

Fremont, John C. *Narrative of the Exploring Expedition to the Rocky Mountains in the Year 1842.* New York: D. Appleton and Company, 1846.

Holliday, J.S. *The World Rushed In.* New York: Simon & Schuster, 1981.

Horn, Huston. *The Pioneers.* New York: Time-Life Books, 1974.

Kelly, Ed. "The Oregon Trail," *Guernsey Gazette,* July 2, 1937.

Mullan, Capt. John. *Miners and Travelers Guide to Oregon.* New York: Wm. M. Franklin, Publisher, 1865.

Munkres, Robert L. *Saleratus and Sagebrush.* Cheyenne: Historical Research and Publications Division of the Wyoming State Archives and the Wyoming State Historical Society Publications Fund, 1974.

Nixon, Oliver. *How Marcus Whitman Saved Oregon.* Chicago; Star Publishing, 1895.

The Old Oregon Train Centennial Series, press releases from Portland, Oregon, 1923. Wyoming State Archives.

Ollis, Lester. Interview with Mrs. Lutie Van Dyke. Wyoming State Archives.

Parkman, Francis. *The Oregon Trail.* New York: New American Library of World Literature, 1950.

Phillips, Paul C. *Overland From Indiana to Oregon.* State University of Montana, Missoula, 1929.

Reinfeld, Fred. *Pony Express.* Lincoln: University of Nebraska Press, 1966.

Rhett, James. Letter to Brigham Young concerning Chief Washakie and Indian Farm Negotiations, 1854-1857. Wyoming State Archives.

Smith, Jackson, Sublette. Letter to Secretary of War, October, 1829. Published with a message from Andrew Jackson, January 25, 1831. Congressional Documents, 29th Congress, 1st Session, Rt. No. 773, Serial No. 491, page 41.

Spaulding, Kenneth A. *On the Oregon Trail—Robert Stuart's Journey of Discovery*. Norman: University of Oklahoma Press, 1953.

Steele, John. *Across the Plains in 1850*. Chicago: Caxton Club, 1930.

Trails West. Prepared by Special Publications Division. Washington, D.C.: National Geographic Society, 1979.

Unruh, John D., Jr. *The Plains Across*. Urbana, Illinois; University of Illinois Press, 1979.

"Wagon Train Burned Near Warm Springs During Trail Days," *Guernsey Gazette*, July 2, 1937.

Ware, Joseph. *The Emigrant Guide to California*. Union Office, 1849. Princeton: Princeton University Press, reprinted 1932.

Wyoming State Tribune, July 26, 1936.

Chapter Five

Bragg, William F. "Wagon Box Fight, August 2, 1867." Unpublished manuscript #185-B. Wyoming State Archives.

Bourke, Capt. John C. "MacKenzie's Last Fight with the Cheyenne," *U.S. Army Recruiting News*, 1929.

Brown, Dee. *Bury My Heart At Wounded Knee*. New York: Holt, Rinehart, Winston, 1971.

———. *Fort Phil Kearny*. Lincoln: University of Nebraska Press, 1971.

Bueker, Thomas R. "Letters from a Post Surgeon's Wife," *Annals Of Wyoming*, Published by Wyoming State Archives, 1981.

Capps, Benjamin. *The Great Chiefs*. Alexandria: Time-Life Books, 1975.

———. *The Indians*. Alexandria: Time-Life Books, 1973.

Carrington, Henry B. *Absaroka: The Land of Massacre*. New York: J.B. Lippincott & Co., 1868.

———. Official Report of the Phil Kearny Massacre to Assistant Adjutant General, Department of the Platte, Omaha, Nebraska Territory, January 3, 1867. Wyoming State Archives.

"Chronological List of Battles and Skirmishes" (between the military and different tribes of Indians in Wyoming), *Annals Of Wyoming*, July, 1942.

Cook, James H. *Fifty Years on the Old Frontier*. New Haven: Yale University Press, 1923.

Carley, Maxine, and Virginia C. Trenholm, *The Shoshones: Sentinels of the Rockies*. Norman: University of Oklahoma Press, 1964.

"Custer Battlefield National Monument." Pamphlet prepared by the U.S. Department of the Interior. Washington, D.C.: U.S. Government Printing Office, 1961.

Del Monte, H.D. "Washakie: Life of Chief Washakie and the Shoshone Indians." Manuscript written in Lander, 1947. Wyoming State Archives.

Flannery, L.G. (Pat). *John Hunton's Diary, 1876-1877*. Lingle: Guide-Review, 1958.

Gibson, Samuel. Letter to the Editor of the *Buffalo Bulletin*, February 27, 1917.

Guthrie, John. Eyewitness Account of the Fetterman Incident. Unpublished manuscript. Wyoming State Archives.

Heitman, Francis B. "Chronological Listing of Battles, Actions, etc. in which Troops of the Regular Army have participated and Troops engaged in what is now Wyoming," *Historical Register and Dictionary of the United States Army*, Vol. 2. Urbana, Illinois: University of Illinois Press, 1965.

Hill, Burton. "Great Indian Treaty Council of 1851," *Nebraska History*, March, 1966.

Hollingsworth, J.C. Letter concerning the Fetterman Incident. Wyoming State Archives.

Hunton, John. "The Grattan Massacre." Unpublished manuscript. Wyoming State Archives.

Jameson, Jesse. "Military Garrisons in Wyoming," *Casper Tribune*, February 19, 1961.

Lowe, Percival. *Five Years A Dragoon*. Norman: University of Oklahoma Press, 1965.

Luce, Edward S. and Evelyn S. *Custer Battlefield National Monument*. Washington, D.C.: National Park Service Historical Handbook Series No. 1, 1949.

McDermott, Jack. "Indians, Treaties, and Wars," *Torrington Telegram*, August 8, 1966.

Madsen, Brigham. *The Northern Shoshone*. Caldwell, Idaho: Caxton Printers, Ltd., 1980.

Meriwether, David. *My Life in the Mountains and on the Plains*. Norman: University of Oklahoma Press, 1965.

Moore, J.K. Letter to A. Coutant concerning the Fetterman Incident. Wyoming State Archives.

Murphy, William. Letter to A. Coutant concerning the Wagon Box Fight, November 1, 1916. Wyoming State Archives.

———. Letter to W.M. Camp concerning the Wagon Box Fight, April 3, 1917. Wyoming State Archives.

Nadeau, Remi. *Ft. Laramie and the Sioux Indians*. Englewood Cliffs, N.J.: Prentice Hall, Inc., 1967.

Neihardt, John G. (Flaming Rainbow). *Black Elk Speaks*. Lincoln: University of Nebraska Press, 1961.

Nevin, David. *The Soldiers*. Alexandria, Virginia: Time-Life Books, 1974.

Pope, Ernest. Letter to A. Coutant concerning the Fetterman Incident. Wyoming State Archives.

Powell, Capt. Letter to Adjutant General, Ft. Phil Kearny, August 4, 1867, concerning the Fetterman Incident. Wyoming State Archives.

Report of Assistant Surgeon, H.S. Schell, concerning Ft. Laramie, 1869. Wyoming State Archives.

Records of Bureau of Indian Affairs, Administration of Indian Affairs at the Upper Platte Indian Agency, 1846-1870. Washington, D.C.: National Archives General Services Administration.

Report concerning the Grattan Massacre. United States Senate Executive Document #91, 1855-1856.

Report to Secretary of War Jefferson Davis concerning the Massacre of Brevet Second Lieutenant John L. Grattan, Senate Executive Document #91, 1st session, 34th Congress, 1855-1856.

Report on the MacKenzie Fight, Senate Document #306, 72nd Congress.

Rickey, Don Jr. *Forty Miles a Day on Beans and Hay*. Norman: University of Oklahoma Press, 1963.

Robbins, Jim. "A New Look at Custer's Last Stand," *American West*, Vol. 22, No. 4, July-August, 1985.

Smith, B.F. (27th Infantry). Report to Adjutant General, Ft. Phil Kearny, August 3, 1867, concerning the Fetterman Incident. Wyoming State Archives.

Smith, Harry. "History of Company C," *Buffalo Bulletin*, March 4, 1937.

Thompson, John C. "In Old Wyoming," *Wyoming State Tribune*, May 22, 1945.

In addition, information was found in numerous articles in the following newspapers:
Bismark Tribune (Extra), July 6, 1876.
Bismark Tribune
Buffalo Bulletin
Casper Tribune-Herald
Cheyenne Leader (1868-1876)
Daily Sentinel Tribune
Denver Post Empire Magazine
Missouri Republican
Montana Post
Riverton Chronicle
San Francisco Chronicle
Sheridan Press
Thermopolis Independent Record
Torrington Telegram
Wyoming State Tribune

Chapter Six

Athearn, Robert G. *Union Pacific Country*. Chicago: Rand McNally & Co., 1971.

Basinger, W.S. Letter to Mrs. Frank D. Casselman, August 31, 1933. Wyoming State Archives.

"Brief History of the Union Pacific," pamphlet published by Department of Public Relations, Union Pacific Railroad. Wyoming State Archives.

Cheyenne: The Magic City of the Plains. Cheyenne: Centennial Historical Committee, 1967.

Davis, John P. *The Union Pacific Railway*. Chicago: S.C. Griggs & Co., 1894.

Dial, Scott. *A Place to Raise Hell: Cheyenne Saloons*. Boulder: Johnson Books, 1977.

Dodge, Grenville. "How We Built the U.P. Railroad." Washington, D.C.: United States Government Printing Office, 1910.

Geddes, Lambertson and Vivian. "100 Years in the Wild West," *Rawlins Daily Times*, August 1, 1868.

Harlow, Alvin. "He Built the Union Pacific," *Trains*, June 1948.

Ridencur, Shelly. "Tales of the Platte Valley Pioneers," *Rawlins Daily Times*, August 7, 1982.

Sherman, W.T. Letter to Grenville Dodge, January 16, 1867, concerning construction of the Union Pacific Railroad. Wyoming State Archives.

Wheeler, Keith. *The Railroaders*. New York: Time-Life Books, 1973.

"Wyoming and the Union Pacific Celebrate Centennial, 1868-1968." Pamphlet published by the Union Pacific. Wyoming State Archives.

In addition, material found in these periodicals was very helpful:
Carbon County Journal (particularly August 3, 1917)
Laramie Boomerang (July 3, 1928)
Leslie's Weekly (1877)
Rock Springs Rocket
The Wyoming Eagle

Chapter Seven

Allard, William Albert. "Cowpunching on the Padlock Ranch," *National Geographic Magazine*, Vol. 144, No. 4, October 1973.

Arland, Victor. Letters to M. Camille Dadant, 1884-1888. Arland Collection, Harold McCracken Library, Buffalo Bill Historical Center, Cody, Wyoming.

———. Letter to Mr. Henning, Jan. 30, 1917. Arland Collection, Buffalo Bill Historical Center.

"Attempt to Repeal Suffrage in Wyoming." Unpublished manuscript, Wyoming State Archives.

Avery, Rachael Foster. "Some Results of Women Suffrage in Wyoming," *Political Equality Series*, Vol. 1, No. 4. Philadelphia: Published by the National American Women Suffrage Association, 1896.

Baker, N.A. "Female Suffrage Bill," *Cheyenne Daily Leader*, December 11, 1869.

———. "Women's Rights," *Cheyenne Daily Leader*, November 10, 1869.

Ballard, J.J. "On the Trail Through Wyoming," Unpublished manuscript. Wyoming State Archives.

Bryan, L.J. Letter to Secretary of the Wyoming Stockgrowers Association, January 1, 1892, concerning rustling. University of Wyoming.

Burger, Nellie W. "Remembering the Hard and Happy Days of Homesteading," *Buffalo Bulletin*, August 16, 1979.

Canton, Frank. *Frontier Trails*. Cambridge, Mass.: The Riverside Press, 1966.

Canton, Frank M. Papers, 1919-1928. Stevens Collection, University of Wyoming.

Collins, Dabney Otis. "Skin Game in Old Wyoming." *Denver Post*, November 17, 1974.

Cunningham, Eugene. *Triggernometry*. Caldwell, Idaho: Caxton Printers, Ltd., 1971.

Denny, Hazel. *Veteran, District 13: Homesteading In Goshen Hole*. Philadelphia: Dorrance & Co., 1976.

Engebretson, Doug. *Empty Saddles, Forgotten Names: Outlaws of the Black Hills and Wyoming*. Aberdeen, South Dakota: North Plains Press, 1982.

"First Women's Jury Drew World Attention," *Casper Star Tribune*, March 30, 1975.

Forbis, William H. *The Cowboys*. New York: Time-Life Books, 1973.

Gallatin, W.E. Letter to Alice Smith, Secretary of the Wyoming Stock Growers Association, July 2, 1900, concerning rustling. University of Wyoming.

Graham, Kevin. "Bill Carlisle: A Memorable Outlaw," *Rawlins Daily Times*, August 7, 1982.

———. "Penitentiary Part of Local Lore," *Rawlins Daily Times*, August 7, 1982.

Gundrson, Mary Alice. "Big House Across the River," *In Wyoming*, Dec.-Jan., 1977.

Guthrie, W.E. "Wyoming's Golden Age." Unpublished manuscript (MSS111A). Wyoming State Archives.

Hendricks, George D. *The Bad Men of the West*. San Antonio: Naylor Company, 1959.

Hill, Burton S. "Frank Canton—The Sheriff," Unpublished manuscript, (Coll. no. 1602). University of Wyoming.

Hill, Charles S. "20,000,000 Acres Free Government Land in Wyoming," Pamphlet published by Wyoming State Board of Immigration, Cheyenne, 1920.

Hosokawa, Bill. "Homesteading," *Denver Post*, June 2, 1954.

Kelly, Charles. *The Outlaw Trail*. New York: Devin-Adair Co., 1959.

"Lawmakers and Lawbreakers." Unpublished manuscript, Wyoming State Archives.

Lee, Edward M. "The Woman Movement in Wyoming," *The Galaxy*, Vol. XIII, January-June 1872.

McAuley, Phil. "The Day Big Nose Really Blew It," *Casper Star Tribune*, April 1, 1981.

Horan, James D. *Desperate Men*. New York: G.P. Putnam's Sons, 1885.

Jones, Ralph F. *Longhorns North of the Arkansas*. San Antonio, Texas: Naylor Co., 1969.

Kendrick, John B. "The Texas Trail," *Wyoming Tribune*, September 16, 1916.

Laberteaux, F.H. Letter to H.B. Ijams, May 21, 1895, concerning rustlers. University of Wyoming.

Legislative Record: Council Bill No. 70, 1869, An Act to Grant to the Women of Wyoming Territory the Right of Suffrage. Wyoming State Archives.

Laws of Wyoming, 1869. Chaper 31, Sections 1 and 2. Published by the Wyoming Legislature, Cheyenne, 1869.

Nelson, Mildred E. *Subject Index of the Cheyenne Leader*, 1867-1890. Cheyenne: Wyoming State Archives, 1947.

Nevin, David. *The Expressmen*. New York: Time-Life Books, 1974.

Nickerson, H.G. "Gives Esther Morris Credit for Suffrage," *Wyoming State Tribune*, February 27, 1919.

Nye, Bill. "The Annual Wail," *Laramie Times*, Oct. 7, 1879.

Parker, Glenn. "The Swan Land and Cattle Co., Ltd." Unpublished manuscript, University of Wyoming.

"Party Platform," *Cheyenne Daily Leader*, September 3, 1870.

Patterson, Richard. *Historical Atlas of the Outlaw West*. Boulder: Johnson Books, 1984.

Pence, Mary Lou. *Boswell: The Story of a Frontier Lawman*. Published by the author, 1978.

"Pioneer of Women's Suffrage in Wyoming," *Chicago Tribune*, June 17, 1895.

Place, Marion T. *American Cattle Trails, East and West*. New York: Holt, Rhinehart & Winston, 1967.

Redford, Robert. "Riding the Outlaw Trail," *National Geographic Magazine*, November, 1976.

Reiter, Joan Swallow. *The Women*. Alexandria, Virginia: Time-Life Books, 1978.

Richards, Bartlett. Letter to H.B. Ijams, Secretary of the Wyoming Stock Growers Association, concerning rustling, July 13, 1894. University of Wyoming.

Rollinson, John K. *Wyoming Cattle Trails*. Caldwell, Idaho: Caxton Printers, Ltd., 1948.

Sandoz, Mari. *The Buffalo Hunters*. Lincoln: University of Nebraska Press, 1978.

————. *Old Jules*. Lincoln: University of Nebraska Press, 1935.

Scharff, Virginia. "The Case for Domestic Feminism," *Annals of Wyoming*, Vol. 56, No. 2, Fall, 1984.

Sheeks, Ben. Letter to Dr. Grace R. Heberd regarding events concerning passage of the Women's Suffrage Bill. Wyoming State Archives.

Stewart, Elinore Pruitt. *Letters of a Woman Homesteader*, Lincoln: University of Nebraska Press, 1979.

Tanner, Ogden. *The Ranchers*. Alexandria, Virginia: Time-Life Books, 1977.

Thompson, John C. "In Old Wyoming—Vigilantes," *Wyoming State Tribune*, February 12, 1940.

Wister, Owen. *The Virginian*. New York: The Macmillan Co., 1911.

"Wyoming in Pictures and Prose," pamphlet published by the Department of Immigration, Cheyenne, 1908.

"Wyoming: Its Resources and Attractions," pamphlet published by the Union Pacific Railroad, 1903.

Wyoming Stock Growers Association Collection. University of Wyoming.

"Women—Their Role in Winning the West," *The Laramie Sunday Boomerang*, May 31, 1970.

Other useful information came from the *Billings Gazette*, along with the *Cheyenne Daily Leader* and the *Wyoming Eagle*.

Chapter Eight

Bartlett, J.S. *History of Wyoming*. Chicago: S.T. Clarke Publishing Company, 1918.

Barton, Wayne. "The Great Diamond Hoax," *In Wyoming*, December-January, 1977.

"Big Nose George," *Cheyenne Daily Leader*, March 23, 1881.

Carey, Joseph M. Telegram to Governor John Meldrum proclaiming Statehood, July 10, 1890. Wyoming State Archives.

Carter, William. *Ghost Towns of the West*. Menlo Park, California: Lane Magazine and Book Co., 1971.

Chisum, Emmett D. "Crossing Wyoming by Car in 1908: The New York to Paris Automobile Race," *Annals of Wyoming*, Vol. 52, No. 1, Spring, 1980.

"Coal Towns Near the Tracks Kept Steam Train Running," *Casper Star Tribune*, March 23, 1980.

Cody, William F. Letter to Rev. Joseph W. Cooke, May 23, 1896. Buffalo Bill Historical Center.

————. Letter to Frank?, December 21, 1895 concerning his opinion of Basin County. Buffalo Bill Historical Center.

————. Letter to Hinkle?, May 28, 1902, concerning building an irrigation dam and canal. Buffalo Bill Historical Center.

Conrow, Robert. *The Great Diamond Hoax*. Boulder: Johnson Books, 1980.

Dillinger, Earl. "The Way It Was," Unpublished manuscript, 1925, Wyoming State Archives.

Emmons, W.H. "Tom Horn," *The Post Bureau*, Cheyenne, Wyoming, October 14, 1903.

Ervay, J.E. Letter to Alice Smith requesting Tom Horn's services, December 2, 1901. University of Wyoming.

Fadner, Ada M. "History of Mining in the Snowy Range," Unpublished manuscript, 1941. Wyoming State Archives.

Fisher, Vardis, and Opal Laurel Holmes. *Gold Rushes and Mining Camps of the Early American West*. Caldwell, Idaho: Caxton Printers, Ltd., 1968.

"Francis E. Warren and the Johnson County War," *Leslie's Weekly*, November 24, 1892.

Gage, Jack. *The Johnson County War*. Casper: Prairie Publishing, 1959.

————. *Ten Sleep and No Rest.* Casper: Prairie Publishing, 1959.

Gould, Lewis L. "Willis VanDevanter and the Johnson County War," *Montana: The Magazine of Western History,* Vol. XVII, No. 4, October, 1967.

Grant, H. Roger. "Wyoming's Electric Railway Project," *Annals of Wyoming,* Vol. 52, No. 1, Spring 1980.

Hague, Harlan. "Eden Ravished," *The American West,* May-June, 1977.

Harpending, Asbury. *The Great Diamond Hoax.* Norman: University of Oklahoma Press, 1958.

Hedgepeth, Don. "Wyoming Cow Country," *Spurs Were A-Jingling,* Northland: Northland Publishing Co., 1975.

Heisler, John T. Letter to Wyoming Stockgrowers' Association, June 8, 1894. University of Wyoming.

Homsher, Lola M. *South Pass, 1868: Journal of the Wyoming Gold Rush.* Lincoln: University of Nebraska Press, 1960.

Hunt, Lester C. "Legislative History of Women's Suffrage in Wyoming," Unpublished manuscript. Wyoming State Archives.

Jackson, Clarence S. *Picture Maker of the Old West: William H. Jackson.* New York: Charles Scribner's Sons, 1947.

Kongslie, Olaf. Unpublished manuscript concerning plays and entertainments in early Wyoming, WPA Subject 1356. Wyoming State Archives.

Longer, William F. Coroner's Inquisition Report on the Death of Dud Champion, May 24, 1893. University of Wyoming.

Mall, Alice J. "Buffalo Bill and the Enduring West," *National Geographic Magazine,* July, 1981.

Mercer, A.S. *The Banditti of the Plains.* Norman: University of Oklahoma Press, 1963.

Mokler, Alfred Jarvis. *History of Natrona County, 1888-1922.* Chicago: The Lakeside Press, 1923.

Phillips, David R. *The Taming of the West.* Chicago: Henry Regnery Co., 1974.

Rapp, Charles. Notes, letters, and diary, 1875-1878. Buffalo Bill Historical Center.

Richards, Jarvis. Letter to H.B. Ijams, Secretary of the Wyoming Stockgrowers' Association, May 2, 1894, concerning alleged rustling activity. University of Wyoming.

Smith, Helena Huntington. "The Gentlemen Battled the Cowboys," *Long Island Press,* May 23, 1965.

————. *War On The Powder River,* New York: McGraw-Hill, 1966.

Stuart, Berkeley. "Life in Cambria," Unpublished manuscript, 1979. Wyoming State Archives.

Thomas, Chauncey. "Buffalo Bill's Last Interview," *Outdoor Life,* Vol. XXXIX, No. 5, May, 1917.

Thompson, John Charles. Address before the Westerners, Denver, 1945, concerning Tom Horn. Wyoming State Archives.

Thorpe, Russell. Interview with Mike Shonsey, included in the Agnes Wright Spring Collection, Wyoming State Archives.

Trachsel, Herman H. and Ralph M. Wade. *The Government and Administration of Wyoming.* New York: Thomas Y. Crowell Co., 1962.

Wallace, Robert. *The Miners.* Alexandria, Virginia: Time-Life Books, 1976.

"The War Ended," *Cheyenne Daily Leader,* April 14, 1922.

Wentworth, Edward N. Letter to Agnes Wright Spring, March 26, 1948, concerning the Johnson County War. Agnes Wright Spring Collection, Wyoming State Archives.

Wyoming. WPA Writer's Project. New York: Oxford Press, 1941.

Yost, Nellie Snyder. *Buffalo Bill.* Chicago: The Swallow Press, 1979.

In addition, material from the following periodicals was very helpful:
Annals of Wyoming, April, 1968.
Daily Sun-Leader, December 22, 1899.
Laramie Boomerang, June 2, 1904.
Newcastle Newsletter, August 17, 1939.
Rawlins Republican, December 10, 1929.

Chapter Nine

Biographies of Uinta County Servicemen, Published by Uinta County Memorial Association, 1920. Wyoming State Archives.

Canary, Frank. Collection (H 79-41) including World War I papers. Wyoming State Archives.

Daughters of the American Revolution War Service Records, World War I. Published by Daughters of the American Revolution, 1919. Wyoming State Archives.

Dyment, C.V. *Interesting Historical Review of Ninety-First Division.* Published by Robert Boyd Stewart, Post 11, American Legion, Lovell, Wyoming.

Echternach, A.V. "War" Editorial in *Cheyenne State Leader,* April 7, 1917.

Elkar, Edith Francis. Collection including diary, letters, and expense records. Wyoming State Archives (B-817).

Guy, Eva Goldsmith. Collection including letters and papers, Wyoming State Archives (C-1454).

Henderson, Vivian. Collection of Historical Records of World War Soldiers. Wyoming State Archives.

"How Wyoming Women Helped Win the War as told by Mrs. Gray," *Wyoming State Tribune*, December 28, 1918.

Jones, Dewey. Collection (MSS-938) including letters and papers. Wyoming State Archives.

Letters from the Front. Collection, WPA-684. Wyoming State Archives.

March, Francis A. *History of the World War*. Chicago: The United Publishers of the U.S. and Canada, 1918.

"Men from Wyoming in World War I," *Laramie Boomerang*, July 11, 1976.

Mentzer, R.S. Collection (H-62-10), including letters and papers. Wyoming State Archives.

Mereness, Newton D. *American Historical Activities During the World War*. Annual Report of the American Historical Association for 1919, Vol. I, page 137-294. Washington D.C.: U.S. Government Printing Office, 1928.

Newspaper Clippings, Collection H60-98. Wyoming State Archives.

Newspaper Clippings and War Series Printed Material, Collection H60-111. Wyoming State Archives.

Plattner, Carl. "World War I—Red Cross," Unpublished manuscript, WPA subject 1270, Wyoming State Archives.

Olsen, Theodore, "Editorial" *The Wyoming Student*, November 1918, University of Wyoming, Wyoming State Archives.

"1,000 Lives Lost When Ship Goes Down" *Cheyenne State Leader*, May 8, 1915.

Parks, Ray. "The War to End All Wars: A Veteran of the Great War Remembers," *Wyoming Horizon, Casper Star-Tribune*, December, 1984.

Spring, Agnes Wright. "Interesting Statistics on Defense Activities in Wyoming in World War I," *Annals Of Wyoming*, March, 1918.

War Service, University Of Wyoming, 1917-1918. University of Wyoming Bulletin, Laramie, 1918.

Wyoming Men in War; World War I Service Records and Induction Lists, 1914-1919. Wyoming State Archives.

World War I Collection H71-11. Wyoming State Archives.

World War I, pamphlet published by the American Legion, 1926. Wyoming State Archives.

Also helpful were numerous articles in the *Cheyenne State Leader* from 1917 to 1918.

Chapter Ten

Adams, Gerald M. "The Air Age Comes to Wyoming," *Annals of Wyoming*, Vol. 52, No. 2, Fall, 1980.

Bille, Ed. "Bustling Days of Salt Creek and Teapot Dome Oil Fields," *Sunday Eagle Tribune*, July 23, 1978.

"Blackwater Creek Fire in Shoshone National Forest Kills 14," *Cody Enterprise*, August 24, 1937.

"Carrie Nation Starts Sensational Campaign," *Cheyenne Daily Leader*, June 17, 1908.

Casper Star Tribune, issues from January 1, 1932 to December 31, 1932.

Civilian Conservation Corps, Lake Guernsey Park, Camp Br9, 1934-1937. Microfilm collection H-254. Wyoming State Archives.

Clary, David A. *The Place Where Hell Bubbled Up*. Washington, D.C.: National Park Service, 1972.

Coffman, J. Collection including scrapbooks and record of CCC Camp Br9. Wyoming State Archives.

Craighead, Karen and Derek, William S. Ellis, and George B. Hartzog. "Yellowstone's Hundreth Birthday: A Four-Part Report," *National Geographic Magazine*, May 1972.

"The Day the Marines Landed In Wyoming," *In Wyoming*, June-July, 1978.

"Era of Jobless Transients Recalled," *Laramie Boomerang*, November 29, 1981.

Fenwick, Red. "They Took to the Woods and Came Out Men," *Denver Post Empire*, June 20, 1965.

Giddens, Paul H. "The Naval Oil Reserve: Teapot Dome and the Continental Company," *Annals Of Wyoming*, Spring, 1981.

Hendrickson, Gordon Olaf. *People of the High Plains: Wyoming's European Heritage*. Cheyenne: Wyoming State Archives, 1977.

———. *Wyoming Works Projects Administration Directory, Federal Writer's Project Collection Inventory*. Cheyenne: Wyoming State Archives, 1977.

Hill, James. "My CCC History, Memory Book, 1937." (H69-37) Wyoming State Archives.

Howard, Helen A. *War Chief Joseph*. Caldwell, Idaho: Caxton Printers, Ltd., 1952.

Jost, Loren. "Some Riverton People Couldn't Stomach Prohibition," *The Riverton Ranger*, March 29, 1984.

Donahue, Jim. "Drainage Districts and the Great Depression," *Annals Of Wyoming*, Vol. 53, No. 2, Fall, 1982.

"Hoover and Congress Debate Food Relief, 1930-31," *Red River Valley Historical Review*, Vol. VII, No. 4, Fall, 1982.

Jones, Walter R. *History of the Sand Bar*. Casper, Wyoming: BASo, Inc., 1981.

"Kemmerer Was Known for Bootleg Liquor during Years of Prohibition," *Casper Star-Tribune*, April 22, 1976.

Knox, Kirk. "Teapot Dome Case Among Most Famous in History," *Wyoming State Tribune-Eagle*, July 24, 1977.

Kongslie, Olaf B. "What the Civilian Conservation Corps Has Done for Our Young Men," Unpublished manuscript, WPA Subject 1362. Wyoming State Archives.

Larom, Larry. Collection, including letters and papers from 1923-1940. Buffalo Bill Historical Center.

McPherren, Ida. "A Tragic Blunder," Unpublished manuscript, Wyoming State Archives (696).

Mokler, Alfred J. "Oil History in Wyoming," manuscript written for Federal Writer's Project, Platte River Empire District. Wyoming State Archives.

————. "The Teapot Dome," manuscript written for Federal Writer's Project, Platte River Empire District. Wyoming State Archives.

"Moonshine Raids," *Deaver Sentinel*, January 16, 1925.

"An Old Timer Remembers," *Republican Basin*, May 1, 1979.

Perkins, Van. *Plight of the Farmer: Crisis in Agriculture*. University of California Press, 1969.

"Prohibition: The Night the Town Went Dry," *Cheyenne Eagle*, September 10, 1984.

Rand, Ralph. "Times May Be Tough Today, But It's Not Like The Dirty Thirties," *Laramie Boomerang*, July 20, 1939.

"Reduced Relief Rolls," *Kemmerer Gazette*, May 1, 1942.

"1940 Relief Act," *Greybull Standard*, July 20, 1939.

Roes, K.T. "Earl Durrand's Story to be Told Once Again," *Powell Tribune*, September 16, 1979.

Rothstein, Arthur. *The American West in the Thirties*. New York: Dover Publications, Inc., 1981.

Saban, Vera. "Barnstormers," *In Wyoming*, Vol. VIII, No. 4, October-November, 1975.

Sniffin, Bill. "The Legend of Earl Durrand," *In Wyoming*, Vol. 7, No. 2, Winter 1974.

"Speakeasies, Dance Halls Sparked Casper," *Casper Star-Tribune*, March 25, 1979.

"State Convention in Casper to Ratify 21st Amendment and Repeal 18th Amendment," *Goshen News*, June 1, 1933.

"Still Found," *Crook County Monitor*, December 15, 1921.

Sutton, Morris. Collection H84-27 relating to CCC. Wyoming State Archives.

Whisenhunt, Donald W. "The Transient in the Depression," *Red River Valley Historical Review*, Vol. 1, No. 1, Spring, 1974.

Willmore, Archie. Interview regarding Prohibition and Moonshining, *Wyoming Eagle*, April 27, 1976.

Wilson, Howard Lee. "Top of the World Broadcasts: Wyoming's Early Radio," *Annals Of Wyoming*, Vol. 43, No. 1, Spring 1971.

"Work Done by CCC," *Casper Tribune*, October 4, 1935.

"W.P.A.," *The Wyoming Press*, November 17, 1938.

Chapter Eleven

American Guidebook. Published by Ladies Auxillary, VFW Post 2221.

"At Fast Pace; 65 Students Enrolled," *Casper Tribune-Herald*, December 18, 1941.

Bangerter, Lowell A. "German Prisoners of War In Wyoming," *Journal of German-American Studies*, Vol. XIV, No. 2, June, 1979.

Cooper, Jean E. Collection H85-8 including papers and World War II information, Wyoming State Archives.

Crowley, Mrs. Frank J. Scrapbooks H71-42 of World War II information, Wyoming State Archives.

"Douglas P.O.W.s from Kansas Camp," *Douglas Enterprise*, December 31, 1946.

"Douglas P.O.W.s Work Timber," *Encampment Valley Roundup*, March 23, 1944.

"Education in Wyoming During World War II," *Wyoming State Tribune*, July 30, 1943.

"839 German P.O.W.s from Kansas Camp," *Douglas Budget*, September 28, 1944.

Esmay, R.L. (Wyoming Council of Defense). Letter to Chairmen of County Defense Councils, Circulars No. 15-45 concerning blackouts, censorship, spies, etc. Wyoming State Archives.

Esmay, R.L. Letter, December 30, 1941, to all County Defense Council Chairmen concerning censorship. Wyoming State Archives.

Ewig, Rick. "Home Front Relocation," *Buffalo Bones, Torrington Telegram*, November 30, 1983.

"Farm and Factory Work Both Stressed," *Wyoming State Tribune*, June 30, 1943.

"Feeding and Equipping the Army," *Denver Post*, July 14, 1942.

"Girls of Sheridan High School Demand Part in War Effort," *Sheridan Press*, Oct. 11, 1942.

"Goshen County Unites for Fight on the Home Front," *Torrington Telegram "The Album"*, February 2, 1985.

"Goshen Beet Growers Hire War Prisoners," *Casper Star Tribune*, September 2, 1943.

Goelet, Gallatin. Letter to Chairmen of Local Defense Councils concerning volunteer services in the war effort, December 13, 1941. Wyoming State Archives.

"Heart Mountain Relocation Center," *Powell Tribune*, July 12, 1984.

"Italians Replaced by Germans in Ag Work," *Laramie Daily Bulletin*, April 25, 1944.

"Italian Prisoners Harvest Crops," *Douglas Enterprise*, December 7, 1943.

Larson, T.A. *Wyoming's War Years, 1941-1945*. Laramie: University of Wyoming Press, 1954.

"Plane Plant to be Sold to City for $1," *Northern Wyoming Daily News*, December 6, 1945.

"Ration Stamps and Women," *Lander Journal*, February 21, 1980.

State Summary of War Casualties. Washington D.C.: Office of Public Information, Navy Department, August, 1946.

"3,000 Sign Protest Against Barbed Wire and Gun Towers" *Heart Mt. Sentinel*, November 21, 1942.

"10,000 Japs will be at Cody Camp Before Winter," *Wyoming State Tribune*, August 25, 1942.

"250 Italian P.O.W.s at Veteran in an Old CCC Camp," *Laramie Daily Bulletin*, November, 1944.

Rationing. Washington D.C.: United States Food Administration, Home Card 1918; U.S. Government Printing Office.

War Services Program. WPA Collection H71-7. Wyoming State Archives.

Wording, Maxine. "Rationing," *Wyoming State Journal*, February 21, 1980.

"Wyoming Men Most Fit In Nation," *Douglas Enterprise*, September 31, 1943.

"Wyoming Schools Shift Studies to Meet War Needs, Report Reviewed," *Wyoming Eagle*, November 13, 1942.

Chapter Twelve

"Boom of Mixed Blessing," *Time*, August 5, 1974.

Carlson, William. Remarks at special meeting of University of Wyoming Faculty Senate, October 23, 1969, concerning Black 14. University Wyoming.

"Energy Transforms a Cow Town," *In Wyoming*, August-September, 1975.

Ewig, Rick. "Wyoming Not Immune to Cold War Rhetoric," *Torrington Telegram*, August 27, 1983.

Farney, Dennis. "The Lonesome Land," *The Wall Street Journal*, October 3, 1969.

"Jeffrey City," Advertisement appearing in *In Wyoming*, August, 1974.

Larson, T.A. "Larson Lists Wyoming's Most Important People and Incidents," *Torrington Telegram*, April, 1984.

Logan, John and Donna Witters. *Directory of Mining and Manufacturing in Wyoming, 1981 and 1982*. Cheyenne: Wyoming Department of Economic Planning and Development, 1982.

McAuley, Phil. "I'll Be Perfectly Honest With You," *Wyoming Horizons*, Nov. 1981.

Murdock, Steve. "The Real World Comes To Wyoming," *The Nation*, November 17, 1969.

Mathews, Samual. "The Night the Mountains Moved," *National Geographic Magazine*, March, 1960.

Mittes, David. "Wyoming: The Saudia Arabia of the Western States," *Annals Of Wyoming*, Vol. 51, No. 2, Fall, 1978.

"New Life in Wyoming," *Time*, September 23, 1957.

"Prosecutor," *The New Yorker*, November 28, 1977.

Putnam, Pat "No Defeats, Loads of Trouble," *Sports Illustrated*, October, 1969.

Richards, Bill. "Powder River Basin: New Energy Frontier," *National Geographic Magazine*, February, 1981.

———. "The Untamed Yellowstone," *National Geographic Magazine*, August, 1981.

Shell, David. "The New Hunger for Coal Brings A Boom To Wyoming's Sweetwater County," *The Smithsonian*, July, 1974.

Special Vietnam Moratorium Edition, *The Branding Iron* (University of Wyoming Campus Newspaper), October 15, 1969.

"Wyoming's Wonderful Women," *Saturday Evening Post*, August 1, 1959.

Wyoming Oil And Gas. Casper: Petroleum Association of Wyoming, 1982.

INDEX